Using

Access 95,

New Edition

Using

Access 95,
New Edition

— Bob Schneider —

Using Access 95, New Edition

Library of Congress Catalog No.: 95-71458

ISBN: 0-07897-0185-5

97 96 95   6 5 4 3 2 1

Interpretation of the printing code: the rightmost double-digit number is the year of the book's printing; the rightmost single-digit number, the number of the book's printing. For example, a printing code of 95-1 shows that the first printing of the book occurred in 1995.

Screen reproductions in this book were created using Collage Plus from Inner Media, Inc., Hollis, NH.

Composed in *ITC Century, ITC Highlander,* and *MCPdigital* by Que Corporation.

Credits

President and Publisher
Roland Elgey

Associate Publisher
Joseph B. Wikert

Editorial Services Director
Elizabeth Keaffaber

Managing Editor
Sandy Doell

Director of Marketing
Lynn E. Zingraf

Senior Series Editor
Chris Nelson

Title Manager
Bryan Gambrel

Acquisitions Editor
Fred Slone

Product Development Specialist
Faithe Wempen

Editors
Noelle Gasco
Chris Haidri
Lynn Northrup
Nanci Sears Perry

**Assistant Product
Marketing Manager**
Kim Margolius

Technical Editors
Brian C. Blackman
Dan Dietschy

Acquisitions Coordinator
Angela C. Kozlowski

Operations Coordinator
Patricia J. Brooks

Editorial Assistant
Michelle R. Williams

Book Designer
Ruth Harvey

Cover Designer
Dan Armstrong

Production Team
Angela D. Bannan
Claudia Bell
Heather Butler
Chad Dressler
DiMonique Ford
Amy Gornik
Damon Jordan
Paula Lowell
Julie Quinn
Regina Rexrode
Bobbi Satterfield
Tim Taylor
Jody York

Indexer
Mary Jane Frisby

To my parents, who have supported me in whatever I've attempted—even when they thought it made little sense.

About the Author

Bob Schneider, CPA/MBA, writes on businesses ranging from child daycare to electrical auto parts. He was Senior Editor at Morgan Stanley and Senior Writer at AIA, a Tokyo Public Relations Firm. He now helps people select and use great software.

Acknowledgments

A complete roster with adequate acknowledgment of all who brought this book to fruition would take many pages, so let me just mention a few people who were key:

Faithe Wempen and Kevin Kloss, Product Development Specialists, who provided incisive feedback and criticism of each chapter. Nanci Sears Perry, Production Editor, who worked under impossible deadlines to put this book to press. Fred Stone, Acquisitions Editor, who was unfailingly supportive and pulled many of the final pieces together. Dan Dietschy and Brian C. Blackman, Technical Editors who offered important criticism to ensure the book's accuracy. Don Roche, Jr., Associate Publisher, who gave me the contract for this book and built my confidence. A very special thank you is due Chris Haidri, who reviewed many chapters and made substantial improvements in all facets of my work.

I'd also like to thank two members of the San Francisco PC Users Group, Harold Heringhi and Butler Crittenden, who through the years have freely given of their time to address my computer-related questions.

We'd Like to Hear from You!

As part of our continuing effort to produce books of the highest possible quality, Que would like to hear your comments. To stay competitive, we *really* want you, as a computer book reader and user, to let us know what you like or dislike most about this book or other Que products.

You can mail comments, ideas, or suggestions for improving future editions to the address below, or send us a fax at (317) 581-4663. For the online inclined, Macmillan Computer Publishing has a forum on CompuServe (type **GO QUEBOOKS** at any prompt) through which our staff and authors are available for questions and comments. The address of our Internet site is **http://www.mcp.com** (World Wide Web).

In addition to exploring our forum, please feel free to contact me personally to discuss your opinions of this book: I'm **75230,1556** on CompuServe, and I'm **bgambrel@que.mcp.com** on the Internet.

Thanks in advance—your comments will help us to continue publishing the best books available on computer topics in today's market.

Bryan Gambrel
Title Manager
Que Corporation
201 W. 103rd Street
Indianapolis, Indiana 46290
USA

Contents at a Glance

Contents

Part 2: Tables

3 Tables: The Basic Building Blocks of Your Database

4 The Art of Database Maintenance

5 Faster, Better Ways to Make Tables

How can I get rid of what I just put in my table?

see page 56

How to make table rows taller.

see page 63

*How do I add
a field with
Field Builder?*

see page 77

6 **Relationships: How Database Tables Relate to Each Other**

*Unraveling
the mystery of
many–to–
many
relationships.*

see page 94

*What kind of
data type is
"Lookup
Wizard?"*

see page 102

Part 3: Finding Stuff

8 How to Find What You Are Looking For

Exactly how do I use a wild card?

see page 128

Part 4: Queries and Filters

9 Questions About Your Database with Queries

10 It's Only an Expression

Access can get you the answers fast if you came up with the right query.

see page 140

You can do basic calculations in your queries.

see page 165

11 Filters: A Temporary Viewpoint

What's Advanced Filter/Sort good for?

see page 180

Join tables to get the information you need.

see page 184

12 Queries Using More Than One Table

13 Totals Queries Add Things Up—and More

Part 4: Queries and Filters

Put your data in a form to give it more breathing room. And it will be easier to manipulate too.

see page 219

Please tell me how to move a text box with the label attached.

see page 241

16 A Tour of Some Selective Properties

*How do I select
more than one
control at once?*

see page 244

*I really want to
change the look
of my text.*

see page 259

Part 6: Reports

17 Reports: Data Quick and Easy

*I want to
print mailing
labels.*

see page 293

18 How to Change the Look of Your Report

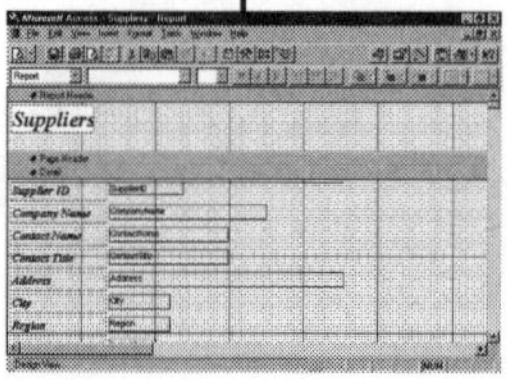

*How do I move
an object to
another Access
database?*

see page 318

Part 7: Finishing Touches

19 Negotiating Exports and Imports

20 Change Your Data with Action Queries

Update queries are great when you want to change many records in a field.

see page 348

Part 8: Appendix

A Where to Go for More Help

Tell me about some on-line services.

see page 358

Introduction

Right now this book is clean and tidy, its pages unspoiled. I don't want it to stay that way. In two months, I want you to have a note-filled, pages-turned-down, *Post-Its*-packed mess of a book, with doodles in the margins and half of yesterday's tuna sandwich wedged in Chapter 16.

So here's my problem: How do I keep this book in your hands and out of the closet?

You put Access on your computer to make and maintain powerful databases both effectively and efficiently. Now you want to learn the best—and the fastest—ways to accomplish that goal. You want direct, succinct, clear advice on how to perform specific tasks and how to solve particular problems.

Each page of this book has been written and edited with your needs in mind. The material is organized to make it easy to find answers to your questions fast. The book is filled with analogies from common experience so that challenging concepts can be quickly absorbed. Real-life, step-by-step examples are liberally employed, accompanied by Access screen shots (almost one on every page) for easy comparison with your own work.

You paid hard-earned money for this book. More important, you're putting your time and energy into it. You deserve value. I hope this book finds a place on your desk, in your briefcase, or next to your favorite chair.

A thumbnail sketch of the contents

Most of this book is devoted to the basics of creating and using the major parts of an Access database—tables, queries, forms, and reports. There's also a few chapters at the end on related topics, like how to import information from (and export it to) other programs. An appendix offers advice on where to go for more help. Let's take a very brief look at the different parts of this book.

Part I: Starting Off

The objective of the first few chapters is to help you feel comfortable in the Access environment. In the first chapter, you get a little taste of what a database is. And, in Chapter 2, "A First Walk Around Access," you open Access and create the file for your first database.

Part II: Tables

Chapters 3 through 6 cover tables, the most basic structures in a database for holding information. You'll learn how to create tables and put data into them. I'll discuss relationships, which will give you a better sense of the power and beauty of relational databases. I'll also show you how to find and replace specific pieces of information you have entered in tables.

Part III: Finding Stuff

You can find individual pieces of information in your table by using the Find command. Sometimes you know exactly what you want to search for; other times you have some idea, but you don't know the specifics. Chapter 8 will each you how to find data under both conditions. You'll also learn how to replace the data you just found.

Part IV: Queries and Filters

Queries are the subject of Chapters 9 through 13. You use a query to ask for information that meets certain standards or guidelines, and Access retrieves it from your database. Often this requires using **expressions**, which gives you and Access a common means of communication. You'll also learn how to ask Access to perform simple calculations (like a total) on your data.

Part V: Forms

Forms present your data more attractively than tables can and allow you to manipulate data more easily. But forms are not mere window dressing—they can make your databases much more robust and useful. Chapters 14 through 16 discuss the different kinds of forms you can create and show you how to make them.

Part VI: Reports

When you want to present database information to others, you put it in a report. Chapters 17 and 18 show you how to make effective, great-looking reports quickly. You'll learn about sorting and grouping in reports, which make your data far more compelling for the reader. You'll also learn how to make attractive mailing labels with little bother.

Part VII: Finishing Touches

The final chapters of the book, 19 and 20, tackle important topics that build on your knowledge of database basics. In Chapter 19, you'll learn how to exchange data between Access and other programs through importing and exporting. And in Chapter 20, you will learn how to make large changes to your tables.

Part VIII: Where to Go for More Help

This book doesn't pretend to cover more than the basics of Access. You will have problems that this book won't answer. Appendix A discusses where you can turn when you need more help.

Special book elements

This book contains a number of special elements that are designed to make it easier to read, and to help you find information more quickly.

TIP **Tips describe shortcuts and secrets that show you the best way to get a job done. Tips often help you solve or avoid problems.**

CAUTION **Cautions warn you about potential problems that might arise from a particular action.**

Q&A *What are Q&A notes?*

These are notes cast in a question-and-answer format. Most attempt to propose solutions to problems the reader is likely to encounter.

 *Plain English, please!*

These elements are used to make Access and database terms easier to understand.

Throughout this book, we'll use a comma to separate the parts of a menu command. For example, to open a database you'll choose File, Open Database. That means pull down the File menu and choose Open Database from the list.

What do the underlined letters in the above command mean? You may find pressing these letters while holding down the Alt key a faster way to issue commands. For example, press Alt+F to display the File menu.

Sidebars are interesting nuggets of information

Sidebars provide interesting, nonessential reading, something to read when you're not "doing stuff."

Here you may find more technical details or interesting background information.

Part I: Starting Off

1

A Little Bit About Databases

● In this chapter:

● **What is a database?**

● **Access handles all kinds of information**

● **What are the many business and personal uses of databases?**

You don't need to know Greek symbols or computer languages to learn Access. You don't even have to be good with math . . . . ⊙

T he introduction of computer technology has, in several ways, made life colder and more impersonal. And the information revolution certainly does raise serious issues for personal privacy. But all of that has nothing to do with your own ability to learn and use Access comfortably—and with confidence. You don't have to know database theory or any computer languages. How you want to use Access is your business: you can create databases for telemarketing—or to inspire second graders to read, promote human rights, or home-deliver meals to the elderly.

The purpose of this chapter is to give you an idea of what a database is and how to use one.

What is a database?

Did you ever make up a guest list for a party? You thought about the people you owed invitations to, the people you just met at your child's new day-care center, and the people who just moved in down the block. You also thought about those who drink and those who don't, those who love cigars and those who don't, those who wear fur and those who are animal rights activists, and so on. After working out all the possible combinations of who will get along with whom, you came up with a guest list for the gala affair.

Now, you probably didn't realize it, but what you did was open tables, enter records, import information from other databases, run select queries, sort the results, and save a query as a table. In other words, you used a database.

Here's the point: a database stores and organizes information—a lot of information—and it has the power to expand, update, manipulate, and retrieve it rapidly.

What types of information get put in a database?

Your databases will contain all kinds of information—the names of people in your garden club, the dates you visited the art museum, the number of

Mickey Mantle cards you have, and the cost of your new sofa. If you are using it for your business, you can inventory your entire stock, including parts numbers, list prices, and reorder quantities; record your sales with customer names, order numbers, and delivery dates; and list your purchases (put in supplier names, discounts taken, and taxes paid).

In fact, it's harder to think of what you can't put in a database than what you can. In Access, you can also put in graphical elements, like photos and graphs.

What kinds of databases can I create?

One way to get a feel for the wide range of databases you can create is to look at the tables in the Access Table Wizard (I'll discuss what those are in Chapter 5.) Table 1.1 lists the names of the tables and what kinds of information you might put in them.

Table 1.1   The kinds of databases to create

Database	Kinds of information
Books	Title, Purchase Price
Exercise Log	Activity, Resting Pulse
Household Inventory	Manufacturer, Serial Number
Investments	Security Name, Shares Owned
Plants	Species, Light Preference
Photographs	Date Taken, Lens Used
Recipes	Time to Prepare, Calories per Serving
Video Collection	Year Released, Rating
Wine List	Vineyard, Vintage

How is a database structured?

A database comprises different **objects**—which are structures—for holding, storing, and manipulating your information. This book devotes several chapters to each major object—tables, forms, queries, and reports. To get a feeling of how a database is organized, let's take a very quick look at each object.

Storing information in tables

A **table** is the bedrock of your database. All of your information is stored in tables, which are **grids**. Figure 1.1 shows a table taken from the Northwind Traders database that is included in Access. Each column in the table contains one specific type of information. Each column is known as a **field**. In a wide table, most of the columns are not visible.

Each row contains information about a particular customer, with each field filled out for that customer. Each customer's data is called a **record**.

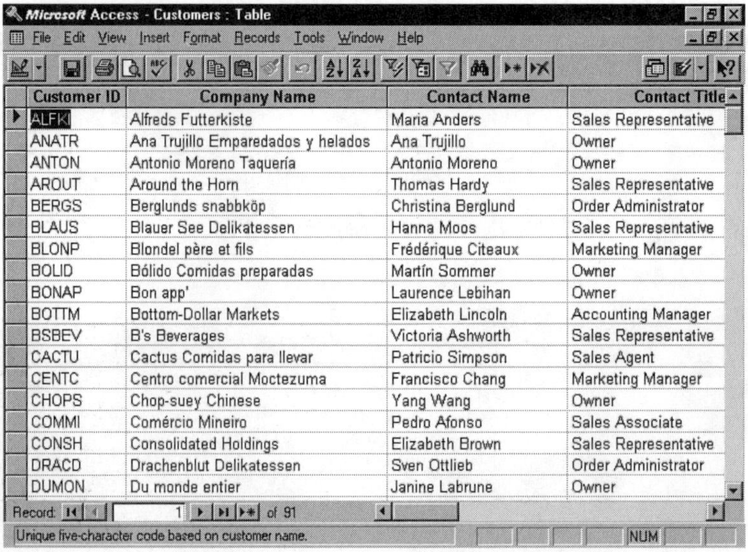
Microsoft Access - Customers : Table
File Edit View Insert Format Records Tools Window Help
Customer ID | Company Name | Contact Name | Contact Title
ALFKI | Alfreds Futterkiste | Maria Anders | Sales Representative
ANATR | Ana Trujillo Emparedados y helados | Ana Trujillo | Owner
ANTON | Antonio Moreno Taquería | Antonio Moreno | Owner
AROUT | Around the Horn | Thomas Hardy | Sales Representative
BERGS | Berglunds snabbköp | Christina Berglund | Order Administrator
BLAUS | Blauer See Delikatessen | Hanna Moos | Sales Representative
BLONP | Blondel père et fils | Frédérique Citeaux | Marketing Manager
BOLID | Bólido Comidas preparadas | Martín Sommer | Owner
BONAP | Bon app' | Laurence Lebihan | Owner
BOTTM | Bottom-Dollar Markets | Elizabeth Lincoln | Accounting Manager
BSBEV | B's Beverages | Victoria Ashworth | Sales Representative
CACTU | Cactus Comidas para llevar | Patricio Simpson | Sales Agent
CENTC | Centro comercial Moctezuma | Francisco Chang | Marketing Manager
CHOPS | Chop-suey Chinese | Yang Wang | Owner
COMMI | Comércio Mineiro | Pedro Afonso | Sales Associate
CONSH | Consolidated Holdings | Elizabeth Brown | Sales Representative
DRACD | Drachenblut Delikatessen | Sven Ottlieb | Order Administrator
DUMON | Du monde entier | Janine Labrune | Owner
Record: 1 of 91
Unique five-character code based on customer name.
NUM

Fig. 1.1
Tables form the foundation of your database.

Viewing information in forms

A **form** allows you to view a single record more easily. The Customers form in the Northwind Traders database contains the same fields as the Customers table. The information in the form is spread out over an entire page for each individual customer. You can see all of the information, and it is easy to read. In figure 1.2, you see all the information for the Around the Horn company in the Customers form. In figure 1.1, you see only part of that record. Many people prefer to use forms for viewing and entering data, since it's easier to focus on specific pieces of information using a form.

Fig. 1.2
You can view a single record more easily in forms.

Company Name

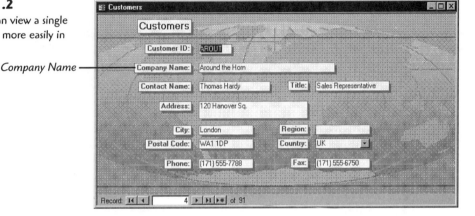

Search for information with queries

Queries are for retrieving information you have entered in tables or forms—in a fairly sophisticated way. You ask Access to show you information that meets certain standards or guidelines, and it gives you the answer. The actual query itself—the data that is retrieved—is presented in a format that is much like a table, as shown in figure 1.3.

Fig. 1.3
A query retrieves information stored in your database.

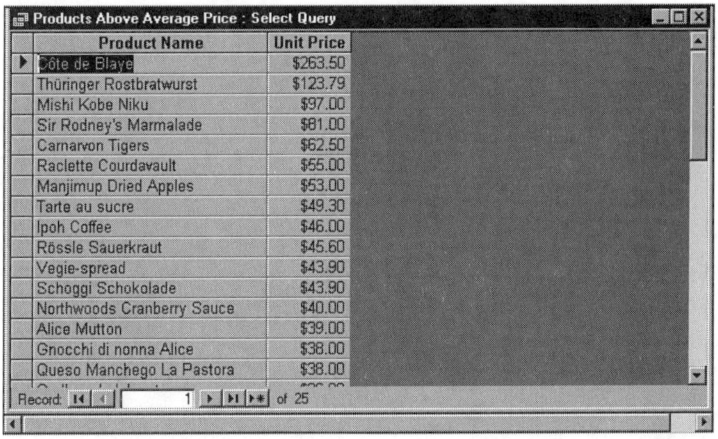

Present it attractively in a report

You can print out a table, form, or query without any problem. But usually you'll use **reports** to print out your information. You can make reports look more attractive than a grid or form. You can also sort and group data in reports, and come up with totals and subtotals more easily than in other objects (see fig. 1.4).

Fig. 1.4

Access offers a variety of ways to present your data in reports.

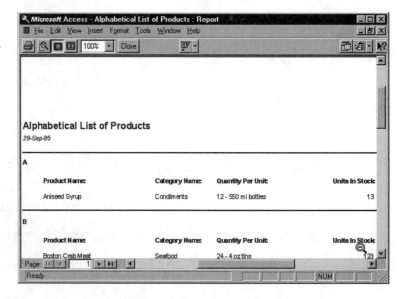

A First Walk Around Access

● **In this chapter:**

- How do I start up Access?

- Creating your first database file

- Poking around the main menu

- What do all these icons on the toolbar do?

- Help, help, and more help

- How can I tell one dialog box from another?

It's time to start up Access and create your first database file . . . . ❯

Is there anyone who doesn't feel nervous about starting a new job? The first day at work is more than a good reason for a panic attack. But by the fourth or fifth day, things start to get a little more familiar. Soon you feel like you worked there all your life.

In the next few pages, you'll have a first look at Access. I'll take you on a walk around the program, show you where a few things are, and teach you a few names. Don't worry about how everything works, or what each button is for. Just try to get a sense of the Access environment.

Some of this stuff will undoubtedly seem strange and foreign, like the first day on the job. But a lot that you'll see—menus, toolbars, dialog boxes— should be more familiar. Remember, you're using a Windows program, and all the Windows conventions apply. So it should be more like the fifth day of work than your first—you're still a little apprehensive, but at least you know how the copier works.

How do I start up Access?

You can launch Access in lots of ways. One easy method is through the Start and <u>P</u>rograms menus of the taskbar.

1 Click the Start button at the bottom of your screen.

2 Point at <u>P</u>rograms, and the Programs menu will appear.

3 Point at Microsoft Access on the Programs menu (see fig. 2.1).

4 Click Microsoft Access to start the program.

Q&A *I don't see Microsoft Access anywhere on the Programs menu. What do I do?*

Take another look at the Programs menu and see if there's an item called Microsoft Office. Point at it with the mouse and another submenu should appear containing Microsoft Access. Choose it, and Access will open.

TIP **If you hold down the mouse button from the time you click the** Start button, you don't have to click Microsoft Access to start it. Keep the button depressed as you look through the menus. Release the mouse button when Microsoft Access is highlighted, and the program opens.

Fig. 2.1
The Windows 95
interface makes
opening programs
a simple affair.

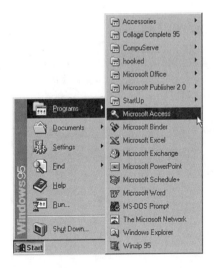

The Access welcome screen

Figure 2.2 shows the Access welcome screen. You have two basic options, do you want to create a new database, or would you like to open a database you've already created? Right now, you haven't created or opened any database files. So you won't see all or any of the files listed in the bottom half of figure 2.2. As you create database files, these will be added to the list of those you can open.

Fig. 2.2
The welcome screen
for Access gets you off
to a fast start.

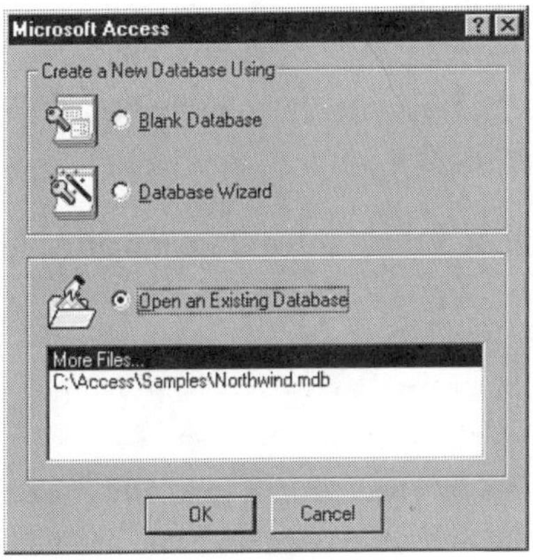

Creating a database file

Right now, you're just going to create the database file—you're not going to put anything into it. Click the Blank Database button (if it's not already selected) and click OK. The File New Database window appears (see fig. 2.3).

Fig. 2.3

Begin to create a new database in the File New Database window.

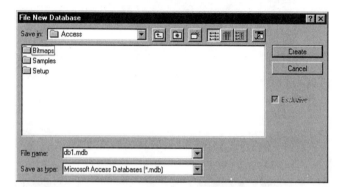

In the Save In box, you can select the folder for your new database (refer to fig. 2.3). The current folder in the figure is Access, which is a good place for the new database you will create. So leave that just the way it is. If you want to change the drive or folder, however, click the Save In drop-down arrow, and then navigate through the desktop hierarchy to choose a different location.

Near the bottom of the File New Database screen, you see the File Name box. In the box is a suggested file name: db1.mdb. The .mdb extension indicates that you are creating a database file. Depending on your settings for viewing file names, you may not see the .mdb extension.

In this book, I have included the .mdb extension after Access file names for the sake of clarity, but you don't need to see it. For example, the Northwind.mdb database may appear simply as Northwind on your computer.

TIP If you would like to see (or not see) file name extensions in the File New Database and other windows, you can easily change the appropriate setting. In the Windows Explorer, click View, Options, and the View tab. The Hide MS-DOS File Extensions for File Types that Are Registered check box controls whether you see file extensions for many programs, including Access. Put a check mark in the box to hide extensions; leave it unchecked and they'll be visible. If you decide to make a change, click Apply and then OK to make it effective.

In the Save as Type box at the bottom of your screen, the setting should read Databases(*.mdb) or Microsoft Access Databases(*.mdb). Again, if you're not viewing file extensions, you will not see (*.mdb) after Databases. Leave that setting as it is to create a new database file.

Because you can now use file names longer than eight characters, let's call the new database My personal stuff.mdb. In the File Name box, type **My personal stuff**. (You don't need to type in the file extension.)

Click Create and Access will create your new database. After a few moments, the Database window appears (see fig. 2.4).

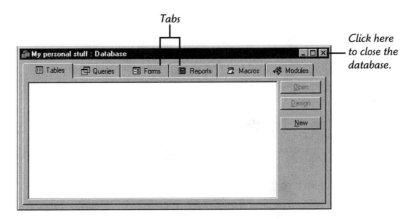

Fig. 2.4
The Database window appears when you create a new database.

Tabs

Click here to close the database.

Q&A *Why did I choose to use a Blank Database rather than a Database Wizard?*

If you choose the Database Wizard option, Access asks you a series of questions and then creates an entire ready-made database for you. Whenever you open the database, Access asks you what you want to do and lets you get right to work. My own feeling is that you need to learn the basics first to use Access with any degree of agility. That means starting with an empty database file and building the database step-by-step on your own—the game plan you will pursue in this book.

What are all these things in the Database window?

The Database window can be thought of as Control Central. It's a little like the table of contents of a book. It gives you the broad overview of what's inside.

Across the Database window you see **tabs** for the various database **objects**, like forms or reports (refer to fig. 2.4). Click any tab and you'll see that it is completely empty. As you create database objects, they will be listed in each tab folder.

In this book I'll talk a lot about tables, queries, forms, and reports. These are the primary objects that make up your database. Right now, don't worry about them. Just concentrate on getting a feel for the Access environment.

How do I open an existing database?

It's hard to get a good sense of the Database window with a totally empty database, so let's look at a database that is already well developed. Open the File menu and choose Open Database. The Open dialog box appears, as shown in figure 2.5.

Fig. 2.5
When you open another database, the current database closes.

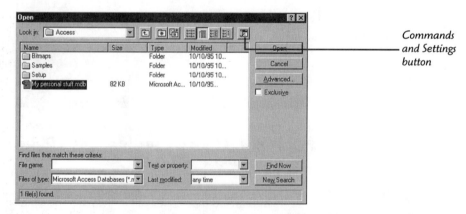

Commands and Settings button

Access comes with a sample database called the Northwind Traders. Later in this book, after you become well-grounded in some database principles, you will use it to do some sample examples. Let's open it and take a look at it.

The file name for the Northwind Traders database is Northwind.mdb. Because it doesn't appear among the databases listed in figure 2.5, let's use the Find command to open it. Databases (*.mdb) or Microsoft Access Databases (*.mdb) should already be selected in the Files of Type box at the bottom of the screen; if not, click the arrow for the drop-down menu and change the selection. Right above it, in the File Name box, type **Northwind**.

Click the Commands and Settings button (the icon farthest to the right in the Look In row), and click Search Subfolders; this setting should now be checked. Click the Find Now button, and Access will find the file for you and highlight it. Double-click its icon, and Access opens the file. Click OK on the Northwind Traders welcome screen, and you'll see the Database window (see fig. 2.6). (If you see the Database window without first seeing the welcome screen, that's fine.)

Q&A ***When I clicked the Find Now button, no files were found.***

Let's do a complete search of all your folders and subfolders. In the Look In box, click the drop-down menu and select your hard drive (usually the C: drive). Click the Commands and Settings icon and make sure Search Subfolders is checked. Click the Find Now button and you should find Northwind.mdb.

Fig. 2.6
The Northwind Traders database contains eight tables.

Table icon ——

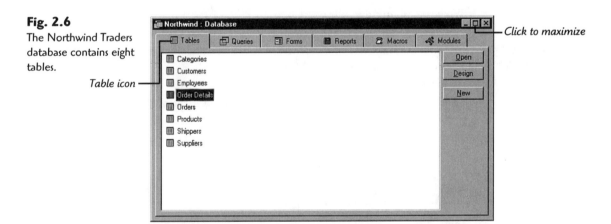

—— Click to maximize

A well-developed database has many objects

Maximize the Northwind Database window. You can see in figure 2.6 that the database contains many objects. For example, eight tables have already been created. Click some of the other tabs—Queries, Forms—to get a feel for what's in them, and then click the Tables tab again. The different tabs are like sections of a textbook, with the different objects in them representing chapters to be opened. Notice that each object type has its own icon on the tab folder.

Remember that, in Access, all the objects of a single database go in the same database file. This shouldn't be very meaningful to you now, but keep the thought in the back of your mind.

A quick overview of Access menus

As in other Windows programs, Access menus change depending on what you're up to. But, also like other Windows programs, they follow a certain order and convention. In fact, if you've ever used another program in the Microsoft Office suite, you'll find the menus quite similar. (And if you haven't, they may still be quite familiar to you from using other applications.)

What's happening in all these menus? I'll go over a few things that you can do specifically in the Database window, but I'll also talk more generally about the menus. This should give you some clues of where to look for specific commands when you're working with other objects.

TIP   **As you go through the menus, take a look at the descriptions of** commands that appear in the Status Bar. In fact, the Status Bar will often contain information that will help you with your work. (The Status Bar is located at the bottom of the Access window.)

The File menu

First, if no table is highlighted, select any table (Categories will do fine) in the Database window by clicking once on its icon. Then click the word File in the menu bar (see fig. 2.7). You can come here to create a new database file, or open an existing one. You can also save your work and print it.

At the bottom of the menu will be the names of databases you recently used. Note the My personal stuff.mdb database. When you want to open a database, look here first. If you find it, there's no need to search for it in the Open window. Simply click it or type its number, and the database opens.

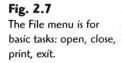

Fig. 2.7
The File menu is for basic tasks: open, close, print, exit.

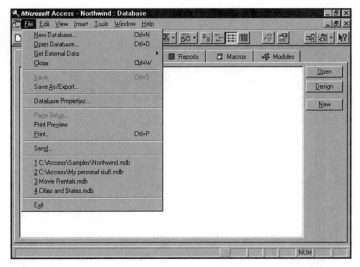

At the bottom of the File menu is the E<u>x</u>it command. That means exit Access itself—*not* the particular window you've been working in. If you want to close a particular window, choose <u>F</u>ile, <u>C</u>lose instead.

 TIP   **There are faster ways to leave Access than using the menu bar.** Probably the best is the keyboard shortcut Alt+F4.

The Edit menu

Now to the <u>E</u>dit menu. Edit is home to three commands cherished by Windows users—Cut, <u>C</u>opy, and <u>P</u>aste. Here you can also <u>U</u>ndo stuff you didn't want to do—it will be the first command at top. The menu is also useful for deleting and finding things.

The View menu

You can choose <u>V</u>iew, <u>D</u>etails to see additional details about your database objects, like the date and time they were created. If you don't need or like such details, select <u>L</u>ist from the <u>V</u>iew menu and they will disappear. You can also choose Large Icons for the Database window, as shown in figure 2.8. Select <u>L</u>ist to get back to a vertical listing.

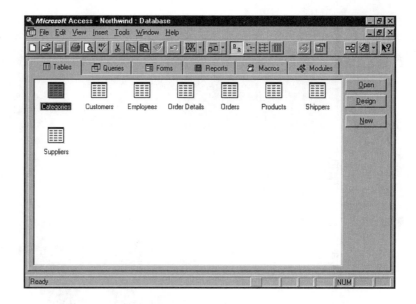

The Insert menu

The Insert menu is, as you would expect, to add things. Often, you will want to add new objects—tables, queries, and so on—when you're in the Database window. Usually, though, clicking the object's tab and then clicking the New button at the right is faster and easier. But remember that the Insert menu is there when you want to put something else into your database.

The Tools menu

Click Options at the very bottom of the Tools menu and you get the screen in figure 2.9. At some point when you're using Access you're going to say, "Gee, I sure wish I didn't have to see this thingamajig all the time," or "Gee, I sure wish I could change the way this looks." If you click the tabs and see the choices, you may find a way to do it. These selections will become much more meaningful to you as you work through the book.

Fig. 2.9
Use the Options
selections to customize
Access.

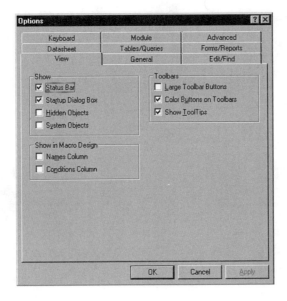

The Window menu

In the Window menu, you can see which windows are open. Right now you can only choose Northwind's Database window, the window you are currently viewing. Only the database itself is open—none of its objects. So only Northwind: Database is listed at the bottom of the menu. The check mark in front of it means that it's selected (not much of a choice when only one screen is open).

If you open a table, then you would have two screens from which to select—the Database window, indicating the database itself, and the table. To demonstrate this, open the Categories table of the Northwind database. Click once on the Categories icon to highlight it (if it isn't already), and then click the Open button. Don't worry about what's in the table you see—we'll discuss that in detail in the second part of this book, which is devoted to tables.

The menu bar changes a bit. You still have a Window menu, though—go ahead and select it (see fig. 2.10). The Categories table is listed at the bottom of the menu and has the check mark in front of it. To switch back to the Database window, you could click 1 Northwind: Database directly on top of it.

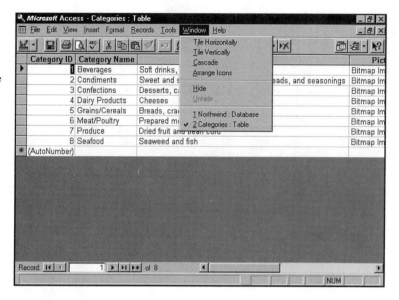

If you want to see both windows at once, you can tile them. Select Window, Tile Horizontally (see fig. 2.11). If you want to see them side by side, choose Tile Vertically. You can also cascade the windows with the Cascade command. Cascading arranges windows in an overlapping pattern so all title bars are visible.

You can open more objects if you want to, as long as all the objects are in the same database.

TIP **When you tile horizontally, the window that is currently selected** goes on top. When you tile vertically, it appears on the left.

When you cascade or tile your windows, they become "un-maximized." To get rid of the tile or cascade, simply maximize one of the windows by clicking the window's Maximize button (the middle button in the upper right-hand corner).

Fig. 2.11
If you want the
Database window on
top, first click it, and
then tile the windows
again.

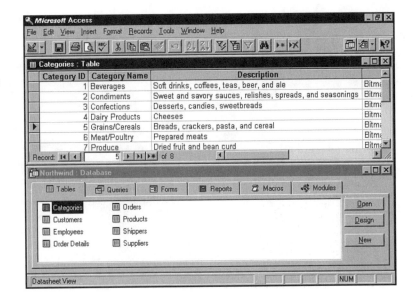

Taking advantage of shortcut menus

One of the new features in Windows 95 is the widespread use of shortcut menus. You get them by clicking the alternate mouse button. (With apologies to the left-handed, for simplicity sake, I'll use the term right mouse button to mean alternate mouse button.)

One rule of thumb that the computer pundits suggest for Windows 95 is, "When you don't know what to do, click the right mouse button." The same point applies to Access. You may find it more convenient to choose from these short menus, rather than use the menu bar or toolbar.

For example, click the right mouse button anywhere in the (white) foreground of the Database window. You get the shortcut menu shown in figure 2.12. Note the little arrow after the first two commands. That means, "Click again, and you'll see more choices." If you click View, you'll see that you have many of the same choices that you had when you clicked View on the menu bar. To cancel the menu without selecting anything, click with the left mouse button anywhere outside of the menu.

Fig. 2.12
Handy shortcut menus appear with a click of the right mouse button.

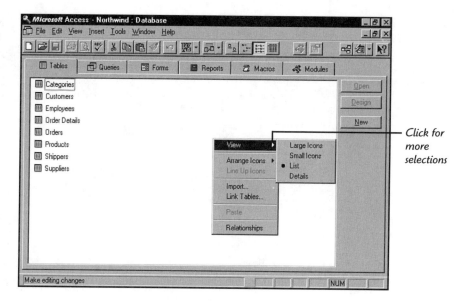

Click for more selections

Now, move the mouse pointer up to the title of the Tables tab and click the right mouse button. You get an entirely different menu. Don't worry about what any of the commands do. The point is you can get "context-sensitive" menus in Access merely by clicking the right mouse button.

Remind me, what are toolbars?

Toolbars are the icons, or buttons, strung along the width of your screen below the menu bar. For the most part, they duplicate commands available on the menu bar. Be aware that toolbars in Access change a lot depending on the screen you are looking at and what you are doing.

Sometimes, it's hard to figure out what an icon does just by looking at it. Take, for example, the New Database icon, the first button on the toolbar. Does this say "create a new database" to you?

But there is a way to find out what any button on the bar does. Simply point the mouse at it and the name of the icon will appear. At the same time, a description of the icon's function appears in the Status Bar (see fig. 2.13).

Fig. 2.13
Rest the mouse pointer over the icon for more information.

Icon name —

Description —

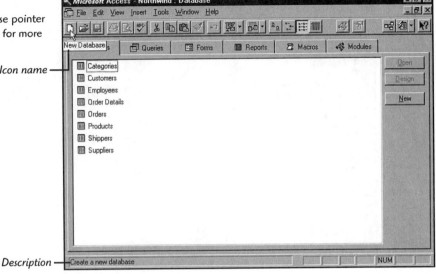

 Q&A ***I tried to find out the name of the icon by pointing the mouse at it, but the name never shows up.***

Don't get impatient. Sometimes you've got to leave the mouse pointer on the icon for a full second or so. Once you get one name to come on, the others show up pretty fast as you move your mouse across the bar.

If you still can't see the names, check that the Show ToolTips option is on. Click Tools, Options, and click the View tab. In the Toolbars section, click to put a check in the Show ToolTips box, and click OK.

Getting Help in Access

Help comes from many hands in Access. The Help menu offers four different approaches for obtaining the assistance you need. You can also use the Help icon.

The Contents tab

Start with help from the Help menu first. Select Help, Microsoft Access Help Topics. The screen in figure 2.14 appears.

Notice that the help topics are divided into a series of "books" (see fig. 2.14). Double-click a book, and a new set of books appears (see fig. 2.15). If you want to close an open book, double-click it.

Fig. 2.14
The Contents tab in Access Help. Note the Print button on the bottom for easy printing.

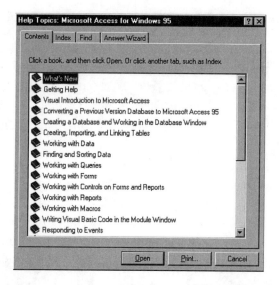

Fig. 2.15
Double-click a book for more choices, or a question mark for help.

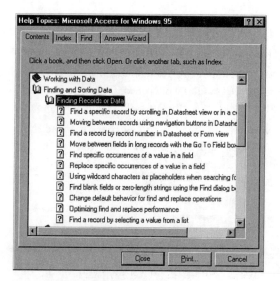

Actually, even though the book metaphor is used, the help system works more like an outline. Just remember that if you see a book, that means there are more choices inside. It's only when you double-click a question mark, called a **topic**, that you actually get some help. But this system undoubtedly helps to organize the material, and makes it easy to go from one topic to the next.

The Help Index

If you have a more specific question about a term, use the Help Index. Click the Index tab in the Help Topics dialog box. In the first line, type the first few letters of whatever you want to find, and Help sends you to that part of the index. For example, typing **que** sends you to queries (see fig. 2.16). You can then double-click any topic to open and read it.

The Answer Wizard

The Answer Wizard is helpful when you have a task in mind and are not sure what term to use. Click Help, Answer Wizard and you see the screen in figure 2.17. Follow the easy directions shown on the screen to find and select related topics. You will find this method quite useful, although it sometimes involves reading and rejecting a number of obscure topics before you find a topic you want to read.

Fig. 2.16
Just type the first few letters of the search term.

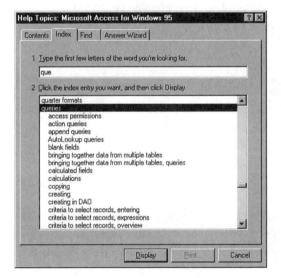

The Find tab

I mention the Find tab last because it's probably the most difficult option to use; it also takes a little bit longer. Frankly, I prefer to use the Help Index or Answer Wizard when I have a specific need that the Contents tab can't help me with.

Fig. 2.17
The topics found from your search are divided into sections. How Do I gives you instructions for a task; Tell Me About provides important support.

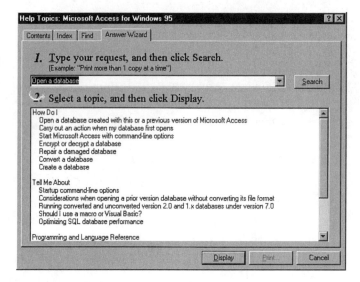

 Find may be useful, however, when you want to know all topics where one or more words appear. You select the word or words, and Access performs the search. You can find instructions on the Find tab for its use.

Using the toolbar Help icon

The toolbar Help icon can be used to find the name and perhaps some explanation of any item on your screen. You'll find the button at the far right of the toolbar. Click the button and then drag it to the item you want some information about, and then click again. You'll get a help box describing the item. It's a pretty neat trick.

 TIP **Suppose you click the Help icon accidentally or decide you don't** need help half-way to its target. You can't just click anywhere to disengage and get rid of the big question mark. You have to take it back where it came from and click the Help button again.

Part II: Tables

Tables: The Basic Building Blocks of Your Database

● **In this chapter:**

- **Why are tables the cornerstones of my database?**

- **First steps in creating a table**

- **What are *fields* and *records*?**

- **Add, rearrange, and delete fields**

- **Primary keys are truly unique**

All of your information goes into tables so that both you and Access can find it. . . . . ⊛

Tables form the bedrock of your database by holding and organizing all of your information. Do you remember coming home on Halloween with 15 pounds of candy in your bag? Mom would tell you to spread all of it out on the kitchen table so you could see everything you got. After you dumped it all out, you'd begin to organize the loot for critical decision-making—what to put in the freezer, what to give Aunt Rose, what to feed the guinea pigs.

Like Halloween candy, information comes to us from many sources, and in many different shapes and sizes. It needs to be organized so we can work with it. We spread out all of our data in tables so we—and Access—can see everything we have and find it quickly. This chapter covers some basics of what tables are and how you create them.

How do I begin to make a table?

Whenever you want to make a table, you have to put it in an existing or new database. Every database has its own file—one file, one database.

Before you can make a table, first create or open a database. You learned how to open a database in Chapter 2; but, to refresh your memory, select File, Open Database. Select the My personal stuff.mdb database that you created in Chapter 2, in the Open dialog box. Click OK, and the Database window will appear (see fig. 3.1).

Fig. 3.1
When you open a database, the Database window appears with the Tables tab selected.

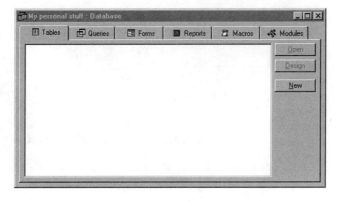

TIP **Here's a fast way to open a database you recently worked on.**
Select the File menu, which lists recently opened files at the bottom. Click your database's name.

The Tables tab, the first tab on the left, should be selected when you open the Database window. If it isn't, click it. Along the right side of the window there are three buttons: Open, Design, and New. You want to make a new table, so click New. (Since you don't have any tables yet, it's your only choice anyway.)

You can create a table in a number of ways (see fig. 3.2). For this example, we'll use Design View, so select it and then click OK. The window in figure 3.3 appears.

The Design view of a table is like an architect's blueprint. Builders plan their creations first before they pour the concrete; you design your table before you pour information into it. Fortunately, it's much easier to change the plan of a table than it is to redesign a 60-story tower. You will often find yourself in Design view changing the structure of your table—even after you thought all the pillars were in place.

TIP **When you first start using Access, all the screens can look alike.**
If you want to know if you're in Design view, click View on the menu bar. There should be a dot before Table Design, first on the list.

Fig. 3.2
The descriptions on the left can help you remember how each table creation method works.

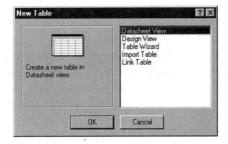

Fig. 3.3
The Design grid always
has three columns:
Field Name, Data
Type, and Description.

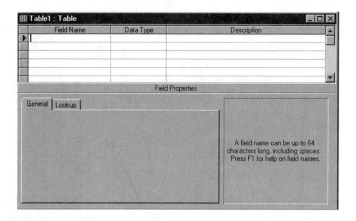

Q&A *I can't find my database to open it. I thought I saved it in the Access folder, but it isn't there.*

Don't worry, it's somewhere on your hard disk. At the top of the Open dialog box, click the Look In drop-down menu and select the hard drive in which Access is installed (usually your C: drive). Click the commands and settings icon and make sure Search subfolders is checked. Then, go to the Find Files That Match These Criteria section at the bottom of the Open dialog window. Type **My personal stuff.mdb** on the File Name line. Click Find Now and Access finds your file. Then click Open, and your database should open.

What is a field?

Think about your address book for a moment. You have entries for friends and loved ones, as well as for the window washer you used once in 1984 and haven't seen since. For each person, you have key information—the person's name, his street address and telephone number and maybe his city, state, and ZIP if he lives out of town.

Suppose you organized whatever information you have in your address book in rows and columns for easy reading (see fig. 3.4). Each type of information would go in a different column—one for their name, one for their address, and so on. In a database table, each of those columns would be called a **field**. So field is really just a fancy name for column. Remember, though, that each field contains one particular piece of information.

Fig. 3.4
The fields are the columns going down; the records are the rows going across.

First Name	Last Name	Street Address	City	State	ZIP	Telephone
John	Bartel	47 Quigby Lane				234-6677
Andrea	Donaldson	511 Winston	Monroe			254-7896
Laura	Cramer	72 Pine St.				234-5678
Jean	Sheinfeld	56 Winthrop				234-7563
Tom	Ehrlich	462 West Cove	Hawthorne	MD	20814	301-622-8976

If columns are fields, rows are...

Take another look at figure 3.4. Each row is one complete entry in your address book. Not all of the information is filled in for all of the rows, but that's fine. You've shown all the information you have and presumably need. In a database table, each of the rows is called a **record**. Each row contains information about the people in your life.

How do I name fields in a table?

Let's go ahead and make a table of your address book. When you're through, you'll have a table that looks like the one in figure 3.5. (It won't have any records in it yet—you'll learn how to enter them in Chapter 4.) For now, don't worry about the first column, or the first field, called ID. We're going to take it real easy and slow for the next few pages—I'll explain the ID field and everything else.

The first field could simply be First Name. In the design grid (which you encountered back in figure 3.3), type **First Name** directly under the column Field Name, as shown in figure 3.6.

 TIP Remember, when you're in Design view, you're not putting any of your data into the table. All you're doing is deciding what the table will look like. You'll put your information in afterwards.

Fig. 3.5
Putting your address
book in an Access
table will make finding
stuff a lot simpler.

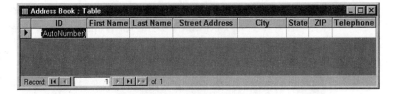

Fig. 3.6
Type the name of the
first field in the upper
left-hand corner.

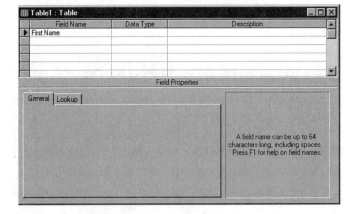

 Q&A *Why are you putting First Name in the first field? I want to be able to alphabetize everyone by Last Name. And do I really need separate fields for things I hardly use, like State and ZIP Code? Nearly all my friends live nearby.*

Those are excellent points. But within a couple of chapters, you'll see why they shouldn't concern you. You'll be able to view and use your table exactly as you want it.

What do I do after I name the field?

Press Tab to move over to the Data Type column. (You can also press Enter.) A bunch of stuff happens. First, the Field Properties section at the bottom of the window springs to life. The General tab is selected and lists ten field properties, some of which look fairly technical.

Don't worry—we'll talk a lot about Field Properties in Chapter 7. Right now, let's go back to the top of the table and look at what happened in the Data

Type column. In the first row, the word Text is highlighted. Click the **drop-down** arrow at the right of the box, and you will see the other types of data you can choose from (see fig. 3.7).

Fig 3.7
The Data Type menu offers several choices, of which Text is the most frequently used.

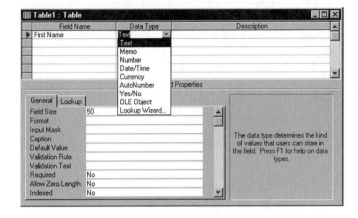

66 *Plain English, please!*

When you click a down arrow in a cell and see selections to choose from, that's a **drop-down menu**. These are great because you have all your choices staring at you, and you don't have to worry about making spelling mistakes. Simply click to make your selection. If you find it easier to just type what you want, though, you can do that too. 99

Look at your choices. Someone's first name would appear to be Text, right? As the **default** selection, Text is already highlighted, so just press Tab to select it. Now you're in the third column, Description. I'll discuss the Description column in a minute. Right now, let's fill in the rest of the field names, along with their data types.

66 *Plain English, please!*

The **default** selection is the choice you automatically get if you don't choose something else instead. In selecting Data Types, for example, Text is the default selection. You can pick some other data type by clicking the drop-down menu and choosing something else. But if you don't bother and just hit Tab, then you get Text. 99

I want to add some more fields

Press Tab again and you're in the Field Name column of the second row, below First Name. You can now create your second field. Take another look at your Address Book in figure 3.4. After the first name, you'll want the last name. To make Last Name your second field, follow these steps:

1 Type **Last Name** in the first column of the second row.

2 Press Tab to move over to the second column, Data Type.

3 Like a first name, someone's last name would also be Text. Text is already highlighted, so don't bother to click the drop-down menu. Just press Tab to select it.

4 You're now in the Description column. Leave it blank and press Tab to move to the next row and enter your next field.

The next field to enter would be Street Address. Type the field name **Street Address** in the first column and press Tab. What would be the Data Type? A street address is **alphanumeric text**, which is considered Text. Press Tab to enter Text, and press Tab again to move to the next field. Now add fields for the City and the State, both of which are Text.

 Plain English, please!

Alphanumeric text is text with both letters and numbers in it. That's not too hard to figure out—the *alpha* is from *alphabet*, and *numeric* is like *numerical*. The stuff on this page is alphanumeric text.

 TIP **You can move around the table design window by either using Tab** or the Arrow keys. If you want to move horizontally, Tab is faster, since it takes you directly from one box to the next. If you want to move straight up or down, use your arrow keys.

When a ZIP code is not a number

Now for the five-digit ZIP code. Surely that takes the Number data type, right?

Well, there are numbers and then there are *numbers*. In Access, you select the Text data type for numbers that accompany text, for example, 1600 Pennsylvania Avenue (a street address). But select the Number data type for numbers you want to do some type of calculation with.

Also, with a Number data type, you can only put in numbers—no hyphens, parentheses, or the odd letter allowed. So, if you wanted to put in a nine-digit ZIP with a hyphen, or you have a friend in London's swanky SW1 district, you'd be out of luck. It's the same thing with telephone numbers—the Data Type is Text. Go ahead and add fields for the ZIP Code and Telephone Number, which are both Text.

What is the Description column used for?

You might think of **Descriptions** as what you would name your field if you had lots and lots of space. Suppose you want something more revealing than Last Name in the second field? Something like "All the people I adore, except for Johnnie Jones, who I only talk to because he gets me tickets to the Steelers games"? You can put all that in the Description column in the last column at the right. When you are actually using the table you have created, that description would show up at the bottom of your Access screen whenever you're in the Name field. That's all a Description does—it is entirely optional.

Let's add a description for the Street Address field. You might want a reminder that "If it's summertime, make sure this is the right address." Click the Description column for Street Address and type in the text, and then press Tab. Don't worry if some of the text moves out of view as you type other text in. It's still all there.

Figure 3.8 shows what a table design for the address book would look like after typing in the field names, data types, and a description for the Street Address field. (If you can't see all of it, first maximize the Design window. Then click the vertical scroll bar to see all the fields at top.)

Fig 3.8
You can use the
optional Description
column for special
instructions for data
entry or to elaborate
on the field's purpose.

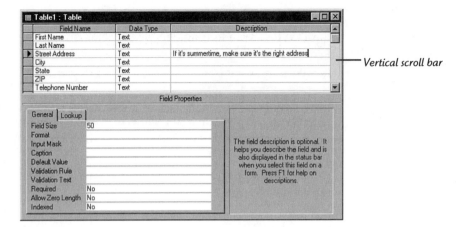

Vertical scroll bar

What if I want to change what I've done?

After you have finished designing your table, you may want to shift some
things around. Unlike the foundation of a 60-story building, a table's structure
is amenable to change. Moving, adding, and deleting fields can all be easily
accomplished with a few clicks of the mouse and sometimes a little typing.

How do I rearrange fields I've already set up?

In figure 3.8, Telephone Number is now the last field. Let's say you want to
see your friends' telephone numbers in the third column of the finished table,
right after their last names. You could move the Telephone Number field up
and put it after Last Name. To do so, follow these steps:

1 To the left of the field names is a small square called the **field selector**
  box (see fig. 3.9). Click it for the Telephone Number field. The entire
  row is now highlighted.

2 Now click the field selector box again and keep the mouse button
  depressed.

3 Drag the entire row up so that it sits right on top of the third field,
  Street Address.

4 Release the mouse button. The Telephone Number will now be right
  after Last Name.

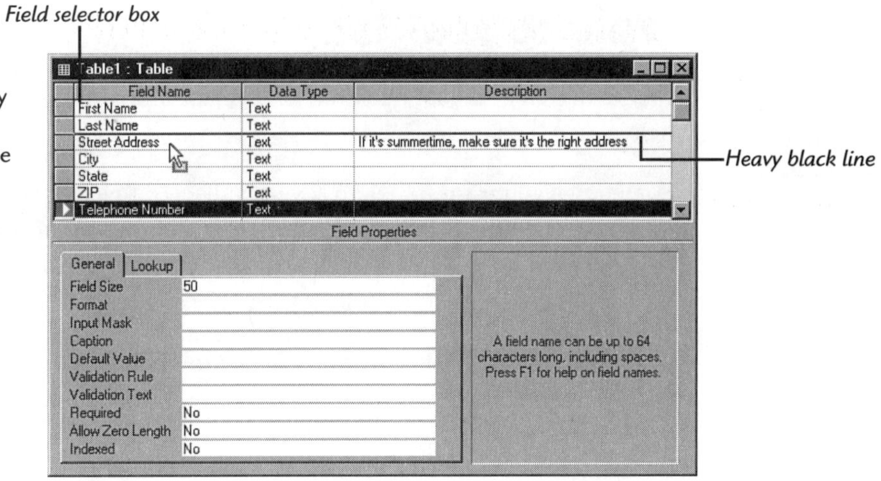

Field selector box

Fig. 3.9
Designate the field by clicking the field selector. Then drag the row, using the heavy black line as a guide.

Heavy black line

Field Name	Data Type	Description
First Name	Text	
Last Name	Text	
Street Address	Text	If it's summertime, make sure it's the right address
City	Text	
State	Text	
ZIP	Text	
Telephone Number	Text	

Field Properties

General | Lookup

Field Size	50
Format	
Input Mask	
Caption	
Default Value	
Validation Rule	
Validation Text	
Required	No
Allow Zero Length	No
Indexed	No

A field name can be up to 64 characters long, including spaces. Press F1 for help on field names.

5 Put the Telephone Number back where it was by clicking Edit, Undo Move.

Moving fields around isn't difficult, but it takes some practice to get good at it. When you move the field up or down, watch the dark horizontal line move with it. When moving up, the line shows where the top of the row will be when you release the mouse. When moving down, it shows the bottom.

Q&A *I just tried to move a field, but the only thing that happened was that each row got a lot higher.*

First, get your rows back to where they were by clicking Edit, Undo Row Height. Now you're ready to start over. When you grab the row to drag it, you want to see a white arrow with a little square around its tail. Drag with a different symbol, and something different will happen. Move the cursor slowly around the middle of the field selector box, away from both the top and bottom, to see the white arrow.

I'm all confused. Didn't you say the fields were the columns going down and the records were the rows going across? So why have you been talking about fields as rows?

Remember, we're just *designing* the table. Each row in Design view represents one field, or one column, in your table. You'll soon see that all the fields in Design view are columns on your table where you can input data.

How do I delete fields?

On the design grid, just click the field selector box of the field you want to delete, and then press Delete.

Sometimes you want to delete several adjacent fields at the same time. You may have used the Shift key to select adjacent files in the Windows Explorer. (If you haven't yet, don't worry about it—it's not hard to learn.) You can do the same thing in Access. Follow these steps:

1 Click the field selector box for the first field you want. Make sure you release the mouse button.

2 Press and hold Shift.

3 Click the last field you want to delete. All of the rows—first, last, and in-between—will be highlighted.

4 Release Shift.

5 Press Delete, as you would for a single field.

Similarly, you can use the Ctrl key to select and delete nonadjacent fields. Click the field selector box for the first field, hold down the Ctrl key, and click each row you want to delete. Release Ctrl, and then press Delete.

 TIP **You can use the same procedure to move several fields at once.** Select them as before, and then click and drag the fields where you want them.

I forgot to include a field

If you forgot a field, choose <u>I</u>nsert, <u>F</u>ield. A row is inserted on top of the row you're currently in, as indicated by the field selector arrow. Then just enter the field name and data type as you always do.

 TIP **Don't forget about the right mouse button. Click it in the row** below where you want to insert a new field. Then click Insert Row, and a new row is inserted. You can also use it to delete a row as well.

I want to get to work already!

Enough design. You're ready to start putting your stuff in the table. First, though, save your work. Click File, Save As/Export, and you see the Save As dialog (see fig. 3.10). The Within the Current Database As button should be selected; if not, click it.

Fig. 3.10
Save your table and give it an appropriate name.

What do you want to name your table? Access suggests Table1, which works if you don't feel like thinking of anything better. But you usually want something a little more descriptive, so you can identify the table later on. Call it Address Book. Table1 is already highlighted, so you can just start typing to replace it with the title you want, and then click OK.

The purpose of a primary key

Before you get to work, Access tells you there is no primary key defined and asks if you want one (see fig. 3.11). Your logical response is, "What's a primary key?"

Fig. 3.11
The text's warning notes the importance of a primary key in defining relationships.

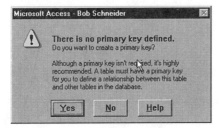

A **primary key** is information that uniquely identifies a record. For example, there are two huge electronics companies unofficially called General Electric, one based in the United States and the other in Britain. If you asked Access to find the yearly sales for General Electric, how would it know which one to choose? Access has to have a way to know you want to select a specific company—a unique piece of information. How can it do that?

Take a look at all the fields you have in your table. In each record, which field contains something that is unique—stuff that can't possibly ever be the same in another record?

People can live in the same state, have the same ZIP code, or live at the same address, so none of those things would make a good primary key. And we've seen that names, whether for companies or individuals, aren't unique. How many Smiths and Browns are there in the world? Even if you used the whole name, both First Name and Last Name together, that wouldn't be unique, would it?

Often the best solution is to simply give each record its own ID number. That's what Access does when you let it assign a primary key for you. It sets up an ID field, and its Data Type is AutoNumber. That means each time you add a record, the counter increases 1, 2, 3, and so on. That number is the primary key for each new record. That makes sense, doesn't it? They're like social security numbers. Often businesses that deal with millions of people identify us by them, because no two people have the same number.

Setting a primary key

 When Access reminds you there is no primary key and asks you if you want one, click Yes. Access sets up an ID field as your first field. If you have a better way and want to set the primary key on your own, first click the field you want to use as the primary key. Then click the right mouse button, and select Primary Key. The field used as the primary key will show a little key symbol in the Field Selector box.

A primary key using two fields

A primary key can also be two fields (not just one) taken together. Here's an example: Let's say the table you were designing was an appointment book for a dentist. This dentist never schedules two patients for the same time. So the primary key could be two fields together—the name of the patient, plus the time of the appointment. Each of those combinations is unique. If you want to designate two fields as the primary key, press Ctrl and select each field; then click the Primary Key button.

Q&A *I'm doing just a small table. Why can't I use the First Name and Last Name fields together as the primary key? It's unlikely that I'll have two people with the exact same name.*

It may be unlikely, or even highly unlikely, but not impossible. Small tables have a way of becoming large tables. Resetting the primary key of a big table can cause you lots of problems once you've got a good-sized database. Try to make certain that your primary key will be unique for each record—for now and always.

A primary key is indexed

Access also automatically creates an index for the primary key. Indexing in a database works much like the index of a book. It helps Access find the location of data and thus speeds up searches. In later chapters, you'll see the importance of the primary key in retrieving data and why it is indexed.

Now, finally, can I put my stuff in the table?

You're all set. To see the table you made and to start putting stuff in it, switch from Design view to **Datasheet** view.

 Plain English, please!

Datasheet may sound strange at first, but it's really quite straightforward. You have data and it goes on something that looks like an accountant's spreadsheet.

 Choose View, Datasheet, or click the Table View icon on the toolbar. It toggles (goes back and forth) between Design and Datasheet View. If you ever forget which is which, just click the drop-down menu arrow and it tells you. Ideally, your table should now look like the one in figure 3.12.

Don't be surprised if your table doesn't look exactly like the one in figure 3.12. First, depending on how you're running your computer—VGA, Super VGA, etc.—your display will differ. You may not even see all the fields on your screen; one or two on the far right may be out of sight. (In the figure, you don't see the full name of the last field, Telephone Number; you can click the horizontal scroll bar to see the full name.) Second, some fields have been resized for a better view.

Fig. 3.12
Switch to Datasheet view of a new table and you see an empty record. In the next chapter, you'll learn how to enter data into it.

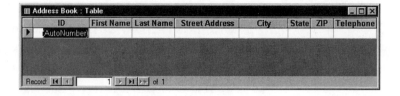

A couple of fields that are out of sight is no big deal; as you enter data across your table, they'll come into view. But if you want to fit more fields on your screen, follow these steps:

1 Select the first field (ID) by clicking in its field selector box. You should see an arrow pointing down in the box with the Field title.

2 Now hold down the Shift key and select the last field, Telephone Number. (If the Telephone Number field is off your screen, click the horizontal scroll bar to get to it.) All your fields should now be highlighted.

3 Choose Format, Column Width. You'll see the Column Width dialog box (see fig. 3.13).

Fig. 3.13
Choose Best Fit for a better looking table.

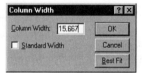

4 In the Column Width dialog box, choose Best Fit.

5 Choose File, Save, if you want to save your changes. Maybe you liked it better the way you had it. Then just choose No when Access asks you, when you close the table, if you want your layout changes saved.

Does your table look better now? It should. It still might not be all you want it to be, though. You may not be able to see all the field titles, or even all the fields. Don't worry about it. In the first place, the fields are all there—you just may not be able to see all of them at one time. And second, this won't be much of a problem after you read the next chapter.

The Art of Database Maintenance

● **In this chapter:**

- **Start putting information into your table**

- **Can't I move around this table faster?**

- **I made a mistake—how do I edit it?**

- **I need wider columns and higher rows**

- **Show me how to hide and freeze columns**

- **How do I delete stuff?**

Entering data into a database can be a thankless chore, but the flexibility of an Access table eases the pain. . . . . ❯

As a kid, did you ever keep score at a baseball game? There was hardly any room to write out anything on the scorecard because all the columns were about three millimeters wide. So you used these really obscure abbreviations, like 5-3 for a groundout to third—or was that a triple to center?

Maybe you've never tried to score a ballgame. But you've probably made a table by hand that wound up looking a mess. You stuck the wrong stuff in the right boxes. You stuck the right stuff in the wrong boxes. You made some columns too narrow...well, you get the idea.

Access has all kinds of features to make sure your tables don't wind up looking like the scorecard of an 18-inning baseball game. This chapter tells you how to enter information in tables and how to make them look neat and tidy.

How do I begin to enter data in a table?

OK, you're ready to get to work. First, you need to open a table, if you don't have one open already. You could work on the Address Book table you designed in the last chapter. It's in the My personal stuff.mdb database you created in Chapter 2.

1 Click File and select the My personal stuff.mdb database near the bottom of the menu. If it's not there, choose Open Database near the top of the menu. Then locate your database, and open it.

2 In the Database window, click the Table tab on the far left (it should be selected already). You'll see the Address Book table listed and highlighted.

3 Click the Open button. Your table will open in Datasheet view, ready to accept entries (see fig. 4.1).

4 Maximize your window if it's not already so. (You can see more this way.)

Fig. 4.1
In Datasheet view you
see an empty record
ready for data entry.

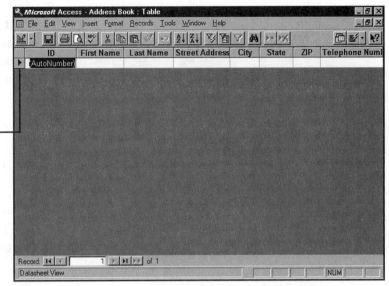

Record selector box. A
triangle shows this row
(record) is selected.

Q&A ***I'm lost. The table says Address Book on top. But the
column headings I see say Field Name, Data Type, and
Description. Isn't that what I was working on last
chapter?***

You've got the right table but the wrong view. In Chapter 3 you designed
the table, so you were in Design view. Now you want to *enter* data, so you
want to be in Datasheet view. Select View, Datasheet to begin entering your
information.

If your first column is an ID like the one in figure 4.1, that field will take care
of itself. No need to type anything here. Each time you enter another record,
the ID will increase by one and uniquely identify your record. (Peek back at
the end of the last chapter if you don't remember why this is so.) Now enter
the information for the first row, or the first record.

1 Press Tab to get to the second field, First Name. The cursor will be
flashing in the box.

2 Type **John**, or **Susan**, or whatever first name you want.

3 Press Tab again to go to the next field, Last Name. Type **Wilson**, or
McDougal, or whatever.

4 Press Tab to move to the next field. Type in the Street Address.

5 Continue entering data across the row by pressing Tab to move to the field, and then typing your data. Don't worry if you have nothing to put in a particular field—leave it empty and tab again.

6 After you finish typing in the last field, press Tab again. You now jump to the beginning of the second record. Your table should look something like figure 4.2.

Fig. 4.2
In the first column, don't let the term AutoNumber bother you—it just means that field will take care of itself.

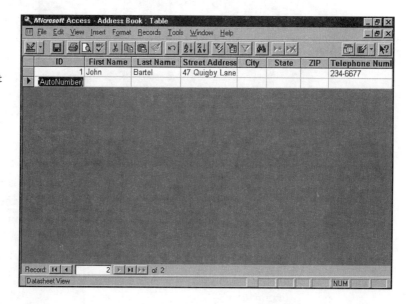

 TIP **You can press Enter to go from field to field, if that's easier for you.** If you skip a field, go back by pressing Shift+Tab.

Record status at a glance

Let's add a few more records following the same procedure. Note the symbols in the record selector box (to the left of the first field) of your table (see fig. 4.2). These symbols change along with the record's status. You've finished a record and pressed tab, so there's a pointer in the selector box of the next record. This symbol shows the record you're now in.

As soon as you start making additions or changes, the symbol changes to a pencil. That means you're now editing this record, and some of the changes may not be saved yet. A star symbol indicates a new, blank record at the end of the datasheet. You don't have to worry about running out of space at the bottom—you can keep on adding record after record.

Q&A *What's the story? The records in your table aren't in any kind of alphabetical order. Sure, there's the ID, but what good does that do?*

Tables are the building blocks of your database. Their primary function is to store your information so you can manipulate it later. Soon you will be learning all kinds of ways to sort your data. Don't worry if things aren't in alphabetical order right now—you'll be alphabetizing them, and more, in a little while.

How do I save my data?

Most of the time, computer books and manuals are constantly imploring you to save your work. But when you enter data in Access, your work is saved automatically. Press Tab in the last field of a row and move to a new record—the data you've just entered in that previous row is now saved. When you close a table, any work that hasn't been saved is automatically saved for you. Even if the power goes off, your data is still safely saved to disk.

CAUTION **Access saves your work for you when you enter *data* in tables.** But when you modify the *design* or *layout* of a table, those changes aren't automatically saved. You have to tell Access specifically that you want to keep them. Access will prompt you before letting you exit and ask if you want design changes saved, so you don't have to worry too much about it. If you're spending a long time on designing a table, you'll want to save regularly. That way you can be sure you don't lose any of your work.

I can only see part of this really long address

If you have a long entry in one cell and you want to see the whole thing, Zoom it up by pressing Shift+F2. In record #6, John Cyborg lives at 53

Crescent Way North. Part of the address is out of view. By using Zoom, you can see the full address at once (see fig. 4.3).

Fig. 4.3
As you can see from the size of the box and the scroll bars on the side, Zoom can handle a *lot* more data than shown here.

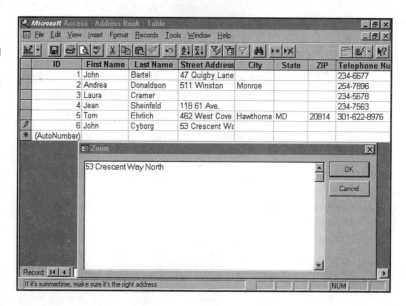

Using Keyboard Shortcuts

Access has many keyboard shortcuts to help you get from here to there. Some may be familiar to you from your experience with other Windows programs. (If not, that's no problem.) Table 4.1 summarizes ways to get you moving around Access faster. Don't bother to memorize them all—you'll pick them up over time as you use the program more.

Right now, getting around quickly may not seem like such a big deal. Your tables may be small, and you may just be entering data record by record. Once you start editing them and changing stuff around, you'll appreciate some additional navigation techniques.

TIP   **Remember, you always have the mouse to get where you want. If** you can't remember the keyboard strokes, or you just like using the mouse better, you can always click the cell you want.

Table 4.1 Getting around Access

Where you want to get to	How to get there
The next field	Tab or Enter
The previous field	Shift+Tab
The next record	Down arrow
The previous record	Up arrow
The first field of the current record	Home
The last field of the current record	End
The first field of the first record	Ctrl+Home
The last field of the last record	Ctrl+End
Down a page (i.e., a whole bunch) of records	Page Down
Up a page (i.e., a whole bunch) of records	Page Up

I want to change some records

Did you forget to put something in a record? Want to change something you've put in? Do you have additional records to enter? Editing records in Access may not always be a joy or a pleasure, but it's easily accomplished.

I want to put something else in a saved record

Suppose you find out that Laura Cramer, ID #3, lives on 72 Pine Street (see fig. 4.3). Click the Street Address field for that record and you'll see the flashing cursor. Type in **72 Pine Street** and you're done.

I just need to change a couple of letters or numbers

Of course, you can use your backspace key to erase data within cells. You can also highlight the text with your mouse and delete it by pressing Delete.

Suppose that Jean Sheinfeld, ID #4, moved up the street, from 118 61 Ave. to 138 61 Ave. Instead of retyping the whole value, just place the mouse pointer after the 11, click, and backspace once. Then just type in **3** and you're done.

I want to get rid of stuff I just put in the table

 Lots of times in life we think, Boy, I wish I didn't do what I just did. In Access, if you make a mistake and catch it fast enough, you can often just Undo it. Access has a bunch of different ways to Undo actions, and then Undo previous actions. You can also Undo what you just undid. Table 4.2 shows how you can accomplish the key Undo tasks easily using a variety of keyboard, menu bar, and toolbar techniques.

Table 4.2   Undoing in Access

What I want to Undo	How to Undo it
The data I just typed in	Press Esc
Something I just did	Click Undo button
Everything in the current record	Click Edit, Delete Record
Everything in the record I just saved	Press Ctrl+Z

How to replace a value in a record

 Suppose you find out Jean Sheinfeld, ID#4, has moved again, this time off 61 Avenue entirely. You want to get rid of her old address and type in an entirely new one. Move the mouse to the far left end of the cell containing the old address. When the pointer changes to a big white plus sign, click. The entire box is now highlighted. Then just type in the new address, **56 Winthrop**.

 *Plain English, please!*

A **value** is information that happens to be in any particular cell. It can be text, or numbers, or whatever else.

I want to shift some things around

Sometimes you'll want to move or copy certain information from one part of a table to another. Like any Windows program, you can use Cut, Copy and Paste. Each has a button on the toolbar. You can also use the Edit menu or shortcut keys. If you forget what these or any other icons do, use the trick you learned earlier—leave the mouse pointer on the icon for a second or so, and it will tell you what it does. Table 4.3 summarizes the ways you can Cut, Copy, and Paste.

Table 4.3   Cut, copy, and paste

Command	Menu Bar	Toolbar	Shortcut Key
Cut	Edit, Cut	✂	Ctrl+X
Copy	Edit, Copy	📋	Ctrl+C
Paste	Edit, Paste	📋	Ctrl+V

Cut, copy, and paste are not available all the time under all circumstances. For instance, you can't paste until you've cut or copied something. Let me go over a few ways to use these commands.

I want to move information in one cell

Suppose you typed **John** in the Last Name field of a record and you want to put it in the right place, in the First Name field. Double-click John to select the text, then click Edit, Cut (or click the cut toolbar button). Click anywhere in the First Name field and select Edit, Paste or click the Paste button.

 TIP   **What if you want to replace text when you Paste? Instead of** simply clicking in the box where you'll paste, highlight the text that's there. When you Paste, the old text will be replaced with the new.

You can move just part of a name too. Suppose you typed Billy Walston in the Last Name field and want to move the Billy part to the First Name field. Just highlight Billy with the mouse, then Cut. Click in the First Name field and Paste. You can follow the same steps to copy data. Just choose Copy instead of Cut.

Q&A *I highlighted the text with my mouse, but when I try to Cut, Access won't let me.*

Did you highlight just the text, or is the entire cell black? If you selected the entire box, it won't work. Just select the text by moving the mouse pointer through it. For an entire word, double-click it, then Cut.

I want to copy data from several cells

You can copy data from several cells to the same number of cells on your table. Suppose Tom Ehrlich and John Cyborg live in the same city and state, and have the same ZIP Code. You could just Copy those three values from Tom's record to John's.

1 Select the cells to Copy by dragging the mouse pointer across them (Begin at the left of the first cell where you see the white cross).

2 Copy to the Clipboard using your favorite method.

3 Highlight the cells where you want to paste by dragging the mouse pointer across them (see fig. 4.4). If there's data in these cells, you can copy right over it. Make sure you've highlighted the same number of cells as you copied to the Clipboard.

4 Select Paste, using your favorite method.

I want to move an entire field

After working with a table for a while you may want to change the field order. Perhaps it would be nice to have the Telephone Number field go right after Last Name. You can move entire columns, or fields, in the table very easily.

Fig. 4.4
Highlight the area for the new data before you paste. You can paste over existing data.

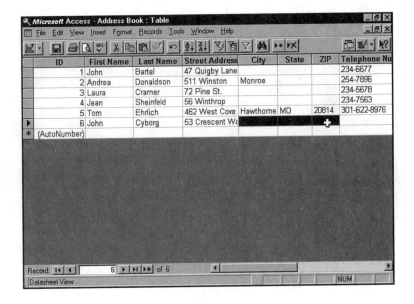

For instance, to move the Telephone Number field, follow these steps:

1 Position the mouse pointer at the top of the field you want to move. Click when you see the vertical black arrow to highlight the entire column (see fig. 4.5).

2 Point the mouse again at the middle of the field title (don't get too close to the borders!). Click again, and keep the mouse button depressed. You'll see a little box around the tail of the white arrow.

3 Now drag the field where you want it. Notice the heavy, solid, vertical bar that jumps between fields as you drag (see fig. 4.6). That would be the far edge of the field if you released the mouse at that point. Release the mouse button.

Did the field wind up where you wanted it? No? It should still be highlighted, so try dragging it again. You could also try dragging it back where you started from.

Fig. 4.5
When you see the vertical black arrow, you can select the field.

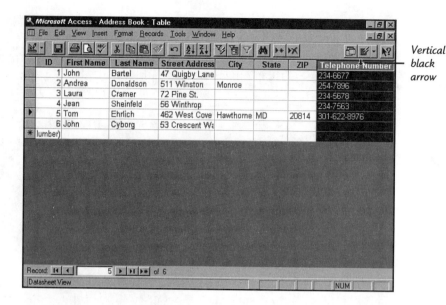

Vertical black arrow

Fig. 4.6
The heavy black vertical line shows the new left border for the field in motion.

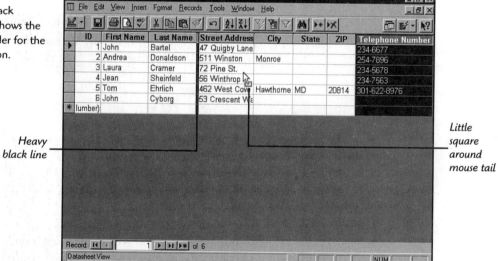

Heavy black line

Little square around mouse tail

I want to change the way my table looks

Access has many features to make your table look just as you want it. You can make columns wider or narrower, and rows higher or shorter. You can hide columns you don't want to see, and show ones you do.

Make the column wider

Remember how you had to Zoom up the Street Address in one record to see the whole thing in one glance (refer to fig. 4.3)? Suppose you widen the Street Address column so that you can see all the data in the records.

1 Move the pointer just at the border between Street Address and City. You should see a double-arrow with bar pointer, like the one in figure 4.7.

2 Click and hold your mouse button. The vertical black line in the figure will appear. That's the guide that tells you how wide your column will be when you release the mouse.

3 Drag to the right to open up enough room for the full street address of John Cyborg, 53 Crescent Way North.

4 Try readjusting the widths of other fields, making them narrower and wider as you see fit.

Fig. 4.7
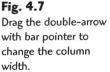
Drag the double-arrow with bar pointer to change the column width.

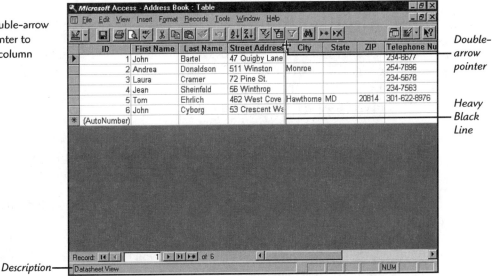

Is there an easier way to adjust a fields width?

You can adjust the column width of a field so there's just enough room to see all the data. And you can do it without hunting around for funny-looking symbols and dragging stuff. You've seen the Best Fit command before—now use it for a single field. Select the field where you want to see every last character. Choose Format, Column Width. Then click the Best Fit button in the lower right-hand corner of the Column Width dialog box, and click OK.

 CAUTION **Note that Best Fit is not a permanent solution to the field width dilemma.** If you choose it, and then type a value that won't fit, you'll have to select Best Fit again.

If you don't like dragging fields, you can also change the column width by typing in a new measurement in the Column Width box (see fig. 4.8).

Fig. 4.8
In the Column Width dialog box, you can choose Best Fit or type a specific measurement.

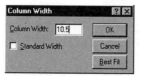

I don't need to see all these fields all the time

Let's say you have one of those 36-column, super-sized tables. It's pretty tough to squeeze all those fields on a 14-inch—or even a 17-inch—monitor. Even in the small Address Book table, it's tough to see every last value on one screen. One solution is the Hide command.

By using Hide, you can see those fields that are most important to you. When you Hide fields, they aren't erased and nothing happens to their data. They are just hidden from the screen until you wish to bring them back.

To Hide a field, first select it (as seen in fig. 4.5) by clicking its field selector. Click Format, Hide Columns, and it's gone.

 TIP **Instead of using the menu bar, you can also choose commands** from the short menus invoked by clicking the right mouse button. The Column Width, Hide Columns, and other commands will be available when you select a field and click.

Now you want it back? Click Format, Unhide Columns. You'll see a list of all your fields (see fig. 4.9). The fields that are currently in view are checked at left. To show a hidden field, simply click the checkbox. It now has a check mark and is visible on the table. If you want to Hide some other columns, you can do it in the same dialog box. Then why do you need a separate Hide Columns command on the Format menu? You don't, really—it's just faster and simpler.

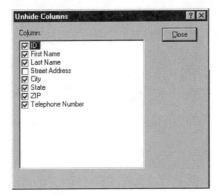

Fig. 4.9
Choose the Unhide Columns dialog box at any time to see which fields of your table are currently in view.

I always want this field to be on-screen, no matter what

As you tab right across a table, the fields scroll out of view to the left. But what if it's important that one or more of those fields remains visible at all times? For instance, in the Address Book table, you might want the First Name and Last Name fields always visible at left, whether you're in the third column or the one-hundred-and-third.

This is easy to do by **freezing** the fields, which makes them always visible. Select the field or fields you want to freeze. Then choose Format, Freeze Columns. As you move right across the table, the fields you froze will remain in view. If you decide you don't have to see them after all, click Format, Unfreeze All Columns. They'll move out of view when they're supposed to.

I'd like to make the rows a little taller

If you have problems reading the rows in your table, you might have more success if you increased the height of each row, so there's more white space between the text lines.

To change a rows height, drag it just the same as you did the width. Place the mouse pointer on the border of any two record selector boxes (see fig. 4.10). Do you see the double-arrow with bar? Click and hold the mouse button. Move it up to make all the rows higher.

The downside of making rows higher in a long table is that you see fewer records on your screen. To make the rows shorter, simply drag in the opposite direction, going down.

Fig. 4.10

When you see the double-arrow with bar, hold down the mouse button. Move it up to make the rows shorter, and down to make them longer.

Symbol for changing row width

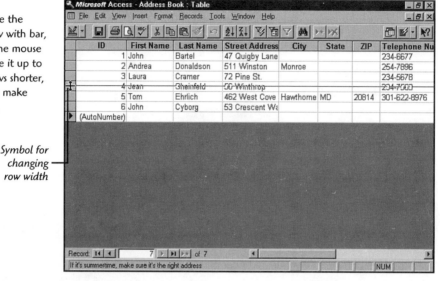

This small type is hard for me to read

Another thing you can do to make reading easier is change the font size. You can also change the font (Arial, MS Sans Serif) and font style (Italic, Bold, and so on).

1 Choose F<u>o</u>rmat, <u>F</u>ont to open the Font dialog box (see fig. 4.11).

2 Select the <u>F</u>ont, Font St<u>y</u>le, and <u>S</u>ize that you find attractive. Take a look at the Sample box. Each time you make a change, the Sample box shows you what your font will look like. Play around with different combinations until you find the right combination for you.

3 Click OK.

Fig. 4.11
Underline the values in your table by checking the Underline box in the Effects section.

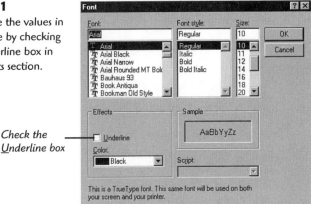

Check the Underline box

I think I could use another field

You've already entered five or six records and then think, "Gee, it sure would be nice to have a separate field for people's nicknames." How could you add an additional Text field?

1 Select the field that you want to follow the new field. For example, select the Street Address field if you want the new field to go between Last Name and Street Address.

2 Click Insert, Column. A new column is inserted between the Last Name and Address fields called Field 1.

3 Double-click on Field 1, and type the new field name.

4 Press Enter. The field is ready for data entry.

The Data Type of a single field created in Datasheet view is, by default, Text. You can change the Data Type of the new field in Design view. Click View, Table Design (or the Table View icon), locate the new field in the list of Field Names, and select another Data Type from the drop-down menu.

TIP **You know how to change the name of any field in Design view.**
But it can be faster and simpler to do it in Datasheet View. Double-click the field name. You can now edit the name. Press Enter when you're done.

I want to add a field description

When you were in the Street Address field, a description appeared in the lower left-hand corner. (Refer to fig. 4.9 to see this.) You can add descriptions for other fields if you'd like. Switch back to Design view, add the Description for the chosen field or fields, and save your changes.

Are you getting some feeling for the dynamic relationship between Design and Datasheet view? While you can enter data only in Datasheet view, some Design functions can be done in both views. To see the structure and the guts of your table, however, you will want to be in Design view. You'll spend more time in Design view when you learn about Field Properties in Chapter 7.

How do I delete records?

You can delete records one by one, a few at a time, or all in one fell swoop. You can even get rid of the entire table.

Deleting a single record

Click the record selector box for the row you want. The entire row will be highlighted. Then press Delete. Access will come back with a complicated message that actually means "Do you really want to delete this record?" Choose Yes.

CAUTION If you have more than one table in your database, deleting records from one may have an impact on the others. These issues will be discussed in Chapter 6.

Q&A *I keep clicking inside the record selector box, but the field isn't highlighted.*

Did your mouse curser change to a black arrow? You have to see that arrow—any other won't do. Move the mouse pointer toward the middle of the box and keep it away from the borders.

Deleting multiple records at a time

Use the Shift key to highlight more than one record at a time. Highlight the first record you want to delete, press and hold Shift, then click the record selector box for the last row you want to dump. The first, last, and all rows in between will be highlighted. Press Delete, and then click OK when you're asked to confirm the change.

Deleting all records in a table

If you're totally disgusted by all of what you've done thus far and just want to start from scratch with a clean slate, choose <u>E</u>dit, Select <u>A</u>ll Records. All the records will be highlighted. Then just press Delete, and confirm the change. You're ready to start over.

 CAUTION **Be sure you really want to delete all records—not just those that** you've added since the last time you opened the table. Select All Records includes all those records you can't see because they've scrolled off your screen.

Deleting an entire table

If you decide the entire table isn't for you, or it's just duplicating another table in your database, you can delete the whole thing. If you're working on the table, close it. Select the table in the Database window and choose <u>E</u>dit, De<u>l</u>ete, then confirm the change.

Needless to say, dumping an entire table is a major step, so be sure there isn't anything in there that you really want to save.

5

Faster, Better Ways to Make Tables

● In this chapter:

- **What are the Access wizards?**

- **A visit with the Table Wizard**

- **Field Builder speeds up adding new fields**

- **Make a table quickly in Datasheet View**

A wizard in Access can do for your databases what an ATM does for your bank accounts—guide you through standard transactions quickly and efficiently . . . . ▷

Automatic teller machines get lots of bad press these days: panhandlers and robbers can lurk nearby, banks haven't saved much money by installing them, and customers who use the machines sometimes find unexpected charges on their next bank statements. Still, it's undeniable that ATMs are convenient. Why? Because they anticipate most of our banking needs, and allow us to finish transactions in a matter of seconds, simply by pushing a few buttons.

An Access **wizard** works that way, too. You press a few buttons to get started, then answer a few questions that the wizard asks. Within a few seconds, out pops anything you need—a brand-new table, a dazzling form, $1,000 in cash…all right, *almost* anything you need.

Of course, an ATM can be less than perfect. It might spit out twenties when you really want tens, or prove inflexible in some other way. Access wizards are more user-friendly, and if a wizard doesn't give you exactly what you want, you can easily go back and change some things.

What's so great about a wizard?

You might have encountered wizards in another program such as Microsoft Word. In Access, you can use a Table Wizard to make great-looking tables efficiently and quickly. Let's spend a moment on the wizard concept so you can see why they're so helpful.

A wizard asks you key questions about the job at hand. Usually, it requests some specific information, but occasionally it asks your preference for how to do something when there are two or three possible ways. The wizard then gives you about 90 percent of what you need to finish your task. You might have to change little things here and there, but most of the work for the job you're doing has been handled by the wizard.

How do I start using the Table Wizard?

When you're ready to create a new table, have the Table Wizard help you. First, open a database by choosing <u>F</u>ile, <u>O</u>pen Database.

1 In the Database window, click the Tables tab, then click <u>N</u>ew.

2 In the New Table dialog box, choose Table Wizard and click OK (see fig. 5.1). Depending on your computer's firepower, you might have to wait a

few seconds for Access to open the wizard. After it does, the Table Wizard appears (see fig. 5.2). Now you can begin to create your table.

Fig. 5.1

Choose Table Wizard from this list to begin making a table.

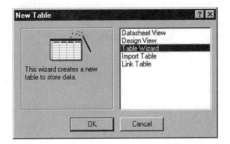

What's all this stuff in the Table Wizard?

There's a lot going on in the first screen of the Table Wizard (see fig. 5.2). At the left, there's a Sample Tables list. When you select a table from this list by clicking on it, notice that the Sample Fields list in the second column changes.

Fig. 5.2

Here's the first screen of the Table Wizard.

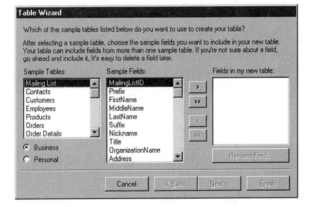

Actually, the tables in the Sample Tables list represent only about half of the tables available to you. Below the Sample Tables list are two option buttons, Business and Personal. Click whichever one isn't already selected, and the Sample Tables list changes to show a different set of tables. You can switch freely between the two lists to find the tables you need.

 TIP **In the Sample Tables and Sample Fields lists, you can press** Ctrl+Home to move to the beginning of the list, or Ctrl+End to move to the end.

Select a sample table and fields

In Chapter 3, "Tables: The Basic Building Blocks of Your Database," we worked through several steps to make an Address Book table. Now, let's create the same table with Table Wizard.

First, select a sample table that's similar to the table you want to make. The Address Book table is for your personal needs, so look at the Personal list. Click Personal, and the first selection in the Sample Tables list—which is already chosen for you—is Addresses. Look in the Sample Fields column, and its fields turn out to be similar to those you'd like to have in the Address Book table.

Now you're ready to select specific fields for your table. There are lots of choices in the Sample Fields list (you can scroll down to see more). You probably don't need many of these fields, but you might find some great ideas here. For this example, let's just select fields that are the same or similar to those we used for the Address Book in Chapter 3 (see fig. 5.3).

Note that with the Table Wizard, you don't have to worry about data types. When you select a Sample field, the wizard assumes it knows what data type you want (and usually does). After creating a table with the wizard, it's a good idea to go into Design view and check to see which data types the wizard has selected.

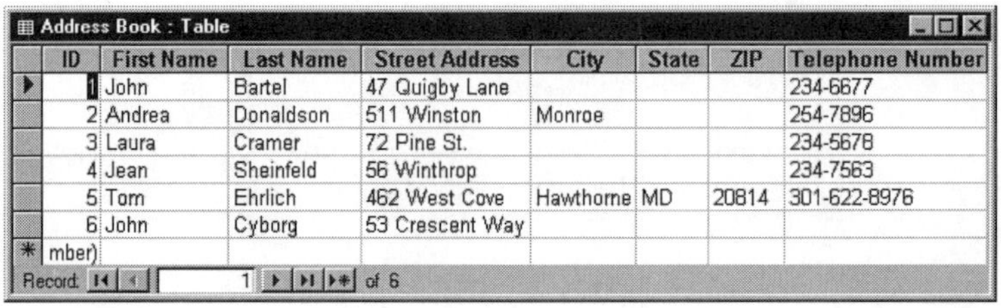

Fig. 5.3

To follow my example, choose fields from the Sample Fields list that match or resemble the fields shown in this figure.

ID	First Name	Last Name	Street Address	City	State	ZIP	Telephone Number
1	John	Bartel	47 Quigby Lane				234-6677
2	Andrea	Donaldson	511 Winston	Monroe			254-7896
3	Laura	Cramer	72 Pine St.				234-5678
4	Jean	Sheinfeld	56 Winthrop				234-7563
5	Tom	Ehrlich	462 West Cove	Hawthorne	MD	20814	301-622-8976
6	John	Cyborg	53 Crescent Way				

The four different arrow buttons to the right of the Sample Fields list are used to select and deselect fields for your table. Table 5.1 shows what each of these buttons does.

Table 5.1 What do these arrow buttons do?

Button	What happens when you click it?
[>]	Adds whatever field is highlighted in the Sample Fields list to the Fields in My New Table list.
>>	Adds all fields in the Sample Fields list to the Fields in My New Table list.
<	Removes whatever field is highlighted in the Fields in My New Table list from that list.
<<	Removes all fields from the Fields in My New Table list.

Right now, we'll use the button at the top, the > button, to select fields for our table. Click FirstName, then click the > button. FirstName is added to the Fields in My New Table list.

Now, select the other fields for the Address Book table. All of them are in the Sample Field list, but the names might vary from what you saw in figure 5.3. For example, the figure shows ZIP Code, but the wizard only offers PostalCode. That's no big deal, but if you want ZIP Code rather than PostalCode, you can change the name easily. Make sure PostalCode is highlighted in the Fields in My New Table list, then click the Rename Field button. Type a new name in the Rename Field edit box, then click OK. The revised field name appears in the Fields in My New Table list.

If you haven't changed any field names, your Table Wizard screen should look like figure 5.4.

Fig. 5.4
For this example you've selected some of the the more common address fields. But the Sample Fields column displays other useful fields that you can choose.

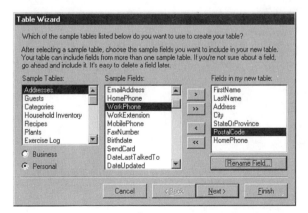

Name your table and select a primary key

Let's move on to other parts of Table Wizard. Click the Next button to get to the next wizard screen.

The wizard asks, "What do you want to name your table?" It offers a suggestion, which you can accept by pressing Tab (see fig. 5.5). If you want to name it something else, just begin to type, and the suggested name disappears. The only real requirements for a table name are that it reminds you what type of data's in there, and that it's not the same as any other table name in that database.

Fig. 5.5
In this screen, you name the table and set the primary key.

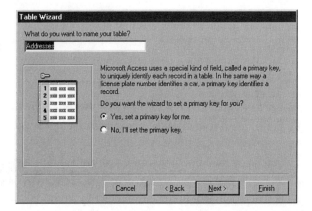

The next issue is how to set the primary key. As we saw in Chapter 3, it's not a good idea to use a person's name as the primary key. You probably want some kind of counter field (i.e., an AutoNumber Field) for the primary key. Access knows all about setting up counter ID fields, and can create one on its own. So let's have the wizard set the primary key for us. Click the Next button to move forward.

CAUTION   **If your database has other tables, you'll see a screen where you** can determine relationships between existing tables and the new one you're creating. You might need to visit Chapter 6 to learn about relationships before you fill in this part of the wizard.

Q&A   ***What if I want to change a field?***

The fields you originally selected aren't carved in stone. After the Table Wizard creates this table, you can always change things around in Design view. If, however, you want to change fields while you're still in the Table Wizard (maybe you've decided, "Oops, I'd better put in a field for fax numbers"), just click the Back button at the bottom of the Table Wizard screen until you arrive at the first screen. You can change the Fields in My New Table list as much as you want. Then click Next to move to the subsequent screens again, or just click Finish.

Putting on the final touches

You've given Access all the information it needs to create a table (see fig. 5.6). It offers three options for how you want the table delivered:

If you want to...	Select this option
View the table in Design view first	Modify the table design.
Start putting stuff in your table right now	Enter data directly into the table.
Create a data entry form	Enter data into the table using a form the wizard creates for me.

Click one of these option buttons, then choose Finish.

Of course, if there's something you need to add or change because the wizard couldn't do it for you, you'll want to head to Design view first. Even if you think the wizard took care of everything, it might still be a useful learning experience to go to Design view and look at the table's inner workings.

Fig. 5.6
Your table's almost done...how do you want it delivered?

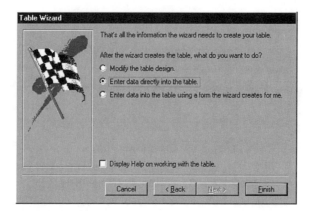

I want to change something the wizard did

Take a look at your new table in Design view (see fig. 5.7). Notice that Access has created a primary key for you; it's named AddressesID. Perhaps you'll use this table to keep track of members in your neighborhood association, and MemberID would make more sense than AddressesID. You can change any undesirable field name; just double-click to highlight it, then type a new name, and press Enter.

You can type text in the Description column to help you remember what kind of information belongs in a particular field. These descriptions are optional, and the Table Wizard doesn't create them for you.

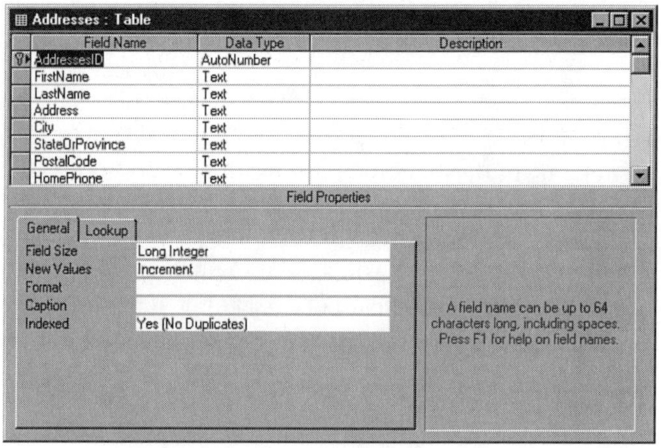

Fig. 5.7
In Design view, you can change some of what the wizard did.

Finally, look at the data types the wizard has assigned to each field. The primary key is AutoNumber, and the rest of the fields are Text. That's probably what you would've selected on your own.

If you now want to begin to enter data in your table, you can switch to Datasheet view by clicking the Table View icon or choosing View, Datasheet. Save your changes if you have made any.

Adding a field with Field Builder

Table Wizard is a great convenience. From time to time, though, you might make a table without a wizard. Or, you might already have a table—made with or without a wizard—and decide it needs some other fields. Access has a tool named Field Builder that can help you out.

Figure 5.8 shows Field Builder at work. Looks mighty familiar, doesn't it? Field Builder's basically a rerun of the field selection part of the Table Wizard.

Fig. 5.8
The Field Builder contains most of the stuff that's on the first screen of the Table Wizard.

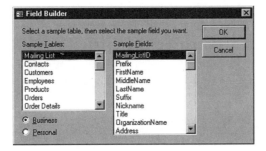

Just as in the Table Wizard, the sample tables here are divided between Business and Personal. You select a sample table from the list on the left, and the list on the right changes to show the fields included in that table. Then, you select fields from this list. The only difference is that you're adding new fields to an existing table, not to a new table.

Here's how to start adding new fields:

1 In Design view, click in the first empty box below your current fields; this ensures that your new field is added at the end. If you want to add the new field between two existing fields, click in the existing field that should follow the new field.

2 Click the right mouse button on the selected line, then choose Field Builder from the resulting shortcut menu. The Field Builder screen appears (refer to fig. 5.8).

3 Select a table from the Sample Tables list (click on it), then click a field from the Sample Fields list.

4 Choose OK.

A nice thing about using Field Builder is that the data type and field properties—both of which are covered in detail in Chapter 7, "Designing Database Tables"—are automatically selected for you.

When you go into a diner and order a cheeseburger, you'll probably get it on a hamburger bun with American cheese; the Grill Wizard (that is, the cook) assumes that's how you want it. If you prefer your burgers with Swiss cheese on an onion bun, you need to make special requests. It's the same way with Field Builder—when you choose a field, you get the most common data type and property settings. If you want to change them, it's not a problem.

 TIP Take some time to browse through the sample tables; you'll get lots of ideas about how to use Access. Haven't you craved a way to keep track of home videos? Been meaning to inventory your valuables for insurance purposes? Make a note of the tables that look useful.

Create a new table in Datasheet view

Computer companies often send people out to demonstrate their products to user groups. When users are impressed with a feature, they reward the speaker with audible oohs, or sometimes a less-enthusiastic-but-still-respectable ah. Occasionally speakers expect an ooh, but only get a slight eh.

On the scale of ooh, ah, and eh, creating a table in Datasheet view is a definite ooh. Here's how it works: you type field names directly on the table, then enter a few actual records. Access looks at what you've done, figures out which data type you want, and assigns the field properties.

Sounds great—where do I begin?

Start by clicking the <u>N</u>ew button in the Tables tab of the Datasheet window. You get the New Table dialog box (refer to fig. 5.1). Choose Datasheet View and get the screen shown in figure 5.9.

Fig. 5.9
The current field titles are just placeholders—you'll replace them with the field names you want.

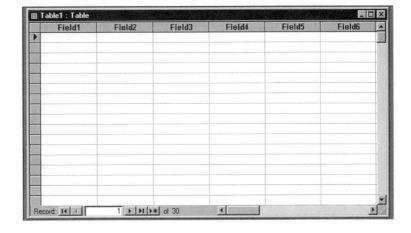

There are 20 columns down and 30 rows across, which should be plenty for starting off a new table. After you save this table, of course, you can add as many fields and records as you want.

Let's make a simple table from the data shown in Table 5.2, which shows the video rentals of a movie lover with eclectic tastes.

Table 5.2   Our fictional friend's recent video rentals

Date	Movie	Cost	Rating
10/14/95	Dumb and Dumber	$2.99	Very Good
11/3/95	The Great Escape	$1.99	Very Good
11/17/95	Tokyo Story	$3.29	Excellent

Start with useful field names

Let's put in the field names first. Double-click in the field selector box of the first column (where it says Field1). The name is highlighted, and a blinking cursor appears.

Type **Date** and press Tab. Add the other field names—**Movie**, **Cost**, and **Rating**—in the following three columns.

Put in the data

Next, enter some records in your table, using the sample data from Table 5.2. Try to use consistent formats (for example, if you put in the first date as 10/14/95, don't type November 3, 1995 for the next one). Of course, if Access doesn't determine the right data type, you can change it later, but you might as well try to get it right from the start. Your finished table should look like figure 5.10.

Fig. 5.10

Be sure to be consistent when putting in your starting data.

Date	Movie	Cost	Rating	Field5	Field6
10/14/95	Dumb and Dumber	$2.99	Very Good		
11/3/95	The Great Escape	$1.99	Very Good		
11/17/95	Tokyo Story	$3.29	Excellent		

Table1 : Table

Record: ◀ ◀ | 3 | ▶ ▶| ▶* | of 30

TIP **Don't worry about the unfilled columns to the right. If there's no** field name or data, Access ignores them.

Save the table

Save your table by clicking the Save icon on the toolbar. Access asks you for a table name. Type something appropriate, like **Movie Rentals**, and press Enter. Next, Access asks if it should create a primary key for you. It's a good idea to let Access create the primary key for you (but if you need to designate a primary key later, you can do so in Design view). Click Yes, and Access creates your table (see fig. 5.11). Notice that the extra columns and rows have been eliminated.

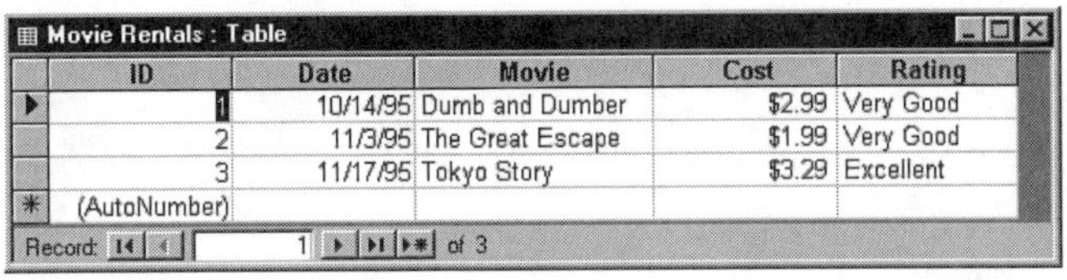

Fig. 5.11
Access created this table based upon the initial data you entered, and included the ID field to serve as the primary key.

Check the settings in Design view

It's time to make sure that the settings Access selected for each field are appropriate. Switch to Design view by choosing View, Table Design. Access should have correctly analyzed your data (see fig. 5.12), and chosen the following data types: Date/Time for the Date field, Currency for the Cost field, and Text for the other two fields. At this point, you can change data types or make other design changes, such as reordering the fields or adding field descriptions.

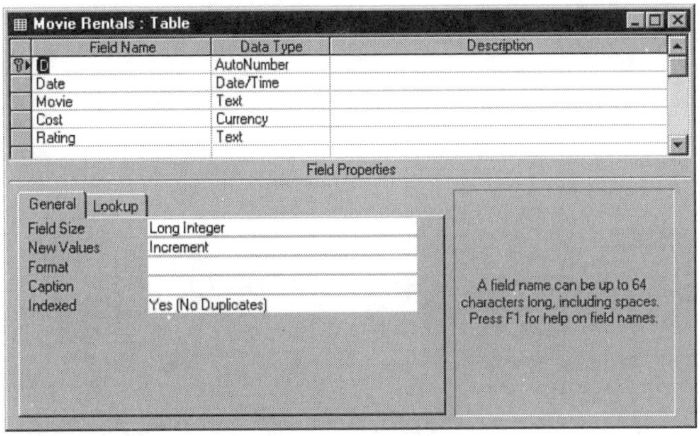

Fig. 5.12
In Design view, you can check the data types selected by Access.

You've made a full-blown table in a couple of minutes with minimal effort. Doesn't that deserve an ooh?

Relationships: How Database Tables Relate to Each Other

● **In this chapter:**

- **One-to-many relationships: the ties that bind**

- **Referential integrity—what's that?**

- **You'll fall for cascade updates and deletes**

- **Unraveling the mystery of many-to-many relationships**

- **Improving your database design**

The well-adjusted table doesn't just sit by itself in a corner of your database. It's eager to get out and establish relationships with other tables . . . . ▶

If Donne had known Access, he might have changed his famous "No man is an island" to "No table is an island." The tables in an active database are like members of a supportive family. Each is a separate entity, fully capable of functioning on its own. But each maintains strong ties with others, allowing them all to work together for the good of the whole.

In this chapter, we focus on **relationships** that bind tables together. You'll learn how to create relationships and about related topics like Cascade Update and Cascade Delete. At the end, you will also take a quick look at database design.

Why bother with relationships?

Relationships integrate your tables and make them much more useful than the sum of their parts. Sure, you can use tables individually, but when you tie them together, you increase their power geometrically. Relationships are also key in keeping your data accurate and your database robust, as you'll soon learn.

What is a relationship, anyway?

You establish a relationship between two tables by selecting a field in each table that contains information common to both tables. Most of the time you'll relate the **primary key** in one table to a matching field in the other table. The next section gives an example that will make these cryptic definitions much more meaningful. Just keep in mind that relationships are created between two tables, and that there's a field in one that has values that also appear in the primary key of the other.

 Plain English, please!

A **primary key** is a field or fields whose values uniquely identify each record stored in a table. **99**

 TIP **The fields relating two tables don't need to have the same field name, but they usually do.**

There are three types of relationships: one-to-many, many-to-many, and one-to-one. The first type is the most important by far, so we'll concentrate on those. Later, we'll discuss many-to-many relationships.

What are one-to-many relationships?

Take a look at figures 6.1 and 6.2. The first displays the initial records of a table listing the 50 states, along with each state capital, state flower, and state bird. The second shows a table listing the largest U.S. cities, which state each is in, and the city's population.

Notice that there's a State field in each table. In figure 6.1, the State field is the primary key. Each state uniquely identifies one record, so no state can appear more than once. In figure 6.2, though, California appears twice and Texas appears three times; in this table, the same state can appear several times.

Because each state can appear only once in the first table, but many times in the second table, you can establish a one-to-many relationship between these two tables. The State field in the American States table is the primary key in the **primary table** (the "one"), and the State field in the Large American Cities table is the **foreign key** in the **related table** (the "many").

 Plain English, please!

> A **primary table** is a table containing the primary key on the "one" side of a one-to-many relationship. A **foreign key** is a field that has the same type of information in the table on the "many" side of the relationship, which is known as the **related table**.

Fig. 6.1
In this table, the State field is the primary key.

State	Capital	Flower	Bird
Alabama	Montgomery	Camellia	Yellowhammer
Alaska	Juneau	Forget-me-not	Willow ptarmigan
Arizona	Phoenix	Flower of Saguaro Cactus	Cactus wren
Arkansas	Little Rock	Apple Blossom	Mockingbird
California	Sacramento	Golden poppy	California valley quail
Colorado	Denver	Rocky Mountain columbine	Lark bunting

American States : Table

Record: 1 of 51

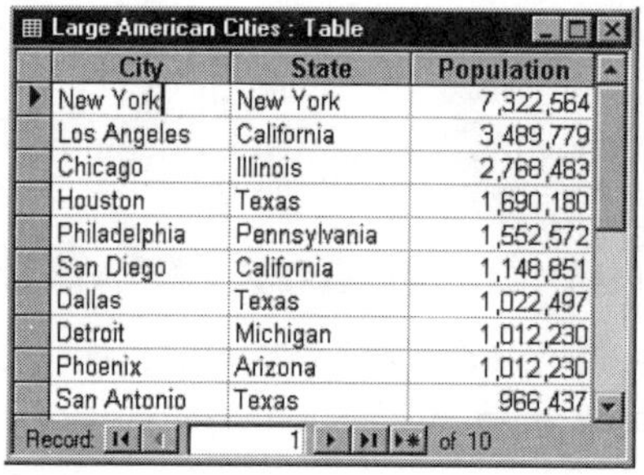

Fig. 6.2
In this table, the same state can appear multiple times.

City	State	Population
New York	New York	7,322,564
Los Angeles	California	3,489,779
Chicago	Illinois	2,768,483
Houston	Texas	1,690,180
Philadelphia	Pennsylvania	1,552,572
San Diego	California	1,148,851
Dallas	Texas	1,022,497
Detroit	Michigan	1,012,230
Phoenix	Arizona	1,012,230
San Antonio	Texas	966,437

Large American Cities : Table — Record: 1 of 10

Q&A *I still don't get why I need to know this, or why relationships are important.*

The answers should become more apparent as you read along, but here's a quick example: Suppose you wanted to know if a particular state capital was also one of the state's largest cities. You could eyeball the two tables for a few minutes, looking for a match. It would be much better, however, to grab information from both tables in a way that would tell you the answer within seconds. To make the tables work together like that, you need to establish a relationship between them. The importance of relationships will become fully evident when you start to create queries in Chapter 9.

Starting up a new relationship

The Large American Cities and American States tables we just looked at represent a very small, not-too-important database. Still, they're fine examples of how to create a relationship.

TIP **You can create these two tables if you want to, but that's a lot of** work. It's easier to follow along using tables from any of your existing databases.

Start by choosing Tools, Relationships. (If you're in the Database window, click the Relationships icon on the toolbar.) The Show Table dialog box appears (see fig. 6.3).

CAUTION **If you've worked with relationships in this database before, you'll** reach the Relationships window instead of the Show Table dialog box. In the Relationships window, choose Relationships, Show Table to get the Show Table dialog box.

You actually can create relationships with queries as well as with tables. For the moment, just make sure the Tables tab is selected.

Fig. 6.3
The Show Table dialog box includes all your tables.

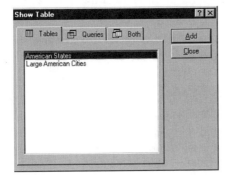

The American States and Large American Cities tables are listed in the Tables tab. Double-click each table to put it in the Relationships Window, then Click Close.

There are two **field lists** in the Relationships window (see fig. 6.4). Each list shows all the fields in one table, with the primary key in bold.

Fig. 6.4
Field lists for the tables you're relating appear in the Relationships window.

To establish a relationship between the two tables, click and hold the mouse button on the State field in the American States list. Drag this State field atop the State field in the Large American Cities list. When you've got one field directly above the other, you'll see a small rectangle; release the mouse button. The Relationships dialog box appears (see fig. 6.5).

TIP **In a large database with several tables, you can set several rela-**
tionships. Use the Show Table dialog box to add whatever tables you need
to the Relationships window, then drag-and-drop fields to establish each
relationship. Later in this chapter, we'll talk more about how to organize
information within a database.

This dialog box shows details of the relationship you've requested, and gives
you further options. The left column shows the table whose field was
dragged (the primary table). The right column shows the table where the
field was dropped (the related table). Under the table names, you see the
fields that represent the primary and foreign keys, respectively (in this case,
both are named State).

Fig. 6.5
Verify your choices in
the Relationships
dialog box.

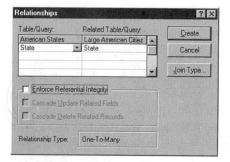

At the bottom of this dialog box, the relationship type is displayed (for this
example, it's one-to-many). Ignore the other options right now, and choose
Create to establish the relationship. A line connects the State fields in the two
field lists (see fig. 6.6).

Fig. 6.6
Access uses a line to
graphically depict each
relationship between
tables.

Q&A *I dragged-and-dropped like you said, but in the Relationships dialog box, Relationship Type says Undefined.*

Have you set primary keys in the tables? (Look at Chapter 3 to learn how to do that.) Access needs to have primary and foreign keys to make a one-to-many relationship.

In the Relationships dialog box, the field names in the two columns are different, and Relationship Type says One-to-One.

When you dragged and dropped, you released the mouse over the wrong field in the related table. For a one-to-many relationship, you must drop the primary field onto a field with the same type of information. You can designate the correct field directly in the Relationships dialog box: click the field in the appropriate table column, click the arrow for the drop-down box, then select the field you need.

Ending a relationship

Unlike many relationships in your own life, you can get rid of a relationship in Access with very little fuss. If the Relationships window isn't already open, choose Tools, Relationships, then click the line for the relationship you want to delete; press the Delete key. When Access asks you if you want to delete the relationship, click Yes.

Making sense of referential integrity

Faced with the chore of explaining **referential integrity**, I wish I could say, "It sounds hard, but it's really quite easy." Well, it's not easy—but it *is* manageable. Let's attack from a couple of angles.

 Plain English, please!

Referential Integrity is a set of rules that protects your data from accidental changes or deletion by ensuring the validity of the relationships between related tables. **99**

First, imagine you're browsing through TV listings, and you notice a great Twilight Zone rerun you haven't seen since 1973. But then you look to see what channel it's on, and—oh, no! It's on static-plagued Channel 62, where Rod Serling sounds like Elmer Fudd, and every summer afternoon is filled with snow. It looks like you'll have to opt for Oprah or Donahue.

The time is right, the episode is one you want to see, and Channel 62 is actually a channel in your area. But you won't watch it, because Channel 62 doesn't come through clearly enough. In your own mental database, it could be said that you enforced referential integrity.

Okay, let's work through an example. Think about the two tables we worked with earlier in this chapter. We established a one-to-many relationship between them, with the State fields as matching keys. Suppose someone with a keen love of baseball but a rather hazy notion of geography tries to add **Toronto** to the Large American Cities table (which is meant for U.S. cities only). When they reach the State field, they type **Ontario**. If referential integrity is enforced between the two tables, that'll never work. Access examines the entry, balks at the fact that there's no Ontario in any record's State field in the American States table, and won't accept the Toronto entry.

Referential integrity also works in the opposite direction. If an Alaskan separatist gets into our database and tries to delete the Alaska record from the American States table, he should be able to do it . But if even one city from Alaska (for instance, Anchorage) is in the Large American Cities table, Access won't let anyone delete the Alaska record from the American States table, because that would violate referential integrity.

Enforcing referential integrity

To establish referential integrity:

1 In the Relationships window, double-click the jagged line that shows the relationship between the two tables. The Relationships dialog box appears.

2 Make sure the <u>E</u>nforce Residential Integrity option is selected (if there isn't a check mark in the box, click to put one there).

3 Choose OK.

Figure 6.7 shows the Relationships window after you set referential integrity. The black line between the two field lists is a lot darker, and there are two new symbols on it. Near the primary table there's a 1, identifying the "one" side of the relationship. Near the related table there's an infinity sign(∞), identifying the "many" side.

Fig. 6.7

A one-to-many relationship with referential integrity.

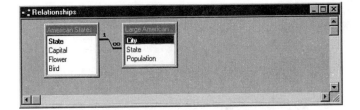

Breaking the rules with cascade options

Let's take another look at the Relationships dialog box (follow the first step in the previous example to call it up). Once you select the Enforce Residential Integrity box, the Cascade Update and Cascade Delete options become available. These options say to Access, "I want referential integrity, but I might need to bend the rules a bit to maintain it." With these options selected, Access makes changes in related tables to preserve referential integrity whenever you change primary key values or delete records in a primary table. These options are discussed in the following sections.

If you want either of these options, make sure it's selected (click its box to place a check mark there if there isn't one already). When you're done selecting the options, choose OK.

CAUTION **When you close the Relationships window, Access asks if you want** to save layout changes. This applies only to how the Relationships window *looks,* and doesn't affect actual relationships you've added or changed. Unless you have a good reason to do otherwise, I suggest you save the layout changes.

Performing cascade updates

Sometimes you'll want to change the primary key of a record in a one-to-many relationship. Suppose the citizens of California decide to change the name of their state to Gold Coast. What happens when you try to replace California with the new name in the State field of the American States table (the primary key)?

If you haven't selected Cascade Update, Access won't let you do this. You get a message saying that you'll violate Referential Integrity rules if you make the change. Why is it a violation? Because it's the primary key in a one-to-many relationship, and California appears in at least one record in the State field of the Large American Cities table (the foreign key).

If you have selected Cascade Update, there's no problem. You can change the state name to whatever you want. As soon as you do, Access updates the State field in the Large American Cities table without you lifting a finger (see fig. 6.8).

Fig. 6.8
When you change a primary key with the Cascade Update option selected, the foreign key is automatically updated.

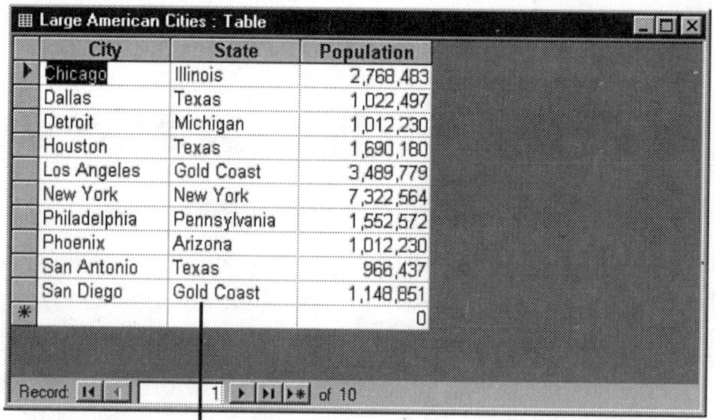

City	State	Population
Chicago	Illinois	2,768,483
Dallas	Texas	1,022,497
Detroit	Michigan	1,012,230
Houston	Texas	1,690,180
Los Angeles	Gold Coast	3,489,779
New York	New York	7,322,564
Philadelphia	Pennsylvania	1,552,572
Phoenix	Arizona	1,012,230
San Antonio	Texas	966,437
San Diego	Gold Coast	1,148,851
		0

Anyplace the State field said "California" is updated automatically.

Performing cascade deletes

Suppose the separatist has his way and we do have to give up Alaska. Remember that if Anchorage or Juneau is in the Large American Cities table, then attempting to delete Alaska's record breaks referential integrity rules, and we get an error message (see fig. 6.9).

Fig. 6.9
You can't delete records in the primary table when referential integrity is enforced.

Microsoft Access

⚠ Can't delete or change record. Since related records exist in table 'Large American Cities', referential integrity rules would be violated.

[OK]   [Help]

If you have selected Cascade Delete, however, you *can* eliminate Alaska from the American States table. Juneau, Anchorage, and any other Alaskan city are automatically eliminated from the Large American Cities table, thus preserving referential integrity. In other words, the Cascade Delete option causes all associated records in related tables to be deleted whenever you delete a record from the primary table.

Relationships in a well-developed database

Let's open a larger database to see how all these relationships can fit together. We'll work with the Northwind Traders database provided with
Access. It might give you some powerful ideas for setting up and organizing
your own databases.

1 Choose File, Open Database.

2 At the top in the Look In box, select the Samples subfolder underneath
the folder in which you installed Access.

3 Double-click the Northwind.mdb icon to open the database.

4 Choose Tools, Relationships to see all the relationships in the database
(see fig. 6.10).

Fig. 6.10
The Relationships
window for the
Northwind database.

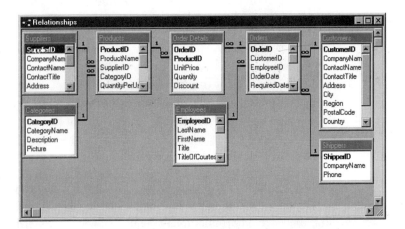

This gives you a good idea how relationships connect different tables in a
database. Notice that one table can have several relationships. The Products
table, for example, has three relationships, and it is a primary table and a
related table in separate relationships.

Note also that the relative positions of the tables are unimportant. For
example, the Customers table has a one-to-many relationship with the Orders
table, even though the Customers table appears to its right. Rather than table
position, look for the 1 and ∞ signs to determine which table is on the "one"
side and which is on the "many."

TIP **Don't be shy about opening tables in the Northwind database to see what they look like. That's exactly what it's for!**

Many-to-many relationships

Consider the operating relationship between products and orders for Northwind Traders. A single order might include several different products, like Grandma's Boysenberry Spread, Tofu, and Sir Rodney's Scones. In the same way, a single product like Sir Rodney's Scones could be included in orders from companies like Island Trading, the Eastern Connection, and Consolidated Holdings. The same product might be part of a second order by Island Trading.

In other words, there is a many-to-many relationship between products and orders. Each product can be on many orders, and each order can include many products. This can cause problems if you're not careful.

Let's say you tried to establish a one-to-many relationship between products and orders. You'd need a field in the Orders table to mirror the ProductID field (the primary key of the Products table). If you had more than one product in an order, you'd need more than one record in an order. Imagine what would happen if you had 30 or 40 different products in one order. You'd repeat the same order information—name, address, ship date, and so on—over and over again. You don't want to do that.

If you try setting up a one-to-many relationship in the other direction—that is, put an OrderID field in the Products table—you'll have the converse problem. A given product might require dozens of records if it was included in dozens of orders, and you don't want to have more than one record per product in the Products table.

A solution to the many-to-many mystery

Figure 6.11 shows how to solve the problem of these many-to-many relationships by creating an entirely new table named Order Details that **indirectly links** the two tables. Order Details contains all the information about specific orders, including which products are included in a given order.

Primary key

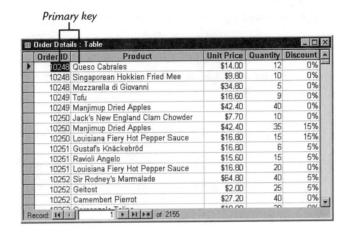

Fig. 6.11
A separate table to contain order details overcomes the difficulty of having a many-to-many relationship between products and orders.

Return to figure 6.10 and examine the field list for the Order Details table. Notice that this table has an infinity symbol on the lines showing its relationships with the Products and Orders tables. Notice also that its ProductID and OrderID fields are both bold; because this table is on the "many" side of two one-to-many relationships, it has two foreign keys. These two keys together serve as the primary key for the Order Details field, because their combination uniquely identifies each record.

Whew! I'm not sure I understand relationships

Don't feel inadequate if you haven't yet mastered the manipulation of many-to-many relationships (or any of this stuff). For most people, it's not something you can read once and have woven into your brain. It's only after working with databases for a while that it starts to sink in. At the outset, you're better off developing a sixth sense for what's going on than trying to remember rules and definitions.

You can avoid wrestling with many-to-many relationships for some time, and on your first few Access databases, Cascade Update and Cascade Delete probably won't be needed. At the very least, though, you need to understand one-to-many relationships, and have some feeling for referential integrity. These concepts are the heart of a **relational database** like Access.

Plain English, please!

In a **relational database**, data is stored in separate tables that have relationships defined between them. The relationships are used to find associated information in the database.

A few words about database design

If your database needs are complicated, try to recruit a database-savvy friend to get you up and running. Of course, if you're building a database for your business or some other critical reason, consider shelling out some bucks to have it set up professionally.

 TIP   If you do get outside help, read this section anyway. Whoever helps you is likely to take you more seriously if you know exactly what you want to accomplish, and are familiar with the necessary tools.

Here's the basic scenario for putting together a new database on your own:

1 *Define the database mission.* Since each database is a separate entity in Access, decide what you want a particular database to accomplish. Is it to manage a small business? Inventory your video collection? Keep track of personal investments? Write out the mission, and keep it in mind through the rest of the design process.

2 *Determine what information you need.* Decide what data you want in your database. If you map out your needs from the start, you'll lessen your chances of forgetting to put in some information you need. Think about where all the necessary information will come from, as well as the logistics and cost of obtaining it.

3 *Divide your information into groups.* Start thinking about what tables you want to have. A key objective is to have information about a single subject in each table.

 TIP   You usually don't gain much by creating separate tables for different time periods. As you'll see in Chapter 20, you can periodically purge old records from tables to keep your databases lean and efficient.

4 *Break down information into its smallest natural component.* This is often a matter of preference. I've said that first and last names should have separate fields, but in some cases you might find it better to treat them as one field. A street address is often one item, but if you were working on projects where house numbers mattered more than street names, you could have a field just for the house number. The same is true for telephone numbers: it's usually one field, but if you needed to, you could make it four fields: country code, area code, exchange, and whatever's left.

5 *Decide what fields to include in each table.* Compare the fields in your tables. In some cases, duplicate fields can be safely eliminated. Other times, you may *want* duplicate fields to establish relationships between tables. Also, keep an eye out for fields that might be better suited in tables other than the ones you originally thought they belonged in.

6 *Determine the relationships between tables.* This step overlaps with the previous one. Look at your tables and decide how they relate to one another, if at all. You might have to add a foreign key to some tables (that is, create a field that exists for no purpose other than relating to a primary key) to make the proper relationships possible.

7

Designing Database Tables

● **In this chapter:**

- Picking the appropriate data type

- Is Lookup Wizard a data type?

- Avoiding extra typing with default values

- Making sure important files aren't skipped

- What's an input mask and how do I use it?

- What about field sizes?

- Choosing a good-looking format for numbers and dates

- Let's do some printing!

You can make better-looking, error-free tables in less time by improving their design . . . . **>**

There are various approaches to setting the table for dinner. For some of us it starts with clearing the table of assorted books, three-day-old pizza, and a worn toy or two with a firm swipe of the left forearm. Next, the soy-sauce-oozing bag from the Peking-O-Rama should be ripped open recklessly, thus ensuring the ruin of any important papers nearby. Separate the cheap chopsticks so that one looks like a toothpick, the other a Redwood. Dinner is served.

But somewhere else, a different kind of table is being set. An elegant table cloth graces the dining room table. Rosenthal China is carefully arranged at each place setting. The water and wine glasses are Waterford Crystal. Light the silver candlesticks, and who knows what the evening might bring?

Designing an elegant database table can be as rich and fulfilling as setting the table for haute cuisine—maybe more so. In this chapter, we're not going to do anything so lavish and so daring, but we are going to go a little bit beyond the Chinese takeout stage. Let's get to work.

A look at data types

You've already learned some distinctions among data types. For example, in Chapter 3 I talked about the difference between numbers that you calculate, like your bowling scores, and numbers that are essentially descriptions, like a ZIP code. By choosing a specific data type, you are making several decisions, including:

- *The type of values* that can be entered in a field. You may not want alphanumeric text in a Number field, for example.

- *The type of operations* that can be performed. You can add, subtract or multiply calories, for example (numeric values), but not people's names (alphanumeric values).

- *The size of the field.* For example, suppose you wanted to have a long description in a field, like a short biography. You could use a Memo field, in which you can put up to 64,000 characters, rather than a Text field, limited to 255 characters.

Table 7.1 summarizes the different data types and the kind of information stored in them.

Table 7.1   A comparison of data types

Data type	What kind of information
Text	Alphanumeric characters
Number	Numbers
Date/Time	Dates and times
Currency	Monetary values
AutoNumber	An incremental number that increases by one each time you add a record
Memo	Alphanumeric characters (usually several sentences)
Yes/No	Yes or No, True or False
OLE Object	Objects Linked or Embedded (OLE) in Access that were created in another program, such as a picture or spreadsheet.
Lookup Wizard	Creates a field that allows you to choose from a list of values.

I think the first four data types in Table 7.1—Text, Number, Date/Time, and Currency—are straightforward. You've already seen the AutoNumber data type at work when I discussed primary keys in Chapter 3. As indicated above, use Memo when you plan to have several sentences in a field, rather than several characters. The OLE Object type is beyond our scope; if you wish, type **Using the OLE Object Data Type** on the request line of the Answer Wizard for a list of related help topics. For a more advanced discussion of OLE objects used in Access, Que's *Special Edition Using Access 95* would be a valuable reference.

That leaves the Yes/No and Lookup Wizard types. Let's take a look at each.

It's either a Yes or a No

Did you ever have to ask a child if he broke the neighbor's window playing baseball? After the stutterings and evasions, you're finally reduced to asking "Look, just give me a yes or a no!" The yes/no data type asks the same question with the same demand for certainty. The new member either paid his dues or didn't, or the package was shipped on time or it wasn't, or the customer is entitled to a discount or not. So the Yes/No data type has only two acceptable values—Yes or No. (You can also type 1 for Yes and 0 for No).

What kind of data type is a "Lookup Wizard?"

Actually, a Lookup Wizard is not a data type—it creates a handy aid for selecting values during data entry. The wizard makes a **lookup column** filled with values that you access from a drop-down menu in a table cell. You can then either select a value from those shown, or you can type in another value.

An example should make things clearer. Think about the City field in a table of names and addresses. Most people we know live in our own town or nearby, so the same town names appear again and again in the table. Let's use the Lookup Wizard to create a lookup column that includes the cities typed most frequently.

1 Open in Design view the Address Book table you created in Chapter 3. (To do that from the Database window, click the Tables tab, select the table, then click the Design button.)

2 Click the Data Type cell in the City field, then click the drop-down menu arrow.

3 Select Lookup Wizard... at the bottom of the list.

4 Access starts the Lookup Wizard. In the first screen, you can choose to select the values from an existing table, or type in the values you want. Select the second option and click Next.

5 In the second screen you create the lookup column. In the box on top, you tell Access how many columns you want; let's use the default value of one.

6 Access then creates a box for you to enter your selections. Type **Belmont** and press Tab. In the same fashion, type **Lincoln** and **Monroe**. Your window should look like figure 7.1.

7 Click the Next button and then click Finish. The wizard creates your lookup column.

Now, when you click any cell in the City field, you will see a drop-down menu for the lookup column. Click it to select from the three city choices (see fig. 7.2).

Fig. 7.1
Often one column will
be enough, but you
can add more to better
classify your choices.

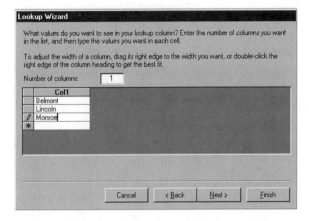

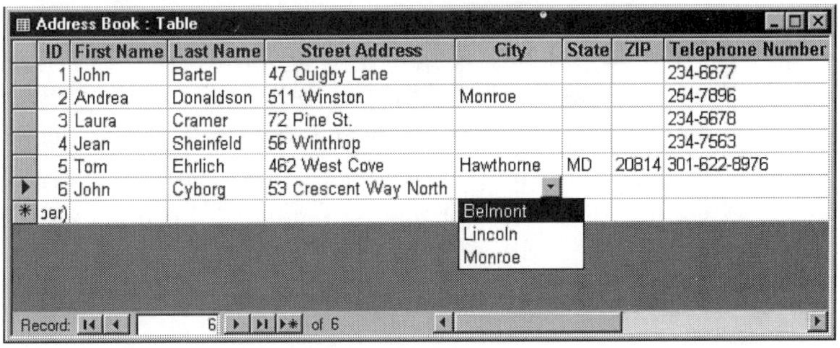

Fig. 7.2
You can choose from
the values in the
lookup column, or
type in another value
of your choice.

Changing data types

At first glance, nothing seems simpler than changing a data type. In Design view, click the Data Type column for the field you want to change; then click the drop-down menu and select the new type. Save the change.

But for a piece of information, a data type is its defining characteristic. Change that and you've changed its essential nature. It can be like telling a poodle that it's now a bulldog.

Sometimes data type changes present no major problems. If all the values in a Text field are either Yes or No, you should have few problems converting to a Yes/No field. Changing from Text to Memo also presents relatively few difficulties. Other switch-overs, such as from Text to Number, can result in data loss. Before attempting data type changes, it's a good idea to backup your data—just in case things don't turn out quite the way you planned.

I usually don't like to send people hunting through Access Help, but in this case, it has an excellent chart that summarizes data conversion issues. In the Answer Wizard type **Data Types** on the request line, click Search, and then select Consequences of changing a field's data type in the Tell Me About section. Scroll to the bottom and click the button for "To view a summary of data type conversion results."

Dressing up your table with field properties

Take a look at the Address Book table in Design view (see fig. 7.3). In Chapter 3 we spent all our time on the top half of the table adding new fields. Now we're going to work on the bottom half—field properties.

These **properties** are for specific fields—not the entire table. When you want to change the properties for a field, you first have to click on it so it's selected. The properties for that field will be displayed below. The properties change depending on the field type—for instance, text fields don't have a setting for decimal places, and memo fields don't have a field size.

Let's look at some of the properties you may find in the general tab and see how they can help you work easier and better.

 Plain English, please!

Remember your chemistry teacher talking about the **properties** of some element, like hydrogen or oxygen? That's kind of the way **properties** is used in databases. It's another word for **features** or **characteristics.**

 CAUTION **It's easy to add a field and set properties for it. But if you want to** change properties of an existing field after you've entered lots of data in it, things become more complicated. For instance, if you have a text field with long entries in some records, and you decrease the field size, some of your data gets truncated. There can be other complications as well. As a general rule, try to set your table properties the way you want them before you begin entering data.

Fig. 7.3
Use the Field Proper-
ties settings at the
bottom of the design
window to make better
tables that are easier to
use.

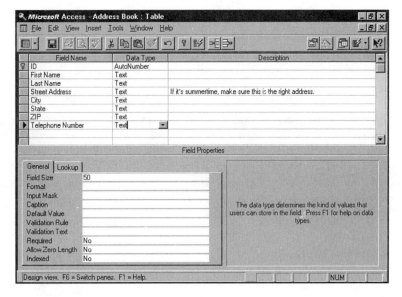

Choosing the right format for your field

When you set the Data Type for a field, you're partially defining how you
want that field's data to look. For instance, if you choose Date/Time as the
Data Type, any numbers you enter will be converted to a date or time format.

But that's only the beginning. To format a field with more control, you can
use the Format line in the Field Properties list. When you select the Format
line, an arrow for a drop-down list appears. Click on that arrow to open the
list and see your options. You'll have different choices depending on which
data type you've selected. In the following sections, we'll look at two data
types that use very specific formats—numbers and dates.

Formatting numbers

First, add a field in your Address Book table called Number of Children and
select the Number data type. (If you don't want that field, you can just delete
it after we're through. A better example of a Number field, actually, would be
Calories in a diet plan, or Number of Units in an inventory reordering table.)

Even though we always input numbers as just numbers, we want to see them
in different ways—as dollars and cents perhaps, or a percentage. Click the
Format property (it's below Field size) for the Number of Children (or any
Number) field, then click the arrow for the drop-down menu.

You will see six different format choices, which are summarized in Table 7.1. If you're in doubt about which format to use, General Number is the default and your most likely choice.

Table 7.1   How do I want to see the numbers displayed?

When I use this format	with this number	I see this
General Number	7243.7	7243.7
Currency	7243.7	$7,243.50
Fixed	7243.7	7244.00
Standard	7243.7	7243.70
Percent	0.595	59.50%
Scientific	7243.7	7.24E+03

Below the Format property in the Field Properties area, you'll see Decimal Places. The default setting is Auto, which is where you will usually want to leave it. The General Number format shows just the number of decimal places you physically enter yourself, which is probably what you want. For the other settings, though, you can choose the number of decimal places from the Decimal Places drop-down list.

What date format should I use?

You might have a field in your Address Book for, say, Date of Last Visit. For this field, you would select the Date/Time data type. Then you could select a format from the Format drop-down list in the Field Properties area.

You can format the date in several ways. Click in the Format property box, then click the drop-down menu, and you will see the choices in figure 7.4. (Remember, you have to be in a field with the Date/Time data type to have this selection.) The right half of the menu shows what the different choices actually look like on your screen.

You don't have to enter the date using the format you chose. For example, if you input September 17, 1995 and have the Short Date format selected, Access accepts the date and displays it as 9/17/95. You could have also entered 17-Sep-95. What format you choose to display the date is a matter of personal choice. If you don't choose any Format and leave it blank, Access will display the date in the Short Date format.

Fig. 7.4
Select the Date/Time format that suits you from the drop-down menu.

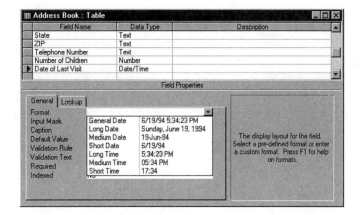

Automatically entering a default value in a field

Each time you've entered data in a table, you've had to type in the entire thing from scratch. But in some fields, you may find yourself entering the same value almost every time. For example, if you were making a table of your Address Book, many of the addresses would probably be located in the same state that you live in.

Rather than type the same name again and again, you can set the Default Value property. Whatever you type for the default will appear as the value for that field in every record—no questions asked. You can type over the default value if it's not appropriate for a particular record.

To set a default for a field follow these steps:

1 Select the field you want to set a default for. For example, in figure 7.5, the State field is selected.

2 Type in the default value on the Default Value line of the Field Properties section. In figure 7.5, the default value is IL.

3 Save your changes. You'll see that IL has become "IL" (which is discussed in Chapter 10).

Fig. 7.5
Set a default value for
a field so you don't
have to keep retyping
the same information.

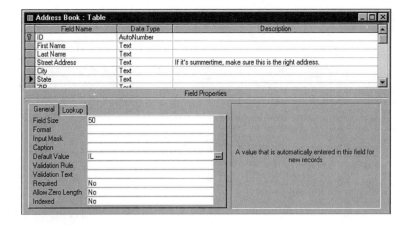

Let's see what the table now looks like in Datasheet view. Select View,
Datasheet or click the Table View icon. As shown in figure 7.6, the default
value of IL is in the State field for the next empty record (that's the one with
the star in the record selector box). Notice that the new default value doesn't
affect any existing records.

So now when you go to fill in that record, you don't have to worry about the
state if it's Illinois. If it's not Illinois, type in the state separately.

Fig. 7.6
The default value of IL
is already filled in for
you in the next empty
record.

ID	First Name	Last Name	Street Address	City	State	ZIP	Telephone Number
1	John	Bartel	47 Quigby Lane				234-6677
2	Andrea	Donaldson	511 Winston	Monroe			254-7896
3	Laura	Cramer	72 Pine St.				234-5678
4	Jean	Sheinfeld	56 Winthrop				234-7563
5	Tom	Ehrlich	462 West Cove	Hawthorne	MD	20814	301-622-8976
6	John	Cyborg	53 Crescent Way North				
*	oer)				IL		

Record: 1 of 6

This field should never be empty

Let's face it—no matter how great Access is, entering a lot of data into it can be a monotonous task. If you're under time pressure, or get interrupted, or if your mind simply skips a beat, you might miss a field and leave out important information. When that happens, the field has a **null value**.

 Plain English, please!

> A **null value** means there is no value in the field. It does not mean "zero." There is simply no value for the field at all.

Fortunately, you can make Access force you (or whoever is doing the data entry for you) to input data in a particular field.

1 In Design view, select the field you want to require data entry. It could be First Name, for example.

2 Click on the Required line of the Field Properties section.

3 The default selection is No. To change it, click the drop-down menu arrow at right and choose Yes.

4 Select File, Save to save your changes.

5 You're done—maybe. If you've already input some records in that field, you'll get the complicated-looking dialog box in figure 7.7. It's a lot simpler than it looks. Access is just saying, "Do you want me to check if there are any null values in the work you've already done? Or should we let sleeping dogs lie?" So choose yes if you want Access to check previous records; choose no to ignore them.

7 Now your table will be saved. You can switch to Datasheet view and input your data.

If you ever forget to put a value in a Required field, you will get the message saying that the field can't contain a null value. Access won't let you save the record until you put something in there.

 To change the Required field property from a no to a yes, as in step 3, you could have just selected the no and typed in yes. But it's a good idea to use the drop-down lists when making selections—even simple ones. First, you avoid spelling errors. Second, you won't input stuff that won't work. Third, you may discover additional choices you didn't know existed.

Fig. 7.7
Access wants to know if it should go back and check for previous wrongdoing.

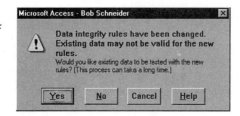

Q&A ***I want to make sure earlier records have no null values. But Access says this may take a long time, which I do not have.***

Go ahead and click Yes. If you've just put in a few records, or even a few dozen, it shouldn't take very long to check. Try to keep things consistent by making sure that the same field properties apply to all your data.

How can I avoid typos and illogical entries?

Just making sure that you fill a field doesn't mean it will be correct, of course. Flying fingers can input some pretty strange things.

Access can't always protect you from putting in the wrong value. But it does have some safeguards to screen some of the really weird stuff out. You can use the Validation Rule property, which is right below Default Value in the list of field properties.

How does it work? Let's say you wanted the Address Book table limited to only people whose last names begin with N through Z. In Design view, click anywhere in the Last Name field. In the Validation Rule box type **>M,** which means only names beginning with a letter after M are acceptable. Save the change, and for this example just click No when Access asks you to look for prior violations. Switch to Datasheet view and try to type **Harrison** in the Last Name field. You won't be able to—you get a message telling you that a validation rule has been broken (see fig. 7.8).

Fig. 7.8
Try to type in a last name beginning with letters A through M, and Access will send you this love note.

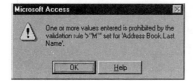

Validation rules take many forms and have many purposes. In a Date/Time field, you could limit values to a certain month or year. In a Number field, you could tell Access not to accept any number above or below some limit. In a Text field, you could insist on entries with three characters. Learning how to create these and other validation rules requires some knowledge of expressions, which are essential to using queries and are thus covered later in Chapter 10. Once you read that chapter, you should be able to create the validation rules you need.

What are input masks, and how can I use them?

There are pursuits in life where innovation and imagination are treasured and esteemed. But entering a nine-digit telephone number into a field calls for uniformity and accuracy, not whimsy and originality. Indeed, most of us appreciate a device that, in effect, tells us, "Look, some people use parentheses for the area code, some people use all dashes—why don't we all just do it *this* way? I'll create the format, and you just fill in the numbers."

In Access, an input mask performs that function. Let's make an input mask for a telephone number using the Input Mask Wizard. First, select the Telephone Number field in the Design view of the Address Book table. Click anywhere in the Input Mask field property box (below the Format property), and then click the ellipsis button to the right of it to start the wizard. Figure 7.9 shows the first screen.

Click the Try It: line to see the input mask for the highlighted Phone Number selection. When you enter data in your table, that mask would appear as soon as you type the first number in an empty Telephone Number record. You can then type the additional digits—no parentheses or hyphens necessary—and the format will match that of the Phone Number in the figure. Additional input masks are available by clicking the Edit List button at the bottom.

I think you'll be able to follow the rest of the wizard's screens on your own to create the input mask you want. Input masks require only a small investment for a large return, and their use is highly recommended.

Fig. 7.9
Input masks aren't just for phone numbers. Use them for ZIPs, social security numbers, dates, and so on.

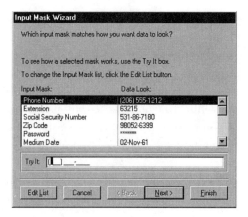

Controlling field sizes

The field size is the number of characters a user is allowed to enter into that field. Field Size is usually the first property in the Field Properties section (depending on the Data Type selected).

There are several reasons for making a field size as small as you can. Sometimes you can curb the potential for error by limiting field size. A field for postal abbreviations of states, for example, should have a field size of only two. If you type **2** in the Field Size box, Access won't let you input FLA (or any other three-character mistake) for Florida.

With smaller field sizes, your tables will also be more consistent and easier to read. For some users, a field like "Comments" is an invitation to write a small book. Curb their worst instincts (and your own) by limiting the field to 50 characters, or however many you think is needed. (Of course, if you need the space, don't be stingy with it.) Fifty characters is the default size for Text fields. To change it, simply highlight the number and type in the maximum you want to allow.

CAUTION   **You can lose data by reducing the size of a Text field that already** has data in it. Access will slice off (truncate, in fancy talk) any characters that exceed the new limit. You'll get a warning about this when you try to save your design changes.

Special field sizes for number fields

Let's take a look at the choices in the Field Size box for a Number field. Click in the Number of Children field, and then click the drop-down menu in the Field Size property. Figure 7.10 shows the choices you would have with a Number type field.

Fig. 7.10
Don't worry about the Replication ID; choose among the other five selections.

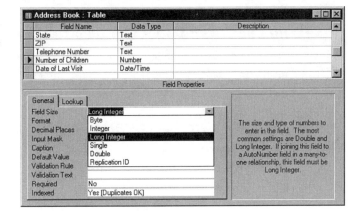

Table 7.2 Field sizes for number fields

Field Size Setting	Range	Decimal Places Allowed
Byte	0 to 255	None
Integer	–32,768 to 32,767	None
Long Integer	–2,147,483,648 to 2,147,483,647	None
Single	-3.4×10^{38} to 3.4×10^{38}	7
Double	-1.797×10^{38} to 1.797×10^{38}	15

Note that the first three settings—Byte, Integer, and Long Integer—allow only integers (whole numbers). In a field where you were counting calories, for example, there would be no need for decimals, so you could select Integer or Long Integer. The Double field size, in contrast, allows up to fifteen decimal places.

CAUTION   **Yes, another warning about losing data. If you have decimals in** any of your numbers, and you change to a setting that only allows integers, you're going to lose your decimals. Access automatically rounds them to the nearest whole number. So be careful how you change the settings.

Q&A   ***Why doesn't everybody always pick the settings that can handle the highest values—Long Integer for whole numbers, and Double for all other numbers?***

Access works fastest with settings that allow the lowest values. But that's mainly an issue if you have really big tables and do lots of number crunching. Usually you'll use the Long Integer and Double selections.

I'm not sure if I get the difference between a Validation Rule and a Field Size. Aren't both used to limit the data you can input in a field?

Yes, that's right. The difference is that Field Size is used to limit the *number* of characters and the Validation Rule is used to limit the *values* of the characters. Of course, the two can overlap. For example, if you set the Field Size property of a number field to 2, there's no way you can write a number bigger than 99 into it.

Isn't it about time I learned how to print?

You'll often want to print out your data in reports, so they'll look great and be easy for others to read and understand. But sometimes you may just want to print out some part or all of a table itself. Here's a few things you can do to get your tables on paper right now.

I don't care what it looks like! Just print it!

Sometimes you just want hard copy of your table immediately. You don't care how it looks, or if it takes six pages to print four records. Just select File, Print, and click OK in the Print dialog box. It might be a mess, but all your stuff will be there.

I only want to print what I've selected

You can select any portion of your table and print it.

1 Point the mouse to the far-left portion of the cell where you want to begin your selection.

2 When the pointer changes to the white cross, press the mouse button and hold it down.

3 Now drag it through the area you want to print.

4 Click File, Print.

5 In the Print dialog box, click the Selected Records button at the bottom of the Print Range section (see fig. 7.11).

6 Click OK, and your selection should be printed.

Fig. 7.11
On the lower right of the window you can choose the number of copies you want to print.

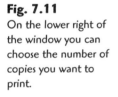

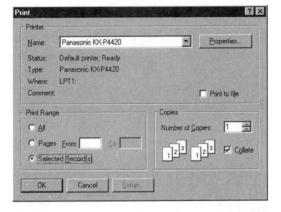

How can I use Print Preview?

It's a good idea to see what your document will look like printed beforehand. You can do that in Print Preview—choose File, Print Preview to get there. Notice that when you drag the mouse over your document in Print Preview the pointer changes to a magnifying glass. When you click, that section of the table zooms up so you can see it. You can change the Zoom level (75 percent, 100 percent, 150 percent, and so on) in the Zoom box on the toolbar (see fig. 7.12).

Fig. 7.12
See what your printed
tables will look like in
Print Preview.

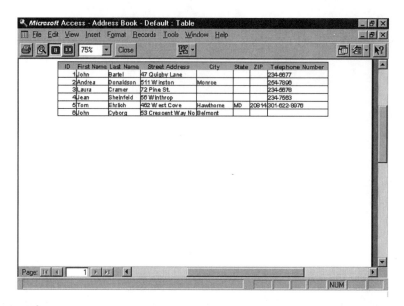

TIP   **Want to forget about printing right now and get back to Data-**
sheet view? Click File, Print Preview again. The check mark to the left of
the Print Preview is removed and you're back where you started.

You can move from page to page, forward or back, by clicking the arrows at
the bottom left-hand corner of the screen (see fig. 7.12). Click the arrow on
the far right to see how many pages it will take to print your table. Don't try
to get a Print Preview of selected records, though—you can't.

How can I print across the wide edge of the paper?

When we get a letter, we expect the length to be greater than the width.
That's Portrait form. But when you're printing a table, you may want it wider
than longer, so you can fit more columns on the page. That's Landscape. With
Portrait printing, you'll fit more records on each page, but not as many fields.
With Landscape, it's the reverse—more fields, fewer records.

Here's how to change to Landscape. In Print Preview, choose File, Page
Setup; then click on the Page tab (see fig. 7.13). Select the orientation you
want and click OK.

Fig. 7.13
Landscape printing
allows you to put more
columns on each page.

I don't need to print all these columns

You may have a table with lots of fields spread out over as many as five
pages. You can reduce the fields you print by using the Hide command that
you learned in Chapter 4.

1 Select the field or fields you don't want to print. (You can select adjacent columns by keeping the Shift key depressed as you drag.)

2 Choose Format, Hide Columns.

3 Print your table.

4 If you want to see these fields again after you Print, choose Format,
Unhide Columns. Check any fields that you would now like to see.

Part III: Finding Stuff

Chapter 8: **How to Find What You Are Looking For**

How to Find What You Are Looking For

● **In this chapter:**

- No more looking for data in all the wrong places

- I can't even spell it—can I still find it?

- Wild cards help you flex Find's muscles

- Find-and-replace: what a team!

- Can I sort things backward?

If it's in there, Access can find it! Access sifts patiently through your information until it finds exactly what you need. . . . ❯

Try telling a record store clerk, "I'm looking for an album, but I don't know the title...or the label...or who sang it...or the names of the songs. All I remember are a couple of words from one song." He'll start to tell you politely that you're out of luck. Then tell him, "It's something like, 'We're Sergeant Pepperoni...'"

"Oh," he'll say. "No problem. That's *Sergeant Pepper's Lonely Hearts Club Band* by the Beatles, 1967. Give me a second and I'll get ya a copy."

We all forget much of what we hear, unless it's distinctive or particularly important to us. For Access, though, any given piece of information is as easy to recall as another.

Access has powerful tools to help you find specific data in your database. You can find things even when you know very little about them—and even when they're not nearly as memorable as Sergeant Pepper. In this chapter, you learn ways to retrieve items you've put in your database, and to replace what you retrieve. Finally, we talk about sorting stuff in alphabetical and numerical order, which makes ferreting out particular data much easier.

Introducing the Find command

You use the Find command to locate specific pieces of information in your database. The great thing about this command is that if you can remember just a little bit, you can find an entire record.

Suppose you made a table of all the guests at your wedding, including their names, addresses, and a description of the gift they gave you. Three years later, the only thing you remember about a certain couple is the opaque goldfish bowl they gave you. When the perfect chain letter or pyramid marketing scheme comes along, you can dig up their name and address. You don't need to remember exactly how you entered "goldfish bowl." Maybe you didn't put in "goldfish" or "bowl" at all; maybe you typed "stupidest trash imaginable." If you remember that you included "stupid," you can still find their names and take your revenge.

Another plus is that the information doesn't have to be unique. Suppose you got a whole bunch of disappointing gifts (all from your spouse's family, of course). If you described each one the same way ("cheap trinket"), you can find all these records later with a single search.

How to find what you need in a table

Finding any piece of specific data in any table is simple—just issue the Find command from the Edit menu, set the options, and click a Find button (Find First or Find Next). The following sections walk you through the process in detail.

Tell Access what you want to find

First, let's tour the Find dialog box. Don't worry if you don't absorb everything immediately. We'll come back and explore all these features with concrete examples. For now, just get a feel for what's out there. Click Edit, Find to reach the Find dialog box shown in figure 8.1.

Fig. 8.1
Use Find to search for stuff.

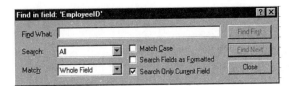

  Even if you're not too familiar with the toolbar, the Find icon is easy to spot; it's a pair of binoculars.

The Find What line is where you type whatever you're looking for. You use Find What even when you don't know exactly what you're looking for. I'll show you in a minute how you do that.

At the right are the Find First and Find Next buttons. You'll usually start your search by choosing Find First, and then find additional matching values by using Find Next.

Decide how you want to search

The line below, Find What is also Search. This is where you indicate how you want Access to search for your data. Click the drop-down list arrow, and click to select All, Up, or Down. Usually you'll want All, but you can search in a specific direction by selecting Up or Down.

CAUTION Be careful if you select Up or Down and begin your search with Find Next. If Access doesn't find matching values in the direction you told it to search, it doesn't reverse itself and search all records. So there may be matches that Access couldn't find because you told it to head in only one direction. It's safest to select All on the Search line and begin your search with Find First.

Tell Access how to match it up

On the Match line, you have three possible settings. Again, you click a drop-down list arrow, then click to select the setting you want.

Field Setting	What it Does
Any Part of Field	This covers all the bases—if what you're looking for shows up anywhere in the field, it's a match, no matter what else is in that field.
Whole Field	What you're looking for has to fill an entire field. If there's anything else in the field, Access won't consider it a match.
Start of Field	This is a match only if what you're looking for comes at the beginning of a field.

Refine your Match options

There are three check boxes in the middle of the dialog box. When you click to select any of these, you control options that further define what Access should consider a match as it performs your search:

- *Match Case.* This option tells Access to pay attention to uppercase and lowercase. If you want to find only fields that exactly match the capitalization you used in the Find What line, make sure this option is selected.

- *Search Fields as Formatted.* The way text is displayed in a field can differ from how it's stored in the table. Choose this option to search for values as they are displayed. See the section "Let's tackle the Search Fields as Formatted option" later in this chapter for more details.

- *Search Only Current Field.* This is the most important option! When it's selected, Access searches only the field that the blinking cursor is currently in. When it isn't selected, Access searches the entire table. (In a big table, even a search in just one field might result in hundreds, or even thousands, of matches.)

Let's look at some Find examples

Let's try to find some things in the Employees table of the Northwind Traders sample database that comes with Access (see fig. 8.2). Open its file, Northwind.mdb, located in the Samples folder below whichever folder Access was installed in.

Let's freeze the ID and name fields so they're always in view. Remember how to do that? Select the ID field by clicking its field selector, then drag as far as the right border of the First Name field. Three fields should be highlighted. Choose Format, Freeze to freeze the three fields. (Refer to Chapter 4 if you need more details, or else follow along without freezing these fields. Remember that you can move through the table by clicking the horizontal scroll bar at the bottom.)

Fig. 8.2
We'll practice hunting for things in the Employees table of the sample database.

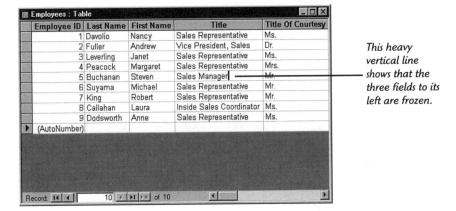

This heavy vertical line shows that the three fields to its left are frozen.

I know exactly what I'm looking for

Sometimes you know exactly what item you want to find. Suppose you want to find the record of the one person at your company whose position is Sales Manager.

1 Choose Edit, Find.

2 Type **Sales Manager** in the Find What line.

3 Select the options shown in figure 8.3. Search should be All, and Match should be Whole Field. Leave the three check boxes deselected.

Fig. 8.3
The options you select in the Find dialog box can mean the difference between a successful search and a dud.

4 Click Find First. Access highlights Sales Manager in Record 5 for employee Steven Buchanan.

5 Click Close to shut the dialog box.

Q&A *Nothing happened when I clicked Find First.*

The Find dialog box might be covering part of your table. Click and drag its title bar to move the dialog box elsewhere on-screen, and you should see the results of the search.

What if I don't know the exact thing I'm looking for?

In the preceding example, we assumed Sales Manager was the employee's title—nothing more, nothing less. Therefore, we selected Whole Field for the Match setting. When Access reached the Title field of Record 5, it found a value that completely matched our search value, so it stopped searching.

Suppose, however, that Steven Buchanan's title had been General Sales Manager. With Whole Field selected, we wouldn't have gotten a match. If you're ever uncertain that what you want is going to be the entire field, you should select Any Part of Field. It's much more forgiving than Whole Field.

What happens if I search only the current field?

One way to make sure Access doesn't find lots of records you don't want is to search only the current field. This narrows the chances of accidental hits.

 Plain English, please!

Accidental hits are records where Access stops during a search because, based on your search options, it thinks you want those records. For example, if you're looking for your friend Florence Smith, you might decide to search for Florence because it's more unique than Smith. If you aren't in the FirstName field and selected Search Only Current Field, you'll find your friend's record, but first you might have to work your way through the records of several people who live in a city named Florence, or a company named Florence's Foodmart, or similar surprises. **99**

Let's redo the search for Sales Manager with the Search Only Current Field option selected. The blinking cursor should be in the Title field. Notice that after you click this check box, the title of the dialog box changes to indicate that the Title field is the only one being searched (see fig. 8.4).

Fig. 8.4
The new title of the dialog box reflects the fact that you've narrowed your search to the current field.

CAUTION   **Be careful when you limit your search to the current field. It's easy** to forget to make sure you're searching the proper field. When you get no results, you might wrongly assume that what you're looking for isn't in the table.

One tremendous advantage of searching only the current field is speed. With only a few dozen records and a sufficiently powerful computer, it's no big deal. With a huge table, though, limiting your search to the current field produces a much faster search, because Access only has to look in one column, rather than a whole table.

I barely remember what I'm looking for

You'll often want to do a search when you don't know precisely what you want. You might want to look up an old acquaintance that lives on Holloway Street. Or was it Holland Street? Or Holland Drive? Oh, that wasn't even Jack who lived on Holland...it was Jay.

When you don't know an exact spelling or can't remember an exact number, use a **wild card**. A wild card in Access isn't all that different than a wild card when playing poker: it makes a match with anything. In your searches, a wild card can stand in for any unknown character or characters. You can use different wild cards for different circumstances.

Q&A   *Why should I use wild cards? Why not just enter the part I know and set Match to Any Part of Field?*

Wild cards can sharply limit the number of accidental hits. If you do just a few searches on small tables, wild cards may not seem useful. But if you're doing searches all day long on large tables, they're a godsend.

How do I use a wild card?

Let's take a simple example from the Employees table. You need Janet Leverling's extension number. You remember that the first digit is 3 and the last two digits are 55, but you can't remember the digit or digits in between. To find Janet's extension, let's use the * wild card, which stands for any number of alphanumeric characters in any combination. Here's how to do the search:

1 Click in the Extension field.

2 Choose Edit, Find to open the Find dialog box.

3 In the Find What line, type **3*55.**

4 Make sure the only check box selected is Search Only Current Field.

5 Click Find First. The value 3355 is found for Janet Levering's extension.

6 Click Close to shut the dialog box.

You could have searched the entire table instead of just the current field. That way, you'd have avoided clicking in the Extension field. The tradeoff is that it would have taken longer, and you might have found values in other fields that would be completely irrelevant.

What other wild cards are there?

Besides the asterisk, the main wild cards are the question mark (?) and the number sign (#). The ? stands for any single alphanumeric character. As you might have guessed, the # stands for any single numeric character.

You can also ask Access to find one of several specific characters by putting them in square brackets. For example, if you wanted Access to find Tom or Tim, you'd type **T[io]m**. Table 8.1 summarizes the capabilities of the different wild cards.

Table 8.1   What matches will different wild cards return?

If you type...	You can find...	But not...
T[ai]mes	Tames, Times	Tomes
T?mes	Tames, Times, Tomes	Thames
T??mes	Thames	Times, The names
3#92	3492, 3792	3-92, 34792
*ton	Layton, 72 Tornton	Layton Drive
ton	16 Tons, 58 Taunton Dr.	Tom

TIP   **To search for one of these characters without it serving as a wild** card, put it in brackets. For example, to find R.F.D. #3, type **R.F.D.[#]3**.

I want to practice using wild cards some more

Let's say you work for Northwind Traders in their London office. One day you return from lunch and the new temp has left you a message. He wants you to call "someone in sales" who hasn't left home yet. After five minutes of looking at the telephone number you finally decipher 70 percent of it. The first three numbers are 555, and the fourth and the sixth are both 4. How do you find out who called? What do you ask Access to find?

You have several choices:

- You could use two number signs [#] as placeholders for the unknown numbers and find **555-4#4#**.

- You could also use two question marks, the placeholders for alphanumeric characters, and find **555-4?4?**

- You could use the star and type **555-4*4***. You could also type **555-4***, since the star wildcard stands for any number of alphanumeric digits. That might mean that, besides the number you need, you would get matches like 555-4378—obviously wrong because you already know the sixth number is a 4. On the other hand, you save yourself the trouble of typing two additional characters in the F*i*nd What line. That's almost irrelevant when you're doing one Find, but significant when you do hundreds.

Now, let's find the number:

1 Click anywhere in the HomePhone field.

2 Open the Find dialog box.

3 In the F*i*nd What line, type **555-4#4#**.

4 Use the rest of the settings shown in figure 8.5.

5 Click Find Fir*s*t. Access finds the telephone number of Steven Buchanan.

All done? Not quite. The temptation when looking for a single value like a telephone number is to find the first match and stop. You should always click F*i*nd Next to see if there are any more matches. In this case, there's one: Anne Dodsworth. Fortunately, the fifth digit in the temp's message looks more like the 8 in Steve's number than the 4 in Anne's, so you're home free. Click Close to shut the Find dialog box.

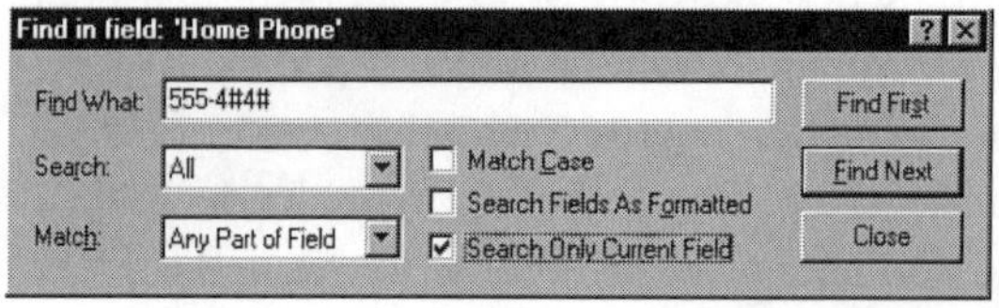

Fig. 8.5
Use the pound sign (#) as a wild card for a single numerical character.

Find in field: 'Home Phone'		? X
Fi*n*d What:	555-4#4#	Find Fir*s*t
Search:	All ▼	☐ Match *C*ase	F*i*nd Next
		☐ Search Fields As F*o*rmatted	
Mat*c*h:	Any Part of Field ▼	☑ Search Only Current Field	Close

Let's tackle the "Search Fields as Formatted" option

I know you've been wondering what the Search Fields as Formatted option does (you can find it in the middle of fig. 8.5). Remember the discussion in Chapter 7 about different ways you could format things like dates and currency? The way data appears in a table—that is, the way it's formatted—can be different from the way Access actually stores the value in the database.

When you search all fields, Access always searches for data exactly the way it appears in your table. When you limit your search to the current field, you have an option—controlled by the Search Fields as Formatted check box—to search for values exactly as they're formatted or to allow matches on values that *are* the same, but aren't formatted the same.

For example, suppose you're searching for a particular date, like the third day of March in 1994. You've selected the Medium Date format, so the date appears on your screen as 3-Mar-94. When Search Fields as Formatted is checked, you won't find it if you put March 3, 1994 in Find What.

Whether to select this option or not is up to you. Many users find it faster to leave the option deselected. For example, you can quickly key in a Short Date (10/3/95) and still find it when it's formatted as a Long Date (October 3, 1995).

How can I replace stuff I've found?

Once you've learned how to find stuff, learning the Replace command is easy. Of course, you can find something, then go ahead and edit it using methods you learned in Chapter 4. But Access has a Replace command which lets you find and fix things simultaneously.

CAUTION **When you want to change hundreds or thousands of records at** once, avoid the Replace command. Just like Find, Replace should be used when you're looking for relatively few records. In Chapter 20, "Change Your Data with Action Queries," you'll learn how to make wholesale changes when I discuss action queries.

To use Replace, you must have a table open. Again, let's use the Employees table of the Northwind Traders database as an example. Choose Edit, Replace to access the Replace dialog box (see fig. 8.6).

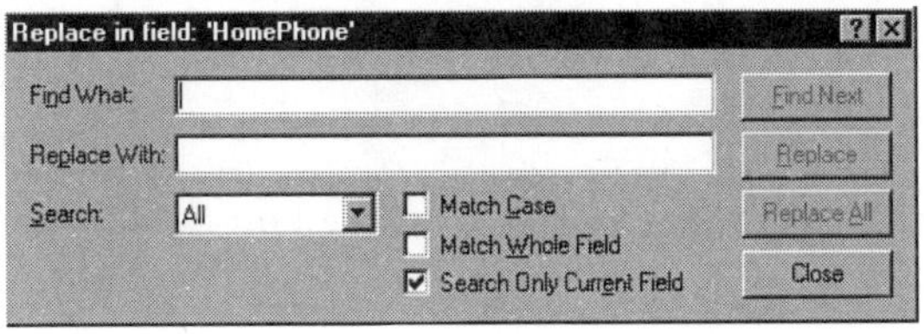

Fig. 8.6
You can use the Replace dialog box to find-and-replace data in one fell swoop.

It looks like the Find dialog box, but it's a little simpler. At the top you have the all-important Fi̲nd What line. Below is a Re̲place With line, where you type the new text that replaces the old. As with Find, you have S̲earch options, but you'll usually stick with All. Here's how the check boxes work:

- Match C̲ase. This is old hat by now. If your Fi̲nd What line says **Pelican** and this option's selected, only `Pelican` is a match, and `pelican` isn't.

- Match W̲hole Field. When this option's selected, the entire value has to match what you typed in the Find What line. If what you typed is only part of the value in the field Access is searching, there's no match.

- Search Only Curre̲nt Field. Leave this option deselected if you want to search the entire table.

Notice the R̲eplace and Replace A̲ll buttons. If you choose Replace A̲ll, Access replaces each match with what you typed in the Re̲place With line. If you choose R̲eplace, you can change the new text for each occurrence. Here's the basic procedure:

1 Type what you want to replace in Fi̲nd What and click F̲ind Next.

2 Type what you want to replace it with in Re̲place With and click R̲e-place. Access replaces the text it found with whatever's in Replace With.

3 Access finds the next occurrence on its own. You can type a new value in Replace With or simply leave what's there. Then click R̲eplace.

CAUTION With Find, it's no big deal if you grab a few values you aren't really looking for—you just ignore them. But the Replace command doesn't leave much margin for error. If you choose Replace A̲ll, Access might replace text you need with junk that you don't really want. Replacing data in only the current field is one safeguard against such a tragedy. Another is to back up your data regularly. A third would be to totally avoid use of Replace A̲ll, but, as we'll see below, sometimes it can be quite useful.

Let's look at a Replace example

Let's change something simple on the Employees table of the Northwind database. Suppose you want to change Sales Representative to Sales Rep everywhere it appears in the Title field. Here's what you do:

1 Click to place the cursor in the Title field.

2 Choose Edit, Replace to open the Replace dialog box.

3 In Find What, type **Sales Representative.**

4 In Replace With, type **Sales Rep**.

5 Make the rest of your settings match those in figure 8.7.

6 Click Find Next, then click Replace All. Access warns that you can't undo this action.

7 Click No, since you don't want to change the sample table.

8 Click Close to shut the dialog box.

Fig. 8.7
Use the Replace All button with care, or you'll change values that should be left alone.

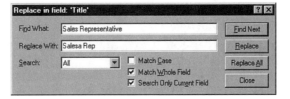

How can I sort the data in tables?

If databases are all that great, why's everything out of order? True, the ID fields are in numerical order, but that doesn't do you much good. Your old-fashioned address book at least kept the A's with the A's and the B's with the B's, and you knew that Helen Aikmann was on the first page, Paul Zygfeld on the last, and Bonnie McAfee somewhere in the middle. Can't this fancy database at least do that? You wouldn't need to use the Find command so often if things were just alphabetized.

Good news! In this section, you'll learn to sort fields of any data type in ascending or descending order. You'll also learn to sort two fields in the same table simultaneously.

 Plain English, please!

> In database speak, **ascending order** means that sorted text fields start from the A's and go to the Z's, sorted numerical fields start from 1 and go to infinity, and sorted date/time fields start from B.C. years and go to A.D. years. As you'd expect, **descending order** means the opposite: Z's through A's, and so on.

You can sort records on any field—this means the order of the records becomes based on the value each record contains in that particular field. When you've decided which field to sort on, click to place the cursor in that field on any record. Choose <u>R</u>ecords, <u>S</u>ort and then choose <u>A</u>scending or <u>D</u>escending.

An easier way to launch the Sort command is to click one of the sort buttons on the toolbar:

 If you want an ascending sort, click this one. Alphabetic values are placed in order from A to Z. Numbers are placed in order from smallest to largest. Dates run from earliest to latest. Currency…well, you get the idea.

 If you want a descending sort, click this one. Now, things are placed in order from Z to A, largest to smallest, latest to earliest, and so on.

For example, you could alphabetize the last names of the Northwind Traders employees. Click the field selector for the LastName field so that the entire column is highlighted. Click the ascending sort button on the toolbar. Access sorts all the records in alphabetical order by the employee's last name. Sorting is considered a design change, and, as you know, Access will ask you if you want to save design changes when you close the table.

I want two fields sorted at the same time

Sometimes you want to sort by more than one field. How does that work? Let's sort two fields of the Employees table. First, we'll sort by the employee's title. Then, within each group of people with the same title, we'll sort by name.

1 You need to move the field you want to sort first (the Title field) to the left of the field you want to sort second (the LastName field). To do this, you need to unfreeze all fields. Click Format, Unfreeze Columns.

2 Click the Title field selector and drag it to the left of the LastName field (see fig. 8.8). If you need a refresher on moving fields, refer to Chapter 4.

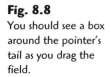

Fig. 8.8
You should see a box around the pointer's tail as you drag the field.

Heavy vertical line ——————

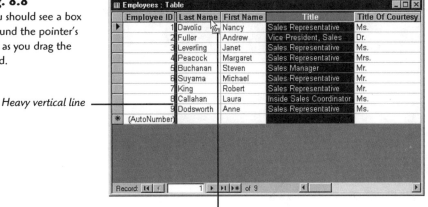

The pointer has a box around its tail

3 The Title field should still be highlighted. You want the Title and LastName fields to be highlighted at the same time, so hold down Shift and click the LastName field selector. Both fields are now selected.

4 Click the ascending sort button on the toolbar.

5 Access has sorted the fields (see fig. 8.9) so that all the employee titles are in alphabetical order. Within each group of employees that have the same title, the names of the employees are alphabetized.

6 Close the table. When Access asks if you want to save design changes, click No. That way, everything's back the way it started.

Fig. 8.9
The titles are sorted now, and last names are sorted within each different title.

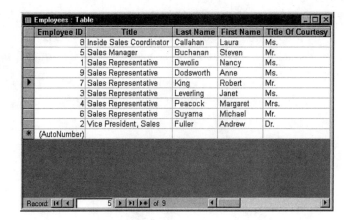

Part IV: Queries and Filters

9

Ask Questions About Your Database with Queries

● **In this chapter:**

- ● **Let's tour the Query Design window**

- ● **Simple queries are a snap!**

- ● **How do I limit my search?**

- ● **On second thought, I'd like to change my query**

- ● **Selecting all fields in a query**

Whenever you need to know something that's in your database, Access can get you fast answers if you come up with the right questions . . . . ●**>**

When you create a query, you ask Access some questions about a database, then refine those questions as much as necessary until Access answers with exactly the data you're looking for. Defining the proper questions requires your energy, but then Access takes care of churning through the database to come up with answers.

We'll spend five chapters learning about the query and its close relative, the **filter.** We'll create simple queries, then get to more interesting ones after learning the ins and outs. So, put on your curiosity cap—it's time to ask lots of questions.

The anatomy of a Query

Before you manufacture any queries, take a quick look at the Query window in Design view (see fig. 9.1). This is where the planning of a query takes place—it's your design and preproduction departments combined into one. When you **run** the query, Access assembles information from the database based on your instructions, then delivers you the final product in a grid that looks like a table.

Let's take a little tour to give you a feel for the query environment. Unlike tables, which you've worked with all your life, the concept of a query is really something new.

Let's start at the top. Most of the menu names—File, Edit, and so on—are familiar to you. Notice an additional menu named Query.

The toolbar looks mostly familiar. The View button at the far left lets you change quickly between Design view and Datasheet view. Cut, Copy, and Paste buttons are farther to the right. But wait! There's a big exclamation point, and something that looks like a first aid symbol, and a Greek letter!

Scan downward and you'll see a box named Customers. Actually, it could be named Videos, Employees, or Pizzerias. This is called a **field list**, and is simply a listing of the names of all fields from one table in the open database. You'll select fields from this list to form part of the query. Additional tables, or other queries, may also be brought into the query design area so that you can choose fields from them.

Fig. 9.1

This is the design area
for a new query.

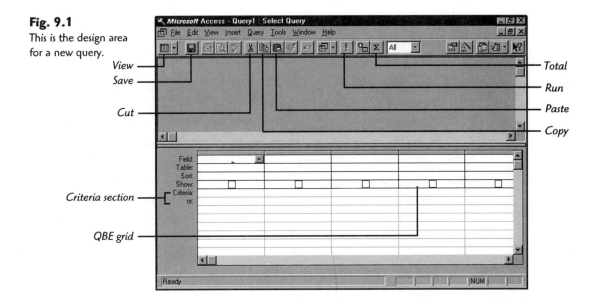

In the middle of the screen is the **Query By Example** grid, more commonly
known as the **QBE grid**. Each row in the grid has a designated purpose:

- *Field.* The fields you use to do your query are placed on this line, each
  in its own box on the grid. Remember that they'll be selected from the
  field list(s) above.

- *Table.* This shows you which table (or query) each field is from. In the
  example we're looking at, your only field list is from the Customers
  table, so the table name would always be Customers.

- *Sort.* In Chapter 8, you learned how to sort fields. You can sort
  the information retrieved in a query the same ways, either ascending
  (A to Z, smallest to largest, earliest to latest, and so on) or descending
  (Z to A).

- *Show.* Do you want Access to show the information it finds in this field?
  Or are you just using the field to perform the query so that you can see
  other parts of each record your query returns? Check this box (that is,
  click it) to indicate the field should be shown; leave the box empty if
  the field shouldn't be shown. For example, in a database of customers,
  when you're specifically searching for everyone in Illinois whose
  account is past due, the State field is needed in your query to limit the

results to Illinois customers; however, you don't want to see Illinois written over and over again in the query results. All you want to see are customer names, past due amounts, and due dates.

- *Criteria.* Here's the most interesting part of the QBE grid. On this line (and the one below it) you limit your search by imposing certain conditions, known as search criteria, that must be met before answers are returned to you. You might want to list only those employees who live in Venezuela, only those pizzerias that generate $100,000 in revenue each year, or only those tropical fish that begin with the letter A. You'll soon learn how to word your criteria so that Access understands them.

That's a very brief overview, but it gets your feet wet. Now, let's go step-by-step through an easy query to see how it's done.

Creating a simple query

A query is used to ask questions about your data. You'll understand what I mean once you see a query in action, so let's go through the process of creating one.

Suppose you've hired a temp to tell all your customers about a special promotion. You sell internationally, so the best way to distribute this type of information is by fax. The fax numbers are in one column of an 11-column table that holds all kinds of information about your customers—names, addresses, and so on.

The temp doesn't need all that information (and you don't want him to have it, anyway). All he needs is the company name, a contact name, and a fax number. How do you provide him just these three columns? A query does the trick.

Let's use the Customers table of the Northwind Traders sample database as the basis for our query.

First, open the database and create a new query.

1 Choose File, Open Database.

2 Locate the Northwind.mdb database in the Samples folder below the folder Access was installed in.

3 Open this database.

4 Click the Queries tab in the Database window.

5 Click New.

Kick off the right type of query

You choose from a list of various kinds of queries in the New Query window (see fig. 9.2). Select Design View in the New Query window, the first on top, and click OK.

Fig. 9.2
Choose Design View in the New Query window.

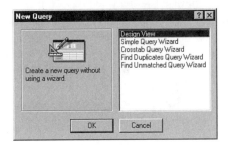

Indicate where information should come from

In the Show Table window, you can indicate where you'd like information to come from (see fig. 9.3). You can get data from tables, other queries, or a combination. In this case, you want to create a query that simply shows information from one table.

Fig. 9.3
Select the tables or queries that are going to provide the data.

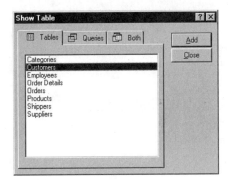

The Tables tab is selected and lists all the tables in the current database. Click the Queries tab to see a list of all the queries. If you want data from both tables and queries, click the Both tab.

For this example, you want data from the Customers table only, so click the Tables tab, click to select the Customers table, and then click Add. A field list appears in the design window. Click Close to get rid of the Show Table window.

Add fields to the QBE grid

The first piece of information the temp needs in our example is the company name. In the Customers field list, position the mouse pointer on CompanyName.

Double-click the field name, and it will be inserted in the next available Field cell on the QBE grid. Immediately, the Field cell at the upper-left of the grid says CompanyName, the table name says Customers, and the Show box is checked (see fig. 9.4).

Next, add ContactName to the field list the same way. To find the Fax field, click the vertical scroll bar on the field list until you reach the end of the list. Double-click the name of the Fax field. Your Design window should look like figure 9.5.

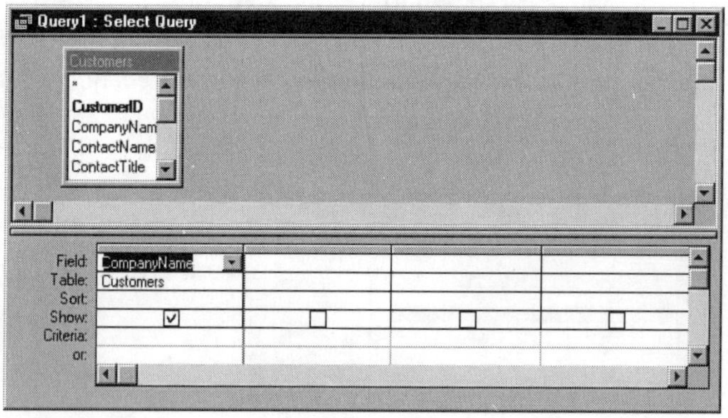

Fig. 9.4
Double-click the field name to place it on the QBE grid.

Fig. 9.5
Make sure all the fields
you want are in the
grid.

Click the
scrollbar
to see Fax

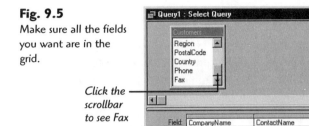

> **TIP** If you don't like what you've done, and want to start all over,
> choose Edit, Clear Grid to begin with a clean slate.

Insert another field at the last minute

You may have noticed a field named ContactTitle in the field list box.
Shouldn't that be included on the fax the temp is sending? You can put it in
the column where ContactName is currently. Simply position the pointer on
ContactTitle in the field list; then, press and hold the mouse button while you
drag the field name onto the ContactName column in the grid. ContactName
slides over to the right to make room.

I'd like to sort the query

If you want to sort the data a particular way, it's easy. You can sort a query
on one or two fields, just as you would any table. To sort our example data by
company name, just click the Sort cell for the CompanyName field. Open the
drop-down list (if it's not already open) and select Ascending. You won't
notice a difference now, but when you run the query, the company names
will be sorted.

What about criteria?

In this example you can leave the Criteria row empty. You selected the only
four fields you wanted from the Customers table, but within those fields you
don't have any desire to discriminate. You want the temp to contact all your
customers, so you need all the names, titles, and fax numbers. Soon, we'll get
to examples where you do use criteria to make sure you don't get results
from every record.

I'd like to change the order of my fields

Take one last look before running the query. Maybe it would make more sense if each contact's title followed his or her name. How do you do this? Just switch the fields around, much like you'd move a field in a table in Datasheet view. Here are the steps:

1 Move your mouse pointer to the column selector for ContactTitle, which is directly above the field's name. When the pointer changes to a down arrow, click to select the column.

2 Press and hold down the mouse button in that spot. A rectangle appears around the pointer's tail.

3 Drag the column to the right. A heavy vertical line shows how far you've dragged it (see fig. 9.6).

4 Release the mouse button when the heavy vertical line is positioned as it is in the figure. The field is moved immediately.

Fig. 9.6
Drag the column, using the vertical line as a guide.

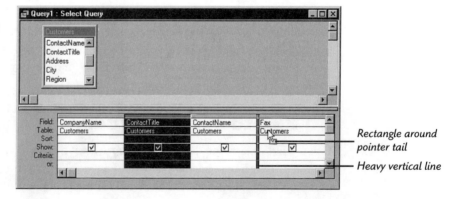

Rectangle around pointer tail

Heavy vertical line

TIP　**You could have achieved exactly the same result by dragging** ContactName one column to the left.

Q&A　***I'm having trouble grabbing hold of the column to drag it. When I click the second time, it loses its highlight.***

Make sure you're clicking the column selector box (the short rectangular box directly above the field name). That's the only place you can grab the column for dragging.

Running a query

It's time to run the query. Click the Run icon (the exclamation point) on the toolbar, or choose Query, Run. The results of your query appear in Datasheet view (see fig. 9.7). Click the vertical scroll bar, or press Page Down, to see more records.

Fig. 9.7
The query results are presented in Datasheet view.

Company Name	Contact Name	Contact Title	Fax
Alfreds Futterkiste	Maria Anders	Sales Representative	030-0076545
Ana Trujillo Emparedados y helados	Ana Trujillo	Owner	(5) 555-3745
Antonio Moreno Taquería	Antonio Moreno	Owner	
Around the Horn	Thomas Hardy	Sales Representative	(171) 555-6750
Berglunds snabbköp	Christina Berglund	Order Administrator	0921-12 34 67
Blauer See Delikatessen	Hanna Moos	Sales Representative	0621-08924
Blondel père et fils	Frédérique Citeaux	Marketing Manager	88.60.15.32
Bólido Comidas preparadas	Martín Sommer	Owner	(91) 555 91 99
Bon app'	Laurence Lebihan	Owner	91.24.45.41
Bottom-Dollar Markets	Elizabeth Lincoln	Accounting Manager	(604) 555-3745
B's Beverages	Victoria Ashworth	Sales Representative	
Cactus Comidas para llevar	Patricio Simpson	Sales Agent	(1) 135-4892
Centro comercial Moctezuma	Francisco Chang	Marketing Manager	(5) 555-7293
Chop-suey Chinese	Yang Wang	Owner	

Record: 1 of 91

Saving your query

You can give each query a name and save it. Click File, Save As/Export. The dialog box in figure 9.8 appears. Access suggests a generic name in the New Name line, but it's better to use something meaningful (for our example, type **Special Promotion**). When you're done typing, click OK. Close the Special Promotion query window.

To check that your query has been saved, look at the Queries tab in the Northwind database window. The query you just created is listed among the queries.

Fig. 9.8
Always use a more descriptive name than what Access suggests.

Save As...

Save Query 'Query1'

○ To an external File or Database

● Within the current database as

New Name: Query1

OK   Cancel

Q&A *What's the big deal about queries? Seems to me you could have done the same thing by opening the table, hiding some columns, and printing it out.*

Yes, but then you couldn't have named and saved it. Actually, there are many more benefits to creating a query—read further to learn what they are.

Using criteria to limit the search

Suppose you decide to do another promotion, but want to limit it to your customers in France. You want Access to give you the same information as before, but only for French companies. Here's how you do it:

1 Click the Special Promotion query you just created in the Northwind database window. Highlight, and choose Design to reach Design view.

2 In the field list box for the Customers table, find the Country field. (Click the scroll bar if it's not visible.)

3 Double-click the Country field so that it's added to the QBE grid.

4 Click the Criteria cell of the column just created for the Country field and type **France** (see fig. 9.9).

5 Now choose Query, Run. The query results appear in Datasheet view.

6 Click File, Save As to save this query with a new name. Type **Special Promotion (France)** and click OK.

You could have created this query from scratch by going through all the steps in the first example, then adding the criteria for the Country field. Instead, you made the new query by modifying your existing one. Whenever reworking an old query can save you time, you should do it!

Fig. 9.9
Use criteria to define the records you want access to retrieve.

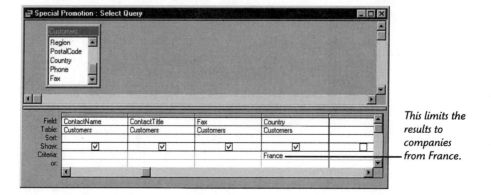

This limits the results to companies from France.

I want to change the way my query looks

You can easily change the way a query appears in your datasheet. In fact, you have most of the same options—hiding and freezing columns, changing the font, making columns wider and rows longer—that you have when using tables. These commands are available from the Format menu in Datasheet view.

Let's also look at a couple of ways you can change what you see in Datasheet view by fiddling with the QBE grid.

Use a certain column, but don't see it

Take another look at the Special Promotions (France) query. You need the Country field in the QBE grid to limit your search to customers in France. But do you need the query results to tell you over and over that each customer's from France? No, your query title already says that. It's better if you keep the Country field out of your query results.

Let's go back to Design view to take care of that. Click View, Query Design to reach Design View. In the Country column, click the Show cell so it becomes empty.

 TIP   **Clicking the Query View button at the left end of the** toolbar switches quickly between Datasheet view and Design view. So as an alternative to running a query by choosing Query, Run, you can simply click the View icon and switch to Datasheet view.

Before you leave Design view, notice that **France** in the Criteria cell of the Country column has quotation marks around it—Access added these. They're nothing to worry about, and they'll be discussed in Chapter 10, "It's Only an Expression."

I don't need this field at all

You might decide you don't need a certain field at all. Go into Design view, click its column selector, and press the Delete key. It's gone.

 CAUTION   **Before you delete a field, make sure your query doesn't need it.** Remember that you might not want to *see* data from some columns, but still might need those fields to form the correct query.

How do I select all the fields for the QBE grid?

Let's go back and visit the temp we hired. Suppose you decide you can trust him fully, and want him to have all the information about your French customers to use for follow-up phone calls after the mailing. Just the French customers, though—no sense giving him your whole mailing list. How can you get every field onto the QBE grid? You could place each one on the grid individually, but that's a huge hassle.

Access provides two methods for making all the fields from a table part of a query. You could get away with using just the first method, but if you stick around to learn both, you can take your pick in different situations.

Use the title bar to select all fields

One way to get all the fields on the QBE grid is to double-click the title bar. Here's how we'd do our sample query:

1 Click the Queries tab in the Database window; click <u>N</u>ew.

2 Select Design View in the New Query window and click OK.

What is this SQL I keep on seeing?

SQL stands for **Structured Query Language**. It's a computer language that's become a standard for relational databases. Instead of dragging fields, checking Show boxes, and so on, you could use SQL statements to tell Access to do everything you want. To get an idea of what SQL looks like, select SQL from the drop-down menu of the View toolbar button while you're in any query.

When you look at SQL, you'll ask...Why bother with that junk? The beauty of Access is that you can work in a graphical environment and in plain English. Why make life so difficult?

Actually, while Access is great for beginners, it's a very powerful application. People who've spent years with SQL and other computer languages sometimes find it easier to use SQL than to learn equivalent Access commands. For some advanced tasks, they simply can't do what they'd like to in Access without the extra oomph of SQL.

This shouldn't bother you a bit. You can do anything *you* want in Access without going within ten miles of SQL statements. When you see it mentioned in Help or in menu choices, just forget it's there. You don't need to know any SQL to use Access successfully.

3 In the Show Table window, click the Tables tab and click on the Customers table to select it. Click <u>A</u>dd, and then click <u>C</u>lose. This adds a field list for the Customers table to the design area.

4 Double-click the title bar of the field list box. All fields in the list are now selected.

5 Place the cursor on any field in the list, click and hold down the mouse button, and drag all the fields (yes, they'll all travel together) to the first column of the QBE grid (see fig. 9.10).

6 Every field of the Customers table is now in the grid. Use the horizontal scroll bar to find the Country field. Type **France** on the Criteria line for that column.

7 Choose <u>Q</u>uery, <u>R</u>un. You'll see information for every field in the Customers table, but only for the records of French customers.

8 Choose <u>F</u>ile, <u>C</u>lose. When Access asks if you want to save your changes, choose No (if you were doing something you cared about saving for future reference, of course, you'd choose Yes).

Fig. 9.10
It's easy to drag all the fields simultaneously onto the QBE grid.

All fields are selected.

Drag them to the first column.

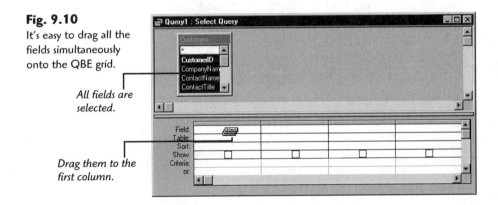

What's that asterisk in the field list for?

The mystery can finally be revealed: you can use this asterisk to select all fields in a table. In our search for French customers, we'd do the same first three steps as we did in the last section, then:

1 Click the asterisk at the top of the field list, press and hold down the mouse button, and drag the asterisk to the first column of the QBE grid.

2 The field name says Customers*, which means that all fields in the table have been selected for the query. You don't see each field in a separate column in Design view, but when you run the query, each one will be retrieved.

3 Now, how do you limit the query to French customers? The Country field was selected as part of the Customers table, but there's no way to indicate criteria for it. What you have to do is to place the Country field on the QBE grid (double-click its name in the field list) so that it has its own column (see fig. 9.11).

4 Now, type **France** in the Criteria box for that column.

5 What about the Country Show box? You already have the Country field represented in Customers*—you don't need to see it again. So click the Show box and make it empty.

6 Choose Query, Run to run the query. You don't need to save it (unless you want to). Just take a look at your results, and see that they look like the results in figure 9.12.

Fig. 9.11
You need to have the Country field in a separate column to set criteria for it.

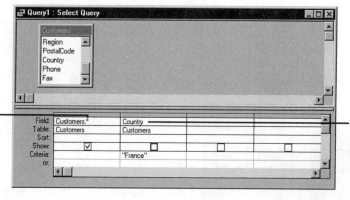

This asterisk means all fields are selected.

Put any fields that require criteria in separate columns; they won't be repeated in the query results.

Q&A   *Why'd you teach me both methods? The first method's obviously better—I can see each field separately on the grid, and set the Show and Criteria lines exactly like I want.*

It's true that the asterisk method has drawbacks, but it has one important advantage. If you add a field to the Customers table *after* you design and run a query involving Customers*, your query is automatically updated to include the new field. With the other method, your query includes only the fields you actually dragged and dropped. The asterisk method also has the advantage of being less cluttered when you add other tables.

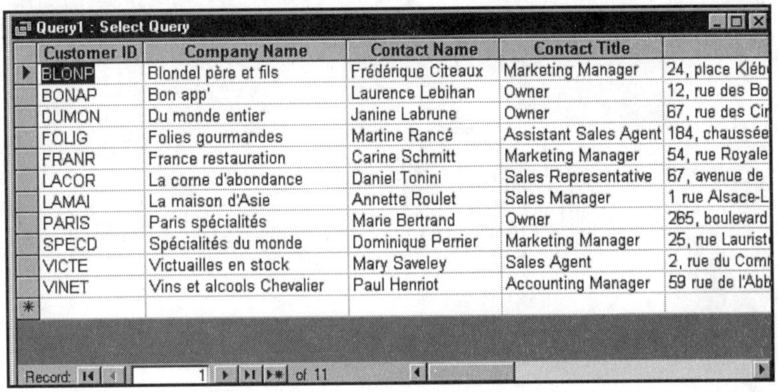

Fig. 9.12
All fields from the Customers table are included in the query results.

Customer ID	Company Name	Contact Name	Contact Title	
BLONP	Blondel père et fils	Frédérique Citeaux	Marketing Manager	24, place Klébe
BONAP	Bon app'	Laurence Lebihan	Owner	12, rue des Bo
DUMON	Du monde entier	Janine Labrune	Owner	67, rue des Cir
FOLIG	Folies gourmandes	Martine Rancé	Assistant Sales Agent	184, chaussée
FRANR	France restauration	Carine Schmitt	Marketing Manager	54, rue Royale
LACOR	La corne d'abondance	Daniel Tonini	Sales Representative	67, avenue de
LAMAI	La maison d'Asie	Annette Roulet	Sales Manager	1 rue Alsace-L
PARIS	Paris spécialités	Marie Bertrand	Owner	265, boulevard
SPECD	Spécialités du monde	Dominique Perrier	Marketing Manager	25, rue Lauriste
VICTE	Victuailles en stock	Mary Saveley	Sales Agent	2, rue du Comr
VINET	Vins et alcools Chevalier	Paul Henriot	Accounting Manager	59 rue de l'Abb

Record: 1 of 11

I want to get rid of queries I've made

Ready to delete unwanted queries (like the ones you added to the Northwind database in this chapter)? Select the Database window, then click the Queries tab. Click to select the name of any query you want to delete, then choose Edit, Delete. When Access asks you to confirm the deletion, click Yes.

10

It's Only an Expression

● In this chapter:

- What are expressions good for?

- Get a quick date with a query

- Wild cards make queries flexible

- No limit on limits: using criteria in more than one field

- Bring some math magic to your queries

Finding records in Access is like finding famous landmarks in a foreign country. You know they're there, and you know it's possible to find them—you just have to figure out how to ask where they are. . . . . ➤

"**W**hat clients did you visit in February?" "What customers do we have in Brazil?" "What movies did you see Michelle Pfeiffer in last year?" Although none of us have trouble understanding these questions, we might have some difficulty recalling the answers. With your computer, it's the other way around: It remembers everything, but has a tough time understanding questions in plain English.

Fortunately, the language Access uses for queries is sort of an English variant, and you shouldn't have trouble picking it up. It combines common English words with a few special symbols that help you make yourself understood to Access.

What are expressions?

You can't turn on your computer and say "Howdy, Access, how ya feelin' today? What customers do I have in Brazil?" Not yet, anyway. What you can do is to use **expressions** that accomplish the same thing. Expressions are a kind of shorthand that you and Access can both understand.

In fact, you've already used expressions. When you typed criteria in a query, those were expressions. If, for example, you're planning to visit a customer in Illinois, and you have a table of business contacts, you might want to list names and addresses of other Illinois contacts (see fig. 10.1). That way, you're all set if there's time to fit other visits in while you're there.

You set up a query based on that table, then drag the fields you want to the QBE grid. (If you want to refresh your query-making skills, turn to Chapter 9.) To limit the results to contacts from Illinois, you type **Illinois** on the Criteria line for the State column (see fig. 10.2).

Illinois, as it's used here, is an expression. An expression doesn't have to be fancy—it can be a single word. In this case, a one-word expression (together with other information in the QBE grid) tells Access, "Take a look at all the records in my Business Contacts table, and show me just the ones from Illinois." As happens in spoken English, one word can say it all in Access. Sometimes, though, one-word questions bring narrow answers. You'll need to learn some fancier expressions to refine your queries.

Fig. 10.1
You might keep your business contacts in a table like this.

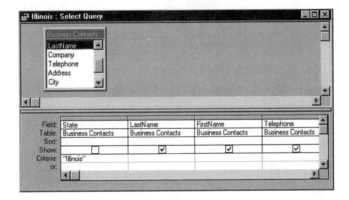

Fig. 10.2
An expression can be as simple as a single word.

Q&A *After I typed Illinois, I pressed Enter and it became "Illinois". Why did Access add quotation marks?*

That's simply a format, known as **standard format**, that Access put your expression in. Similarly, if you type in a date, Access puts pound signs around it—7/16/95 becomes #7/16/95#. Numbers, on the other hand, get nothing: type 100 and Access shows 100.

Using Or expressions

It turns out that everyone you wanted to see in Illinois is unavailable. Since you haven't been to Indiana or Ohio recently, you decide to try your luck with these states. You could run separate queries to find contacts' names in each state, as you did with Illinois. But wouldn't it be easier to do both states in a single query? Of course! You can do so by using an **Or expression**.

Begin your query as you did for the Illinois contacts, but on the Criteria line for the State column, type **Indiana**. Then click the box directly beneath this—the Or line—and type **Ohio** (see fig. 10.3). Click the Datasheet icon, and you'll see the business contacts for both states.

Fig. 10.3
Use the Or line to tell Access which additional records you want to see.

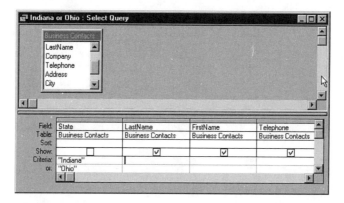

TIP You don't have to put Or criteria on separate lines in the QBE grid. You can type **"Indiana" Or "Ohio"** on the Criteria line; or, if you want to add another state, type **"Indiana" Or "Ohio" Or "Kansas"** on the Criteria line.

A date with Access is easy

In the same way that you asked Access to see the records from certain states, you can enter expressions that request the records from certain calendar dates.

Get me records from a single date

You go to the store to harass them because your new sofa still hasn't been delivered. You don't have your receipt, but the clerk says, "That's OK, we'll find your sofa. Do you know what day you ordered it?" Of course, you do—it was the same day your son had his second-Tuesday-of-the-month soccer game. They look up what date the second Tuesday was, then look up your order, and finally deliver your sofa.

Querying Access for records from a single day is just as easy. Access isn't fussy about how you type dates in as criteria. You want to put in all numbers?

That's fine. Want to write out the name of the month? Go ahead. Here's a sampler of valid ways:

7/18/95

#7/18/95#

18 July 1995

18-Jul-1995

Jul 18 95

Get me records from a range of dates

You can also choose a **range** of dates for your query. Suppose you keep the membership list for your local computer users' group (see fig. 10.4). There's going to be a special meeting for new members, because the president thinks most users are scared of the insides of computers. He wants to get them comfortable opening the backs of their machines and poking around in the guts. He's found just the right guy to give the presentation—a technical whiz who spent years in customer support. All members who joined in 1995 or later are to be invited. Great! Now, how do you find these people?

Fig. 10.4

The table shows data about club members. You can use criteria to select records of members who joined after a certain date.

Mailing List ID	First Name	Last Name	Member Since	Home Phone	Address
1	George	Burns	9/16/93	327-4945	65 Mt. Park
2	Sam	Picard	8/14/92	327-5567	345 Buena V
3	Shirley	Blum	1/3/95	426-5888	53 San Juan
4	Paul	Songrass	10/17/95	426-7712	35 Fruitdale
5	Pamela	Lauden	8/15/92	354-5677	673 River Dri
6	Butler	Morris	7/11/91	426-9832	17 Hollister
7	Drew	Bogner	11/16/95	327-7781	589 Brinckm:
8	Robert	Jackson	2/11/93	354-9922	229 Montrose
9	Sally	Gallinger	2/2/91	344-6883	66 Alvinis
10	Robert	Chan	10/11/88	426-8834	42 Timberly F
11	Walter	Jensen	3/2/95	426-9925	55 N. First S
12	Roy	Pong	10/11/88	327-8751	11 Grand Vie
13	Paul	Arnold	5/15/92	344-7791	699 Willow P
14	Chris	Loring	6/17/93	354-8891	55 Mulberry

Montvale PC Users Group : Table

Record: 1 of 19

You use the **greater than** sign (**>**) to find records after a certain date. You use the **less than** sign (**<**) to find records before a certain date. In a query for the sample problem, you'd type **>12/31/94** as criteria for the Member Since field (see fig. 10.5). (Put in the date any way you feel comfortable.) Click the Datasheet icon. All members who joined in 1995 are shown.

Fig. 10.5
Use the greater than sign to see records of members who joined after a certain date.

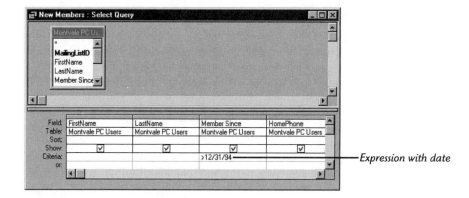

Expression with date

TIP **Put the date in however you're most comfortable. If you don't like >12/31/94, type >Dec 31 94.**

You can further restrict which records are retrieved, by using Between...And. Suppose the club's president wants to limit the guest list to only those members who joined from September to November. You could type **Between 8/31/95 And 11/30/95** as criteria. That would include anybody who joined on August 31, 1995, and November 30, 1995, and all dates in between.

How else can I use the < and > signs?

This stuff's probably looking a little too much like your algebra textbook in high school. And, if you're like most people, that wasn't your favorite subject. Don't worry, there's no Pythagorean theorem waiting to be proved—just some straightforward, useful stuff ahead.

See all the records bigger (or smaller) than some number

Often, you'll want to find values that are greater than or less than a particular number. This can include numbers expressed as currency, or those used as counters (that is, a number ID).

In a table of your favorite recipes, for instance, you can find the dishes that take less than 30 minutes to make. Tell Access to look in the

PreparationTime field for values less than 30 minutes by typing the expression **<30** in the Criteria line. An owner of a small business can find inventory items with a selling price above $100, by typing **>100**. A college recruiter can assign each of her assistants a group of potential candidates, and can divide the HotProspects table between them, by querying it according to IDNumber—Julie gets the list where IDNumber is above 2000, or **>2000**, and Todd takes those that are **<2000**.

 TIP Notice that when you use numbers in expressions you leave out all the extra stuff, like currency signs and commas.

I also want values that are equal to the number

Sometimes you want values that are not only greater or less than some number, but exactly equal to it as well. Let's return to those preparation times for recipes. Cookbook writers don't pinpoint them down to the nano-second—they estimate what's right. As anyone who's ever prepared a TV dinner knows, "cooking times may vary." So, a recipe that'll take you 25 minutes might be listed as 30 minutes in your database.

To make sure you get to see all the 30-minute recipes, add an **equal sign** (=) after the less than sign, so your expression becomes **<=30**. That way, the query returns all recipes taking less than 30 minutes, and also any that take exactly 30 minutes. If you're not particularly hungry and want to try something that takes some time, you can look for **>=30** recipes—those that take 30 minutes or longer.

 TIP You can also use > and < with text. In a field of last names, for example, **>=N** returns all the names that began with the letters N to Z—say, from Nader to Zycoff.

66 *Plain English, please!*

At some point, you might come across the term **logical operators**. These are the symbols and words—And, Or, <, >, =, and others—that are discussed in this chapter. They each show some activity (an operation) being performed. Don't worry about this term too much—the essential thing is learning what each of these words or symbols means to Access. 99

What if I want a range of numbers?

Just as you did for a range of dates, you can use Between…And to define a range of numbers. In a list of product prices, you might want to know all the items that sold for anywhere from $100 to $200. Use **Between 100 And 200** as your expression.

Can I use wild cards in queries?

You've already used wild cards when finding data with the Find command. You can also use wild cards in queries. This helps when you don't know exactly what your criteria should be (for instance, when you're unsure of the spelling). Another good use for wild cards is to expand your query and include additional values. Table 10.1 shows various ways to use wild cards when you query for records. Just type them as shown in the first column of the table. Access displays the expression with the word Like and quotation marks.

Table 10.1   Some ways to use wild cards in queries

What you input	What is displayed	What might turn up
S?lly	Like "S?lly"	Sally, Solly
Th?n?	Like "Th?n?"	Thing, Thank
M*t	Like "M*t"	Malt, Millet, Mojave Desert
*Street	Like "*Street"	Easy Street, 36 First Street
co	Like "*co*"	Macon, 27 Second St., Conoco

 TIP   **When you use wild cards in a query, don't worry about capitalization.** If you type **m*T** instead of **M*t**, you still get records that contain Mojave Desert.

Suppose you run a small flower shop. You discover that a former employee had a problem spelling Johnson; sometimes she spelled it Johnson, but sometimes Johnsen. You want to review all records with either spelling to make sure they're correct. Use the criteria **Johns?n** to have the query return records with either spelling (see fig. 10.6).

Fig. 10.6
You can use wild cards when you're unsure of the spelling of a name.

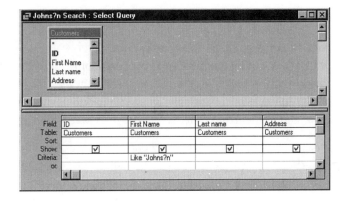

You can also use wild cards to find all the items with a common word or element. For example, several jazz greats recorded "Songbook" albums in the Fifties. Each album was devoted to the tunes of a great songwriter or songwriting team, like Irving Berlin, or Rodgers and Hart. A friend asks you what Songbook albums you have. You know they were all named the same way—The Cole Porter Songbook, The Johnny Mercer Songbook, and the like—so you use the criteria *Songbook to find all the titles.

When would I want to set criteria in more than one field?

So far, you've placed expressions in just one field when creating queries. Often, however, you'll want to put criteria in two columns of the QBE grid. That way, you can better define which data you want to see.

Let's return to our jazz collection. If you need to find all the recordings of Ella Fitzgerald and John Coltrane, that's no problem. Drag the LastName and Title fields onto the QBE grid, then type **"Fitzgerald" Or "Coltrane"** as criteria in the LastName field.

But, what if you want to find albums by those two artists only if you bought them before 1992? Or you want to see everything you own by those two artists, plus all the albums you bought in the 1990s, regardless of artist? In these cases, you'd need to set criteria in two fields, not just one.

Get to know the And criteria

And criteria are used when you want two conditions—from two different fields—to both be met before a record in your table is considered a match. These expressions will go on the same line in the Criteria section of the QBE grid. You're saying, "Show me the records where this-and-that is true in one field, and at the same time, such-and-such is true in another."

Was that sufficiently confusing? Let's try an example. Figure 10.7 shows the Jazz Collection table. Let's say you want to know all the John Coltrane recordings you've bought in the 1990s. Drag the LastName, Title, and DatePurchased fields onto the QBE grid. On the Criteria line, type **Coltrane** in the LastName column. In the DatePurchased column, type **>=1/1/90** (see fig. 10.8). Running this query retrieves all the Coltrane recordings you've bought so far this decade.

Fig. 10.7
Even with small tables it pays to create queries to retrieve the records you want.

Fig. 10.8
Use And criteria in two columns to retrieve only those records where both expressions are true at once.

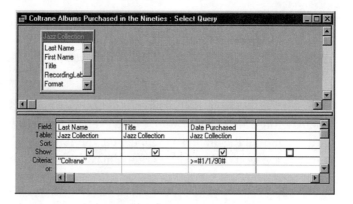

What about true/false queries with an Or expression?

You might want to locate records where an expression in one field is true, *or* an expression in another field is true. In other words, "Show me the records where you have this-and-that in one field, or such-and-such in another." We call these Or criteria.

Take another look at the Jazz Collection table. Let's say you want to know what Coltrane recordings you have, and any recordings that were bought in the 1990s. Take a look at figure 10.9. With And criteria for two fields, both expressions are placed on the same line. This time, however, you're using Or criteria for two fields, so the second expression goes on a different line. Also, just for kicks, let's sort the albums by date, with the oldest listed first. Just select Ascending on the Sort line in the DatePurchased column.

Fig. 10.9
To use Or criteria for two fields you need to put the expressions on different lines.

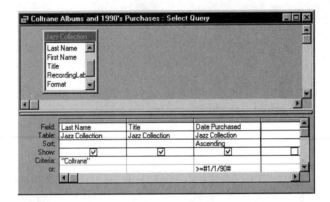

Q&A *I see something called Expression Builder. Should I be using that?*

For doing short queries, it's easier to ignore Expression Builder and just type in expressions as you need them. When you do more complex queries, you might find Expression Builder helpful.

I'd like a little arithmetic in my query

You can do some basic calculations in queries. A business owner might want to see what his selling prices would be after a 15 percent discount. A car collector might want a rough estimate of what each of her vintage Rolls

Royces will be worth four years from now, if their value increases by one-twelfth each year.

Let's look at a full-blown example. Suppose you're the director of a mid-sized public library system. The city manager has said you're allowed a 10-percent increase in next year's budget for buying new books. You want to see how much extra money that means for each branch. Figure 10.10 shows the current book budget.

Fig. 10.10
A small calculation is going to help us learn the impact of a budget increase on the individual branches.

Branch Library Book Budget : Table		
Branch Library	**Location**	**Current Budget**
Franklin Roosevelt	Mt. Ross	$965.00
Hillside	Hillside	$1,615.00
Main	Downtown	$14,345.00
Martin Luther King, Jr.	Andover Terrace	$4,112.00
New Manor	New Manor	$1,400.00
Robert Kennedy	Northside	$4,216.00
South Park	South Park	$2,365.00
Wilson	Seaview	$3,216.00
*		$0.00

Record: 1 of 8

In this case, you don't want to set criteria to get current records. You want to create a new field to show the new budget numbers. Create a new query based on the Book Budget table. Drag all the fields to the QBE grid. In the first empty column on the Field line, type **[Current Budget]*1.1** (see fig. 10.11).

Fig. 10.11
We're creating a new field based on a calculated expression to show the effects of the budget increase.

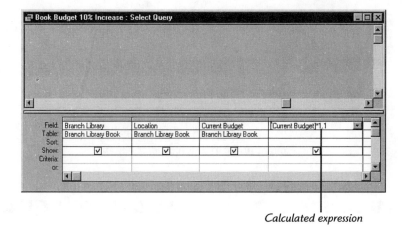

Field:	Branch Library	Location	Current Budget	[Current Budget]*1.1
Table:	Branch Library Book	Branch Library Book	Branch Library Book	
Sort:				
Show:	✓	✓	✓	✓
Criteria:				
or:				

Calculated expression

The * is the **multiplication symbol**, and the **1.1** represents the current budget plus a 10 percent increase in funds. Notice that **Current Budget** is put into brackets, because it's a field name. Figure 10.12 shows the query in Datasheet view. The last column shows what the new budget figures will be.

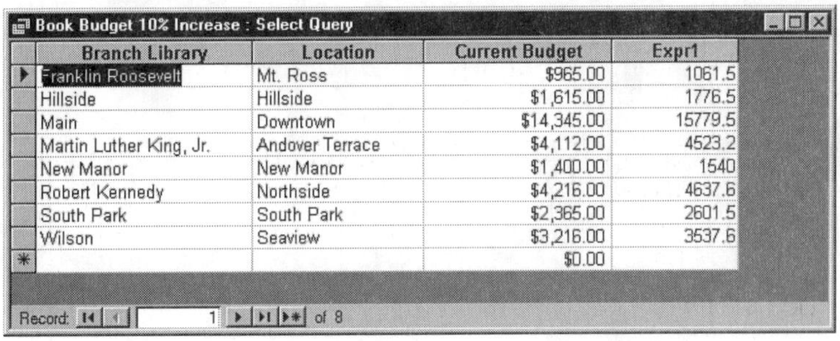

Fig. 10.12

The last column shows the new budget figures. The numbers look right, but they're not in currency format.

Branch Library	Location	Current Budget	Expr1
Franklin Roosevelt	Mt. Ross	$965.00	1061.5
Hillside	Hillside	$1,615.00	1776.5
Main	Downtown	$14,345.00	15779.5
Martin Luther King, Jr.	Andover Terrace	$4,112.00	4523.2
New Manor	New Manor	$1,400.00	1540
Robert Kennedy	Northside	$4,216.00	4637.6
South Park	South Park	$2,365.00	2601.5
Wilson	Seaview	$3,216.00	3537.6
*		$0.00	

Book Budget 10% Increase : Select Query

Record: 1 of 8

Hmmm, not exactly what you want. The new field is named Expr1, which isn't very descriptive, and the data has no dollar signs or decimal points. The numbers look okay, and you could get a quick idea of the budget increases without any further work.

If you want to show this projection to someone else, switch to Design view to make it look better. Then, give the new field a meaningful name by replacing Expr1 with **New Budget:** so that the entire line now reads **New Budget: [Current Budget]*1.1**.

To format the new field as currency, click to select it (if you're not already in the field), and then choose View, Properties. In the General tab, click in the Format box and type **Currency**. Close the Field Properties window. When you switch to Datasheet view, all the new budget numbers will be shown in dollars and cents.

11

Filters: A Temporary Viewpoint

● In this chapter:

- Give your datasheets a filter facelift

- Filter by Selection—create criteria with just one click

- Got the QBE grid blues? Try Filter by Form!

- To give a filter a future, save it as a query

- Filters versus queries: Is there a difference?

What do you call a query that's easy to make, easy to use, and easy to dump? You call it a filter . . . . **>**

Today's consumer culture moves increasingly toward short-term products. Disposable diapers, disposable cameras, disposable contact lenses—what's next? Disposable computers? Boot up once, then throw it away!

Like other trends, disposable items have plusses and minuses. They're often more convenient, and require smaller investments of time and money in the short run. On the downside, however, they sometimes lack the quality and strength of products that are built to last longer.

In this chapter, we focus on **filters**, which are disposable queries. Like other disposable products, filters are quick and easy to use. But they're not as flexible or robust as queries. The filter's so transient that it doesn't even get a name.

Like other disposable products, filters in Access have become better over time. You'll probably prefer to use a filter instead of a query wherever you can.

Where and when can I use a filter?

You can create a filter in a table, a query, or a form. In fact, you can make a filter in any datasheet. In Chapter 8, you learned to sort fields in a table. Now, you're going to filter the values as well, to make sure you see only the ones you want. Open the datasheet first, and filter your information as the need arises. You can do most of what you did when designing a query, but within a datasheet.

 TIP ▼ **This button toggles between applying the filter and remov-**ing it. Use this button when you want to remove a filter and return to your original datasheet.

❝ *Plain English, please!*
We've defined and talked all along about working with tables in Datasheet view. Your queries and forms can be datasheets, too. A **datasheet** is simply a grid with a bunch of information organized in rows and columns. ❞

In what ways can I filter my data?

Let's open a table and see how you begin to filter data. Use the Suppliers table in the Northwind Traders database as a sample. Choose File, Open Database, find the Northwind.mdb database in the Samples folder below the folder Access was installed in, and open this database. In the Database window, select and open the Suppliers table. Notice the three filter buttons on the toolbar shown in figure 11.1.

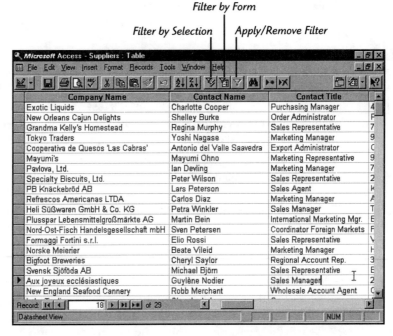

Fig. 11.1
You can use filters within a table or any other datasheet.

Choose Records, Filter. You have three choices for a filter: Filter by Form, Filter by Selection, and Advanced Filter/Sort. To stay on familiar ground, choose Advanced Filter/Sort. You'll see what's shown in figure 11.2. You've seen this before, right? It's essentially the query window in Design view, including the Query By Example (QBE) grid. A field list box—containing all the fields from the Suppliers table—has already been added. In fact, you don't have any other choices. You can't add field lists from other tables or queries to a filter—it's strictly for the table you're working in.

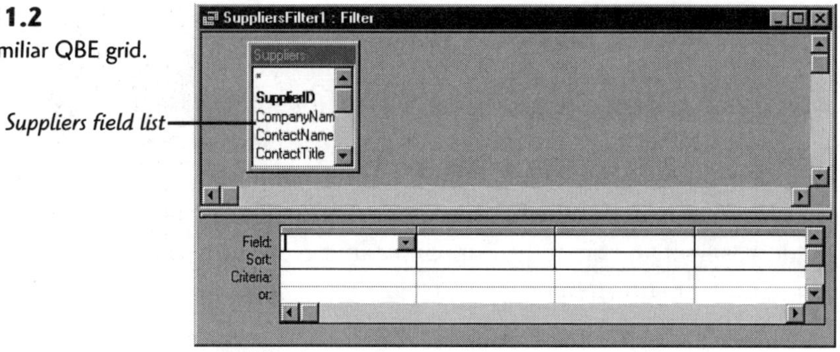

Fig. 11.2
The familiar QBE grid.

Suppliers field list

How do I use Filter by Selection?

Rather than work in the QBE grid, let's start with Filter by Selection. It's not as versatile as the other methods, but it's fast, it's quick, and—you've got to believe me—fun. Its name is apt, because you specify criteria by selecting information in the datasheet. When you filter, only records which meet that criteria are shown. You can refine your filter further by selecting another value and filtering again.

It's time for an example from the Suppliers table. Let's say you want every record where the Contact Title field begins with the word Sales. Simply select Sales where it begins any field (see fig. 11.3), then click the Filter by Selection button on the toolbar. Figure 11.4 shows your results. As you can see, you don't even have to select the whole value in a record—you can just select part of it.

TIP **Even if you prefer using the menu bar, try out some easy alterna-** tives when applying filters. First, the toolbar buttons are terribly convenient. And second, a click of the right mouse button gives you a short menu with the filter commands.

I want to filter what I just filtered

You can refine your filter by making another selection and filtering again. Suppose you want to see just the sales representatives. Select Sales Representative anywhere you see it in the current filter. Click the Filter by Selection button again, and you'll only see records for the sales representatives.

Fig. 11.3
Select all or part of the value you want to use as criteria.

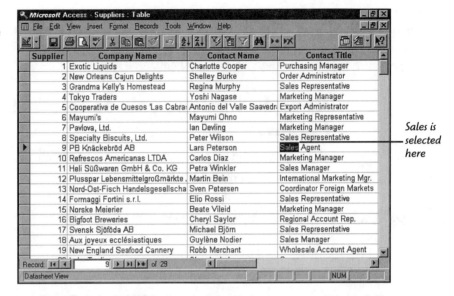

Sales is selected here

Fig. 11.4
The filter shows all the records that begin with Sales in the Contact Title field.

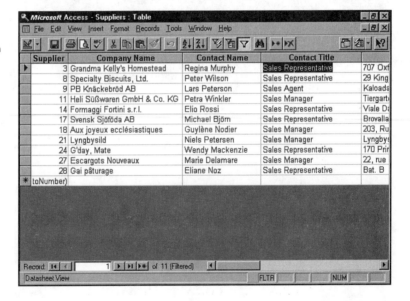

You can sort the records you're viewing in a filter, too. Click the field selector box of whatever field you want to sort on (for the example, use Company Name). Now, click the ascending sort (A–Z) button on the toolbar.

TIP Even though you've filtered your table, you're still in Datasheet view, and all the Format menu commands are available. You can hide, freeze, or resize columns as you wish.

How do I select values to get the records I want?

The flexibility of Filter by Selection is relatively limited, and you can't set criteria using wild cards. But how and where you make the selection for the filter does determine which records the filter returns. Table 11.1 summarizes the different kinds of selections, and shows how each one affects your results.

Table 11.1   The basics of Filter by Selection

What you select	Where it's selected	What is returned	Example
Entire value	Entire cell	Only exact matches	Turkey returns only Turkey
Part of a value	Start of the field	Only records starting with the selected characters	Tur returns Turkey and Turkestan
Part of a value	After the first character	Any record containing those characters	Turk returns Turkey, Aventur, and Saturn

Can I exclude records I don't want to see?

You can filter records by excluding stuff instead of including it. In other words, only records that don't have the selection are returned. Here's how to do that:

1 Open the table you want to filter.

TIP If you're already in Datasheet view and have placed other filters on this table, remove them by clicking the Remove Filter button.

2 Select all or part of a value to serve as criteria.

3 Click the right mouse button on the selected area. A shortcut menu appears.

4 Choose Filter Excluding Selection.

TIP **Click the right mouse button to bring up the shortcut menu again.** Look at all the commands available with a single click in Datasheet view. Try not to forget about this menu!

How do I use Filter by Form?

Filter by Form is more powerful than Filter by Selection. You can set And and Or criteria, and can also use expressions. (Turn to Chapter 10 if these terms are new to you.) Filter by Form offers most features of the QBE grid, and you might find it even easier to use.

Explore the Filter by Form window

Open the Suppliers table of the Northwind database, if it's not already staring at you. Click the Remove Filter button just to be sure no earlier filters are applied. Then, click the Filter by Form button.

CAUTION **If you've been following the examples, there's something in the** Contact Title cell because of a Filter by Selection you did earlier. Access assumes you want to use that again when it opens Filter by Form. To get a clean slate, click the Clear Grid button on the toolbar.

Across the top are all the fields in the Suppliers table. (Remember you can use the horizontal scroll bar to see them all.) At the bottom is a tab labeled Look For and another tab (currently dimmed) labeled Or. Go back to the top and click any empty cell. You'll see an arrow for a drop-down menu; click on it to open a list of every different value that appears in this field (see fig. 11.5).

Enough orientation—let's Filter by Form

Okay, let's try to redo our last filter. We'll select all records where Sales Representative is in the Contact Title field. Click the Contact Title cell, select Sales Representative from the drop-down list (use the vertical scroll bar to find it), and click the Apply Filter button (see fig. 11.6). You get the same results you did when you filtered by selection.

Fig. 11.5

You can use drop-down menus to select criteria.

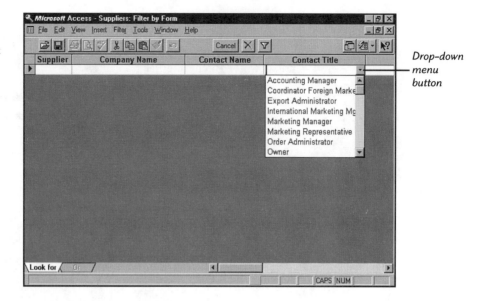

Drop-down menu button

Using a wild card

Let's re-do the first filter we did in this chapter using Filter by Form. If you're still looking at the filtered Suppliers table, click the Filter by Form button. Next, click the Clear Grid button to get rid of previous criteria.

We want to see any record that begins with Sales in the Contact Title field. To tell Access what you want, use a wild card. In this case, you use an asterisk to indicate unknown characters on the right side of Sales, by typing **Sales*** in the Contact Title cell. Click the Apply Filter button, and you get all the records you're looking for. If you had wanted all the records with sales in the field, you could have typed *Sales*.

Using And criteria

Let's build on the previous filter to learn other advantages of Filter by Form. Click the Filter by Form button to return to the Filter by Form window. Don't bother to click Clear Grid this time—when you build on a filter, you want to keep what you already have.

Suppose you want to see any record where the Contact Title begins with Sales, and the supplier is located in the United States. You're now using And criteria—both conditions have to be true for a record to be a match. When we worked in the QBE grid, And criteria were placed on the same row. That's also how it's done in Filter by Form—the criteria for each field are in the same row.

Fig. 11.6
Select your criteria from the drop-down menu.

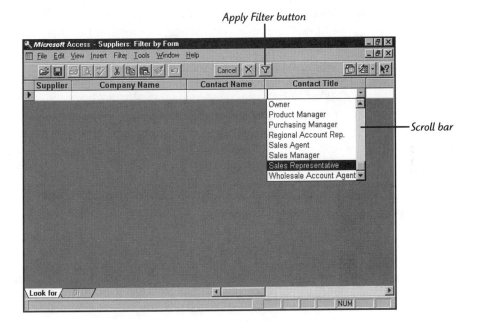

The Contact Title criteria can be left alone. The fact that it says Like "*Sales*" doesn't confuse you, does it? That's just Access handling an expression in its own formal way.

Now, use the scroll bar to move to the Country field at the right. Click in the Country field cell, and click the drop-down arrow to get a list of values. Select USA, then apply the filter. You'll get one match, because Grandma's Kelly Homestead is listed as having a sales representative, and it's located in the United States.

Using Or Criteria

As you learned in Chapter 10, when you use Or criteria, one condition or another can be true for a record to match. In other words, matching records for both sets of values are returned. Now, how do you handle Or criteria in Filter by Form?

Click the Filter by Form button in the datasheet, then click the Clear Grid button in the Filter by Form window. This gets you ready to start a fresh filter.

Recall that when you used Or criteria in the QBE grid, you put the first expression on the Criteria line, but you put the alternative expression on a separate line, the Or line. In Filter by Form, you'll click the Or tab to reach a separate page to achieve the same effect.

As usual, an example should make things clearer. Suppose that besides the records of sales representatives, you also want to find all the records of customers in Germany.

Select Sales Representative as criteria in the Contact Title field. (Remember the steps? Click the field's cell, click the drop-down arrow, select the value to serve as criteria.) When you select the criteria value, the Or tab at the bottom of the window becomes available. Click the Or tab, and you'll see a new screen with a blank Criteria line (see fig. 11.7). The Look For tab is available—you can click it anytime to return to the first page.

Fig. 11.7
Click the Or tab to get a blank screen where you can add other criteria.

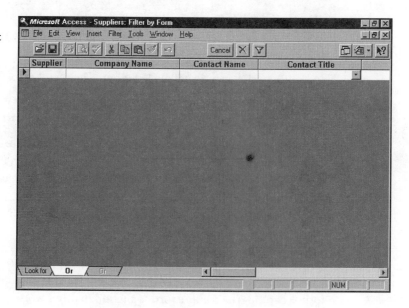

To choose the additional Or criteria, scroll to the Country field, and click the cell for that field. Click the drop-down list arrow that appears, and select Germany from the list. Now, you've told Access to find the following:

All records with Sales Representative in the Contact Title field

All records where the Country field equals Germany

Click the Apply Filter button and Access will find these records.

 TIP   **Did you notice that there's now an extra Or tab available at the** bottom of the window? You can keep on adding Or criteria, one after another.

Using And criteria and Or criteria together

You've already created Or criteria by using tabs to reach different pages. To create And criteria on any page, you just add criteria to another field. Practically any combination of And and Or criteria is possible.

To proceed with our example, click the Filter by Form button. In the Look For page, you're already searching for sales representatives. Instead of clearing the grid, use And criteria to narrow this part of the search. To get Access to look for sales representatives of only U.S. companies, click the Country field, click the drop-down list arrow, and select USA. Table 11.2 summarizes the selected criteria.

Table 11.2   Using And and Or criteria in one filter

Tab	Fields	Value
Look For	Contact Title Country	Sales Representative USA
Or	Country	Germany

What results come from applying this filter? One record from the Look For tab—a U.S. customer whose Contact Title is Sales Representative—and three records of German customers from the Or tab.

 TIP   **Remember that you can use any expression as Filter by Form** criteria. You can also use any of the wild cards you've learned.

Is there a way to see all my criteria at once?

It might be easier to see all your criteria by looking at them in the QBE grid. You can build your filter in the Filter by Form window, but then check the criteria in the QBE grid. If you've got the filter on-screen in Datasheet view, choose Records, Filter, Advanced Filter/Sort. All the criteria are presented in the QBE grid (see fig. 11.8).

Fig. 11.8
You can see your criteria in both the Filter by Form window and the QBE grid.

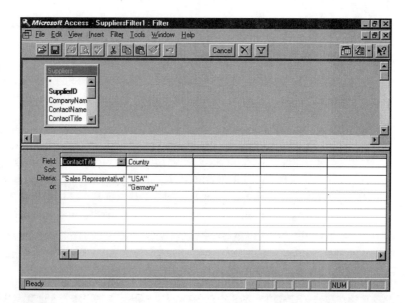

TIP   **To see the QBE grid from the Filter by Form window, choose**
Filter, Advanced Filter/Sort.

What's Advanced Filter/Sort really good for?

Now that you've learned Filter by Selection and Filter by Form, what's so hot about the Advanced Filter/Sort window? Its only real plus is that you get extra sorting capabilities in the QBE format. You can do an ascending sort in one field and a descending sort in another field, and can sort on more than two fields. You probably won't need these abilities too often, but it's nice to know they're there. In Filter by Selection and Filter by Form, you can only sort one or two fields, in either ascending or descending order. (Turn to Chapter 8 if you need a refresher on sorting.)

Is there a way to save a filter?

While I've emphasized the temporary nature of filters, their life-span can be significantly extended, by saving the filter along with the table, query, or form in which it was created, or by saving the filter as a query.

If you choose File, Save Layout in Datasheet view, the filter is saved along with your table, query, or form. Thereafter, it's part of the object. If the filter is applied when you close the object, it's still applied when you reopen the object. If you don't want the filter to be part of the object, don't save your changes before closing the object.

If you want to save the filter as a query, the filter has to be displayed in the Filter by Form window or the Advanced Filter/Sort window. (In other words, if you think you might save the filter, don't use Filter by Selection.) Choose File, Save As Query. Access prompts you for a query name. Type in an appropriate name, then click OK.

Q&A *I'm not sure I understand saving a filter within an object. Does that mean I can save several filters within each object?*

No, you can save only one filter at a time. Let's say you modify the filter, or create an entirely new one. If you save it, the new filter becomes part of the object, and the old one disappears.

I'm still not exactly sure how queries and filters differ

So what is the difference between a filter and a query? When you're using the QBE grid for both, they seem pretty much alike. But there are some differences:

- In a query, you can add fields from more than one object. That significantly increases the power of a query, as you'll see in the next chapter.

With a filter, you're limited to one table, one query, or one form, because you're working directly within an open datasheet.

- A query is a separate object that appears in the Database window. A filter is just part of a table, query, or form. (Unless, of course, you save a filter as a query.)

- A query allows you to decide which fields you want to show in the results. In a filter, all the fields are displayed. (You can hide them later, but they're all shown initially.)

As you can see by the workarounds described in parentheses for the last two items, the only critical difference is that you can use more than one object as a source for a query. That's a big deal, and the entire next chapter discusses creating queries from more than one object.

12

Queries Using More Than One Table

● **In this chapter:**

- **Joins: another type of relationship**

- **Getting in touch with your inner join**

- **When should I use an outer join?**

- **What if they won't let me join?**

- **The Find Unmatched Query Wizard—much friendlier than its name**

Each of your tables contains related data about one subject, but most of your queries need information about more than one subject. You'll have to join the tables to get the results you need . . . . ▶

Thee way you organize information in your database isn't necessarily the way you need to use it. You put data about one subject in a single table, but often you need information from two or more tables to answer your query.

That isn't just a database problem. You come across the same thing every day; for example, after you find a great recipe for strawberry cheesecake in the newspaper, you might want to look at a calorie chart to see how fattening it is. Or, if you own some Amalgamated Widget stock, and read a newspaper article that reports a 15-percent decline in their profits, you need to turn to the stock quotes to see if the news had any impact on the share price.

In other words, one information source—in database terms, one table—often provides just part of the answer. In this chapter, we look at how queries using two or more tables can get you far more satisfying answers to your questions.

Show me an example of using two tables in a query

Let's open the Northwind database again (Northwind.mdb in the Samples folder below the folder Access was installed in). Choose Tools, Relationships to see how the different tables in the database are related (see fig. 12.1). (If this window makes about as much sense to you as a diagram of Finnish sentence structure, visit Chapter 6.)

As you see from the Relationships window, the Order Details table contains information about products sold. Suppose you'd like to run a query showing data from just the Order ID, Product ID, and Quantity fields. No problem, right? To refresh your memory:

1 Click the New button in the Queries tab of the Database window.

2 Choose Design View from the New Query dialog box.

3 Select the Order Details table in the Show Table window.

4 Drag the fields you want from the field list onto the Query-by-Example (QBE) grid. (You can also double-click them.)

5 Run the query.

Fig. 12.1
The Relationships window shows relationships between tables.

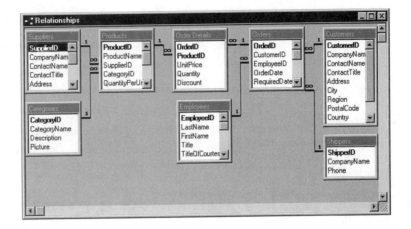

This should be fairly familiar by now—if any of it sounds hazy, take another look at Chapter 9.

> **TIP** **Is it hard for you to figure out what information a table holds just** by looking at its field list? Don't be shy about opening the actual tables and taking a look at them when you need to. Just click the Tables tab in the Database window, select the table you need, and click <u>O</u>pen.

What if you don't want this information for all your orders? Let's say you just want data from orders shipped to Italy. Look at the entire field list for the Order Details table in the Relationships window. Is there any field that tells you which orders went to Italy? Unfortunately, there isn't.

But look at the fields in the Orders table. You can find where a shipment went by using the ShipCountry field in the Orders table (click the scroll bar to see all the fields). So, if you somehow get the Orders table and the Order Details table to work together, you can find out which products were shipped to Italy.

How do I put fields from two tables in a query?

Let's go ahead and make the query. As we do so, we'll take an occasional time-out to talk about information you'll find useful. Here's how to start off:

1 Click the Queries tab in the Datasheet window, and then click the <u>N</u>ew button.

2 Select Design View from the New Query dialog box, and click OK.

3 In the Show Table window, double-click Order Details and Orders, so that both tables are selected.

4 Click the Close button to shut the Show Table window.

TIP   **You can add additional field lists to the query window anytime by** choosing Query, Show Table, and then selecting the tables you need.

Those two tables still have a good relationship

Figure 12.1 shows that the Orders and Order Details tables have a one-to-many relationship. In other words, an Order ID can appear only once in the Orders table, but can appear many times in the Order Details table. When we show both tables in the query window, Access joins the two fields with a join line (see fig. 12.2). The join between the two tables enables Access to manipulate, match, and massage the data between them.

CAUTION   **If referential integrity's not enforced, you won't see the 1 and ∞** signs on the join. You'll simply see a plain, narrow line.

There are a few ways that tables can be joined. The most important are inner joins, which is what you'll use in most queries you do involving more than one source. It's the default type of join, so you don't have to do anything special to get an inner join.

Here's what an inner join tells Access to do: Show me the records from both tables that have the same value in the fields that are joined. You'll see in a minute how this works.

Matching fields

Fig. 12.2
The Orders and Order Details field lists have a join line between them.

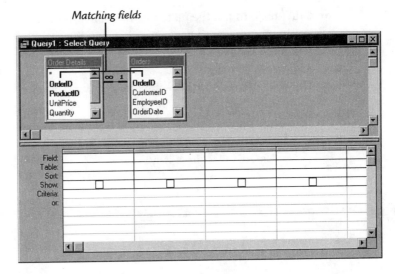

 Q&A *In figure 12.2, the table on the many side of the relationship, Order Details, is on the left; the table on the one side, Orders, is on the right. If it's a one-to-many relationship, shouldn't the order be reversed?*

No, the essential relationship remains the same. Regardless of the order, the ∞ sign and the 1 sign are correctly placed so you know which table is the "one" side, and which is the "many." If you wish, you can change the positions of field lists for easier viewing. I'll show you how to do that a little later in this chapter.

Add the fields to the QBE grid

Next, add the fields you need for the query. Double-click the OrderID, ProductID, and Quantity fields in the Order Details field list. This places those fields on the QBE grid. In the Orders field list, double-click the CustomerID and ShipCountry field. Also include CustomerID, so you'll know which customer the order went to (hopefully, the results will show lots of Italian names). On the Criteria line in the ShipCountry column, type **Italy**. Your grid looks like figure 12.3.

We didn't need to put the matching field of OrderID in our query for it to work. It's enough just to have the join exist. We included that field because we wanted to see its values.

TIP   **If you leave the Show box in the ShipCountry column checked,** this field will be shown in your query and contain the value Italy for each record retrieved. There's really no need to show this field at all; give your query an informative title, like Italian Orders, that lets you know that all orders are in fact from Italy.

So how do a relationship and a join differ?

Good question. When we talk about relationships, we mean the way that two tables relate to one another in general—with no regard to a specific query. When we talk about joins, we mean the way that two tables are linked in a specific query.

This gets confusing, and most of the time there isn't much of a difference. Usually a join is set up between the primary key of one table and a matching field in another table. In our example, it's the OrderID fields in the Orders and Order Details tables, which have a one-to-many relationship. Therefore, any specific OrderID can appear only once in the Orders table, but many times in the Order Details table. (Remember, OrderID is not the primary key of the Order Details table. The OrderID and ProductID fields together make up the primary key.)

But there are differences between joins and relationships. In a query, the two tables can have an inner join or an outer join (we'll get to those in a moment). In both cases, the tables have the same one-to-many relationship, but in a query different records will be retrieved depending on your choice of join. To re-emphasize the point, the join applies to an individual query, while the relationship simply exists between the tables without being associated with any query.

Another point is that Access joins two tables in a query, even if you don't have a relationship set up for them. Remember that even if two tables have the potential for a relationship, they don't actually have one until you create it. Nevertheless, if you show two tables in the query window, Access automatically creates a join, provided that 1) each table has a field with the same name and data type, and 2) one of those fields is a primary key. Those happen to be the usual characteristics of two tables with a relationship.

Fig. 12.3
Select the fields you
need from both tables
to be placed on the
QBE grid.

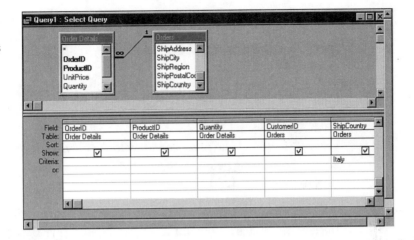

 Q&A *In figure 12.3, the join line now connects to the title of the Orders field list, instead of to the joined field. What's that mean?*

Nothing. When the joined field (in this case, OrderID) skips out of sight, the join line is connected to the title instead. Simply use the scroll bar if you want to show the joined field—better yet, leave it out of sight and don't sweat it.

Run the query

To run the query, click the Run button (the exclamation point) on the toolbar, or choose Query, Run. Figure 12.4 shows the results. If you'd like to save your query, choose File, Save, give your query a name, and click OK.

Fig. 12.4
The query shows the
quantities of products
shipped to Italy.

Order ID	Product	Quantity	Customer	Ship Co
10275	Guaraná Fantástica	12	Magazzini Alimentari Riuniti	Italy
10275	Raclette Courdavault	6	Magazzini Alimentari Riuniti	Italy
10288	Tourtière	10	Reggiani Caseifici	Italy
10288	Scottish Longbreads	3	Reggiani Caseifici	Italy
10300	Louisiana Hot Spiced Okra	30	Magazzini Alimentari Riuniti	Italy
10300	Scottish Longbreads	20	Magazzini Alimentari Riuniti	Italy
10404	Gumbär Gummibärchen	30	Magazzini Alimentari Riuniti	Italy
10404	Singaporean Hokkien Fried Me	40	Magazzini Alimentari Riuniti	Italy
10404	Maxilaku	30	Magazzini Alimentari Riuniti	Italy
10422	Gumbär Gummibärchen	2	Franchi S.p.A.	Italy
10428	Spegesild	20	Reggiani Caseifici	Italy
10443	Queso Cabrales	6	Reggiani Caseifici	Italy
10443	Rössle Sauerkraut	12	Reggiani Caseifici	Italy
10467	Guaraná Fantástica	28	Magazzini Alimentari Riuniti	Italy
10467	NuNuCa Nuß-Nougat-Creme	12	Magazzini Alimentari Riuniti	Italy
10562	Geitost	20	Reggiani Caseifici	Italy
10562	Torte au sucre	10	Reggiani Caseifici	Italy

Record: 1 of 53

I'm still not sure how Access came up with these records

Here's a quick synopsis of what just happened. The Orders table lists all orders only once. By selecting criteria, we told Access not to worry about every order in our Orders table—just find those that were shipped to Italy. Then Access went into the Order Details table and found any record whose order ID matched one of those that went to Italy. In the query results, Access shows data for the fields we placed on the QBE grid for every record it retrieved (see fig. 12.5).

You don't have to put criteria in your query, of course. If you just want to see the country of destination for all orders in the Order Details table, that's possible. Simply leave the Criteria line blank.

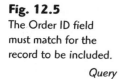

Fig. 12.5
The Order ID field must match for the record to be included.

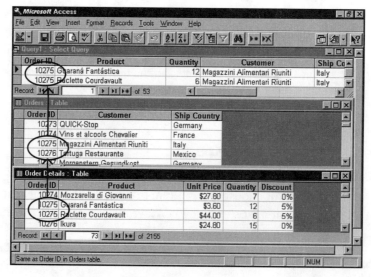

I'd like to try one more example

Imagine that you want to see orders for all employees who have a certain title. Look at the Orders field list in the Relationships window (if you don't have the Relationships window open, click <u>W</u>indow, <u>R</u>elationships to see it, or refer to figure 12.1). There's nothing there to tell you what the employee's title is. But you can use the Title field in the Employees table to identify orders taken by say, the Inside Sales Coordinator. There's a one-to-many relationship between the Employees and Orders tables through the EmployeeID field, so you'll have no problem making a join. Here are the steps:

1 Click the Queries tab in the Database window, and then click the New button.

2 Click Design View in the New Query dialog box.

3 Double-click the Employees table and the Orders table, to add the two tables to the Query window. Notice that they're joined.

4 In the Employees field list, double-click the Title field to add it to the QBE grid. On the Criteria line, type **Inside Sales Coordinator**.

5 In the Orders field list, double-click the asterisk to include all the fields. Figure 12.6 shows how your QBE grid should look.

6 Run the query by clicking the Run button. Figure 12.7 shows the results.

7 Save the query and give it a name, or else click No when Access prompts you to save.

Fig. 12.6
Using the asterisk saves you space when you want to include all fields from a table on the QBE grid.

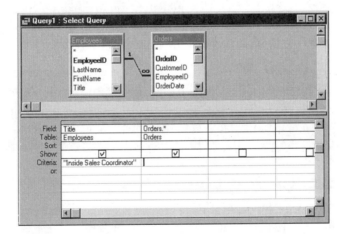

TIP **There's no need for a Title field that repeats Inside Sales Coordinator** ad nauseum, as long as you name the query something like **Orders–Inside Sales Coordinator**. Click on the Show box to remove the check; the Title field will not be shown in your query.

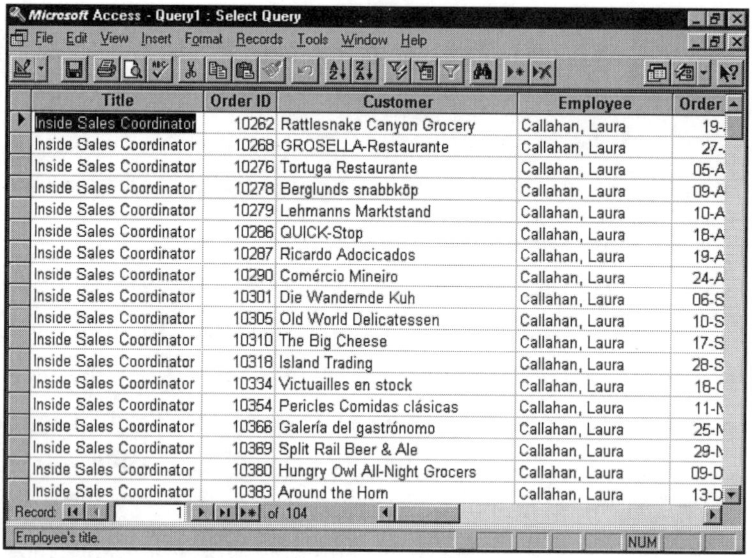

Title	Order ID	Customer	Employee	Order
Inside Sales Coordinator	10262	Rattlesnake Canyon Grocery	Callahan, Laura	19-
Inside Sales Coordinator	10268	GROSELLA-Restaurante	Callahan, Laura	27-
Inside Sales Coordinator	10276	Tortuga Restaurante	Callahan, Laura	05-A
Inside Sales Coordinator	10278	Berglunds snabbköp	Callahan, Laura	09-A
Inside Sales Coordinator	10279	Lehmanns Marktstand	Callahan, Laura	10-A
Inside Sales Coordinator	10286	QUICK-Stop	Callahan, Laura	18-A
Inside Sales Coordinator	10287	Ricardo Adocicados	Callahan, Laura	19-A
Inside Sales Coordinator	10290	Comércio Mineiro	Callahan, Laura	24-A
Inside Sales Coordinator	10301	Die Wandernde Kuh	Callahan, Laura	06-S
Inside Sales Coordinator	10305	Old World Delicatessen	Callahan, Laura	10-S
Inside Sales Coordinator	10310	The Big Cheese	Callahan, Laura	17-S
Inside Sales Coordinator	10318	Island Trading	Callahan, Laura	28-S
Inside Sales Coordinator	10334	Victuailles en stock	Callahan, Laura	18-C
Inside Sales Coordinator	10354	Pericles Comidas clásicas	Callahan, Laura	11-N
Inside Sales Coordinator	10366	Galería del gastrónomo	Callahan, Laura	25-N
Inside Sales Coordinator	10369	Split Rail Beer & Ale	Callahan, Laura	29-N
Inside Sales Coordinator	10380	Hungry Owl All-Night Grocers	Callahan, Laura	09-D
Inside Sales Coordinator	10383	Around the Horn	Callahan, Laura	13-D

Fig. 12.7
The query shows only orders for the Inside Sales Coordinator.

Queries using three tables

Using three tables in a query shouldn't cause you additional problems, provided all the tables are joined. In the first example, you retrieved data about recent orders shipped to Italy. Suppose you also want that query to show the ContactName of the customers who receive them. This information is available only in the Customers table.

You'll need three tables to do this query: Customers, Orders, and Order Details. As you can see from the Relationships window in figure 12.1, the Customers table is joined to the Orders table through the CustomerID field. Doing the query should be a cinch.

Beginning the query

Ordinarily, if you've already created a similar query, you'd just open it up, add the required table, and drag the additional field to the QBE grid. We're going to modify the example a bit, though, and start from scratch:

1 Click the Queries tab in the Database window, then click the New button to create a new query.

2 Select Design View from the New Query dialog box and click OK.

3 Using the Show Table window, add the Customers, Order Details, and Orders tables to the query window by double-clicking each (see fig. 12.8). Click C̲lose.

Those join lines look a bit strange, don't they? Yet they're all as they should be. The CustomerID field is in both the Customers and Orders tables, and they're joined through a one-to-many relationship (it tunnels underneath the Order Details table).

Let's make all the relationships easier to see. Position the mouse pointer on the title of the Customers field list; press and hold the mouse button, and then drag this box to the right of the Orders field list. Now, everything that's going on is much clearer (see fig. 12.9).

Fig. 12.8

The query window displays three field lists and their joins.

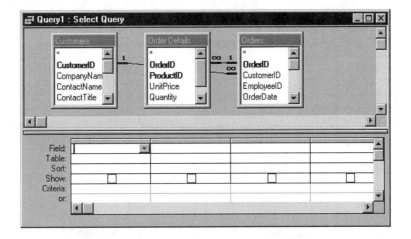

Fig. 12.9

You can drag a field list to a new location to see the joins better.

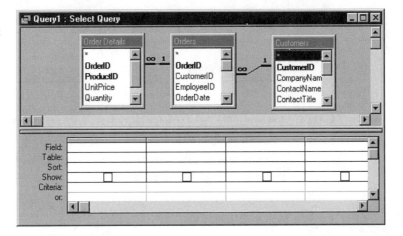

Completing the query

Now, we can finish the query:

1 From the Order Details field list, select the OrderID and ProductID fields so they're placed on the QBE grid.

2 From the Orders field list, select the CustomerID and ShipCountry fields.

3 From the Customers field list, select ContactName.

4 Type **Italy** on the Criteria line for the ShipCountry field.

5 On the Show line, make sure all boxes—except the one for ShipCountry—are checked. Figure 12.10 shows how your QBE grid should look.

6 Run the query by clicking the Run button (or the View button). You see four fields in the query.

7 Choose <u>F</u>ile, <u>S</u>ave to give this query a name and save it.

Fig. 12.10
Put in your criteria and leave the Show box in the ShipCountry field unchecked.

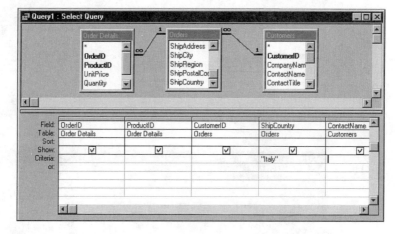

 Q&A *I tried to run the query, but got an error message saying Type Mismatch. What did I do wrong?*

You probably put the criteria in the wrong field. Check your QBE grid again and make sure Italy is in the ShipCountry column.

Using tables that can't be joined

You might be thinking, "This all works nicely if the tables happen to have a field that can be joined. But what about all those tables that don't have a common field? How can I get them to work together?" Don't worry—we've got a solution.

Use a third table to set up a join

In our previous example, we happened to need fields from all three tables to do the query. But what if we only want fields from the Customers and Order Details tables? Those two tables aren't joined, and don't have a common field. Here's what we can do: add the Orders table to our query, just to establish a link between the two tables. There's no need to include any fields from the Orders table in the query.

Let's see the "dummy" third table in action

Now, imagine you want to see a datasheet showing all fields from the Orders Details table, plus the phone number of the shipper who shipped the shipment (this report really needs to be ship-shape). As you can see from the Relationships window, the Shippers and Order Details tables don't have a relationship. We'll include the Orders table in our query to establish a join between Shippers and Order Details:

1 Create a new query.

2 In the Show Table window, add the Order Details, Orders, and Shippers tables to the query window. Click Close to exit the Show Table window.

3 Double-click the asterisk in the Order Details field list.

4 Double-click the Phone field in the Shippers field list.

5 Run the query. You'll see data for every field from the Orders Details table, along with data for the Phone field from the Shippers table.

What are outer joins?

Up to now, we've been working with inner joins—only those records where the joined fields are equal have been included. Let's discuss outer joins, which are used less frequently but are still worth knowing about.

With an outer join, Access includes all records from one side of the join, but only matching records from the other side. That means there can be two kinds of outer joins. You can have all records from Table A and only the matches from Table B, or all records from Table B and only the matches from Table A.

I know that's clear as mud. Let's look at an example that makes things clearer.

Creating outer joins

Suppose you want to know if you have any customers who haven't placed an order. In that case, you want to see the names of all customers in the Customers table, regardless if there are any matches in the orders table. We can then search for customers who do not have corresponding matches in the orders table. (Follow the example, even if you don't understand what we're doing yet.)

Start the query just as you would for a select query:

1 Create a query.

2 Add the Customers and Orders tables to the Query window.

3 Add the CompanyName field from the Customers field list and the OrderID field from the Orders field list to the QBE grid.

Choose a different join

As always, you see the join line between the two field lists at the top of the Query window. That's for an inner join, though, and you want an outer join. Double-click on the join line and the Join Properties window appears (see fig. 12.11).

You have three options. Option 1 is currently selected—that's the default inner join you've been using all along. In this case, you want option 2, which lets you see all the records from the Customers table and only the matches from the Orders table. Select option 2 and click OK.

Fig. 12.11
In the Join Properties window, you select the type of join you need for your query. We've been using the first option, which gives us inner joins. We'll now select a different option that will create an outer join.

Take a look at your join line. It's changed slightly; the line now has an arrow leading to the Orders field list (see fig. 12.12). This shows which kind of outer join you selected. The arrow points to the table from which only records where the joined fields are equal will be retrieved. Remember, all customer records will be included in the query. When we run it, any customer record without a matching record in the Orders table will indicate a customer with no orders. In that case, the customer's name will appear in the first column, with an empty space in the second.

Fig. 12.12
The direction of the arrow on the join line shows the type of outer join selected.

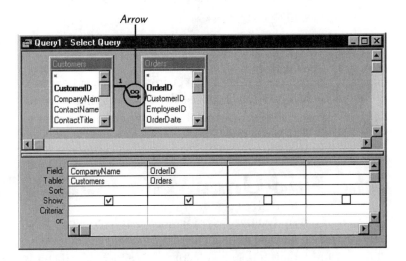

Run the query, then scroll down to record 191 or so in the results. You can see a company that hasn't made any orders (see fig. 12.13). If you search further, you might find other customers who've made no orders.

Fig. 12.13
Use an outer join to find the records without matches.

A company with no orders

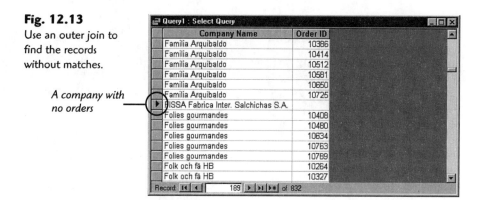

How about the join option we didn't choose?

What if you'd chosen option 3 in the Join Properties box? In that case, we'd have found all orders, whether or not they had customers. If an order didn't have a customer, we'd see the order number in the first column, and an empty space in the second.

That doesn't make sense—why would you have an order without a customer? Well, that's the kind of thing that outer joins are especially good at finding. If there's an order without a customer, it might be a fluke, or it might expose a weakness in your database design—it might even show that someone's been tampering with your database, putting phony orders on your books without any customers for them.

Using the Find Unmatched Query Wizard

If you find all this outer join junk baffling, I have great news: the Find Unmatched Query Wizard does most of what outer joins do. In fact, for finding unmatched records, it's a lot better than the method I explained in the preceding section. If you've absorbed some—or perhaps even nothing—of what we've been talking about, then using this wizard will be a breeze.

Click the Queries tab in the Database window, and then select Find Unmatched Query Wizard in the New Query dialog box, and click OK. The first two screens ask what tables you want to use. (Click the Next button at the bottom of a screen to move to the next one.) You probably can figure out what tables to choose from reading the directions in the wizard, but here's some clarification. For the query where we found a customer without an order, you'd select Customers in the first screen, and Orders in the second. In other words, the first screen's for the table that should give you all records, and the second screen's for the table where you want only records that match.

The third screen (see fig. 12.14) is easier than it looks. Access wants to know the matching fields in your table, but it probably figured them out by itself. Take a look at the equation in the Matching Fields box (above the Cancel button) to make sure it's right, and then click <u>N</u>ext.

Fig. 12.14
It's a quick trip through this screen, because Access usually guesses correctly what the matching fields are.

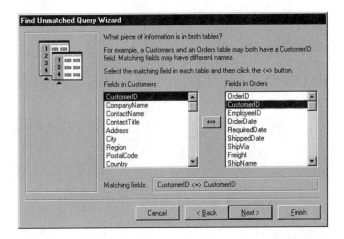

I may be dumb, but I'm not stupid

I don't know about you, but the first time I hear about a new concept like outer joins, the meaning usually blows right past me.

Individually, the words make sense, and I might even understand the sentences, but the idea itself doesn't make sense yet. A former British Chancellor of the Exchequer (similar to the U.S. Secretary of the Treasury) said that he often pulled out a bunch of match sticks and moved them around in order to understand trade issues. The same technique might help you learn about joins.

So, don't expect to fully absorb this stuff in one reading—you need to work with it for a while to have it sink in. You should do whatever you can to make these dull, impenetrable concepts real for yourself. Working through examples helps, but if you need to take out match sticks, pieces of paper, or whatever, and move them around on your desktop, go ahead. If it's okay for the Chancellor of the Exchequer, it's okay for you and me.

In the fourth screen, Access wants to know what fields you want to see in your query. The only fields available are those from the table you selected in the first screen; that is, the table on the "all" side of the join. Why's that? Because we're only interested in records from the first table that have no matching fields in the second. If there's no match, then there's no record to show—just an empty cell. You saw that in the last example, and you'll see it again when we run this query. Select Company Name and click <u>N</u>ext.

That's nearly it. Choose a name for the query, and follow the wizard's instructions to run it. Figure 12.15 shows your results. This is a sweeter deal than the query we created in the preceding section, because here you don't have to go scrolling through many records to find the couple that don't have any matches.

Fig. 12.15
The query shows only the records with no matches.

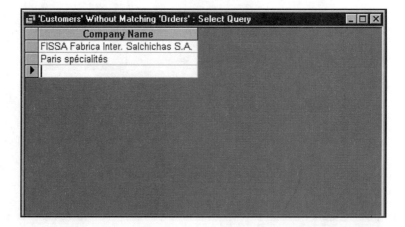

13

Totals Queries Add Things Up—and More

● **In this chapter:**

- **What kinds of calculations can a query do?**

- **Groping at the idea of grouping**

- **Two types of criteria for totals queries**

- **How useful is the Simple Query Wizard?**

Sometimes, actual data that's in your database isn't good enough to answer the questions you have. Let Access do some math and provide the solutions you need! . . . . ▶

You already know how to use queries to locate particular items in your database. You tell Access what fields to look in and what criteria to use, then you sit back while Access fetches values for you.

Sometimes, however, you aren't all that interested in knowing individual values. Sometimes all you really want to know is how much they add up to…or what the highest value is out of a whole bunch of records…or how many records have values in a certain field. Stuff like that.

In situations like this, you can ask Access to do some math for you. As you can imagine, Access handles calculations extremely well. By the end of this chapter, they should be as easy for you as they are for Access.

Starting off

To do things like get field totals or find averages, you need a **totals query**. You start it off just like any other query: Click the Queries tab in the Database window, click the New button, select Design View in the New Query dialog box, and choose the tables you need from the Show Table window; then place the fields you need on the Query by Example (QBE) grid.

 Plain English, please

Queries that perform calculations on groups of records are called **totals queries**. A totals query doesn't always refer to a sum—it can be any of several types of calculations. You can find the average of all values in a field, for example, as well as its minimum or maximum value. **"**

Making a totals query

 Here's where the new stuff starts. After you've started creating your query, choose View, Totals (or click the Totals button on the toolbar). A new row, appropriately named Total, appears in the QBE grid (see fig. 13.1). That's where you tell Access what kind of calculation you want to do. Right now it says Group By in the first column, but don't worry about that. You'll soon learn what that's for.

Fig. 13.1
To do calculations, you
need to see the Total
row in the QBE grid.

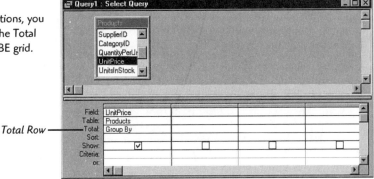

Total Row

TIP   **You can get rid of the Total row as easily as you put it there. Just**
click the Totals button again to make the row disappear.

Adding up one field in one table

Let's start with something basic that is also extremely useful. How do you get
a total for a single field? For example, you might need to total all the freight
costs on Northwind Traders orders (to follow along, open Northwind.mdb in
the Samples folder below the folder Access was installed in). All freight
charges are shown in the Freight field of the Orders table. Let's create a
query to total them up. (If you need a refresher on the basics of creating a
query—steps 1 to 3 below—visit Chapter 9.)

1 Create a query.

2 Use the Show Table window to add Orders to the query window.

3 Add the Freight field to the QBE grid.

Is this getting "sum"what confusing?

Don't let the Totals button intimidate you. In case
you haven't met it before, that funny-looking E is
the Greek letter, **sigma**. In the arithmetic world,
sigma means "total it up" (sometimes it's called

the **summation symbol**). I wish the Totals button
in Access just showed a big T, and didn't imply, "you
need to know calculus to click me." Don't worry,
all you really need to know is basic math.

4 Click View, Totals to insert the Totals row (if it's not already there).

5 Click in the first column of the Total row (where it says Group By). There's an arrow at the right for a drop-down menu—click this arrow to get the list of choices shown in figure 13.2.

6 Select Sum, the second choice in the drop-down menu. That's what you want Access to do—sum up all those values in the Freight field.

7 Click the Run button to see the query results in Datasheet view (see fig. 13.3). Don't dump this query—we'll use it in the next example.

Fig. 13.2
Select Sum to total the values in the field.

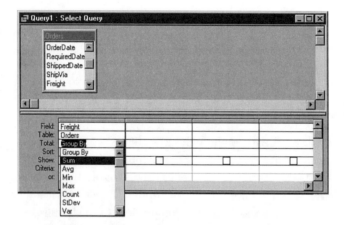

Fig. 13.3
The results of your totals query are shown in Datasheet view.

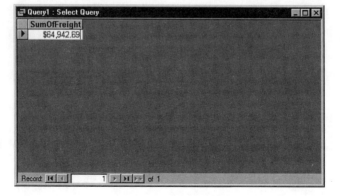

Let's do another example

Okay, let's change the previous example a bit. Suppose you want to know the highest freight charge for any order. Switch back to Design view by clicking the View button at the left end of the toolbar. Click the drop-down menu for the Total row in the Freight column, and change the selection from Sum to Max. Run the query. Your answer should be 1,007.64.

  TIP **From Design view, you can click either the Datasheet view** button or the Run button to see the query results.

What other calculations can I do?

Table 13.1 shows additional selections from the Total drop-down menu and the type of calculation each returns. Most are straightforward, and you'll have no problem with them. Two of them, though—**standard deviation** and **variance**—involve some knowledge of statistics. If you've never taken a statistics course, don't be concerned. Without knowing anything about those two, you can do everything else in this chapter.

 Plain English, please

The calculation methods listed in Table 13.1 are also known as **functions**. I prefer not to use this term, since it makes things sound more difficult than they are. You might, however, bump into this term in Access Help, so it's worth knowing.

The Count calculation needs a few words of explanation. It goes through every record looking at a certain field, then tells you the total number of records that had values in that field. In other words, it leaves out records where that field has a **null value** (has been left blank).

Table 13.1 Selections in the Total Row of the QBE Grid

Drop-down menu choice	What it calculates for a field
Sum	The total
Avg	The average
Min	The minimum (lowest) value
Max	The maximum (highest) value
Count	The number of values (excluding empty cells)
StDev	The standard deviation
Var	The variance
First	The value of the first record
Last	The value of the last record

Become a real groupie

Often, you don't want a grand total for all the records in a field. You want to break the records down into groups, and get totals for each group. To tell Access how to group your records, you use the Group By option in the Total row of the QBE grid.

Suppose you want to know how many orders each employee has made. Therefore, you want to count the orders and group them by employee. Your query needs the names of employees in one column, and the number of orders they made in a second column.

Start off your query the usual way, and add the Orders table to your query window. Here are the remaining steps:

1 Place the EmployeeID field in the first column of the QBE grid.

2 Place OrderID in the second column.

3 Choose View, Totals (or click the Totals button on the toolbar).

4 In the Total row, leave the Group By setting for the EmployeeID column. In the Orders column, click the Total row drop-down menu and select Count. Your grid should look like figure 13.4.

5 Run the query. Figure 13.5 shows the breakdown of orders by employees.

Fig. 13.4
Use Group By in the Total row to group the results.

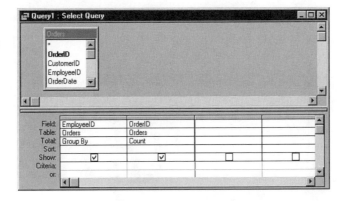

Fig. 13.5
Grouping creates a breakdown of orders according to individual employees.

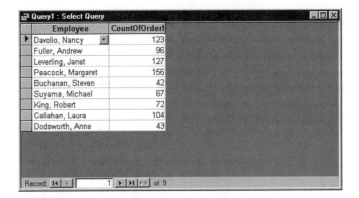

Don't think that the field you group by has to be in the same table as the field you do the count on. For example, instead of grouping by employee, we could have grouped by employee title, a field found only in the Employees table. That could answer questions like, "How many orders did all the sales representatives make?" Here's how to do it:

1 Create a query.

2 Add the Employees and Orders tables to the query window.

3 Place the Title field from the Employees table in the first column of the QBE grid. Place OrderID in the second column.

4 Click the Totals button. In the first column on the Total row, leave the default Group By. In the second column, select Count. Figure 13.6 shows what your QBE grid should look like.

5 Run the query. You'll see total orders for each classification of employee.

Fig. 13.6
You can even group by a field in a different table.

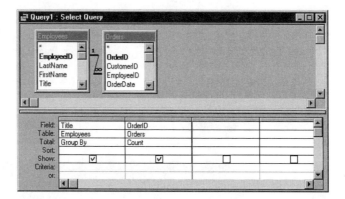

Grouping in more than one field

Once you're comfortable with grouping, you can easily group on more than one field at a time—that is, you can group within the group. You definitely need an example to figure this out!

Northwind uses three different suppliers: Federal Shipping, Speedy Express, and United Packaging. Suppose you want to see the number of orders handled by each shipper for each customer. You can group first by customer, then by shipper. The order in which you place the Group By fields in the grid determines how Access groups the records. Let's do the example:

1 Create a new query. Add the Customers, Orders, and Shippers tables to the query window.

2 Place the following fields on the QBE grid (in order): CompanyName from the Customers table, CompanyName from the Shippers table, and OrderID from the Orders table.

3 Choose View, Totals. In the Total row, leave the default Group By for the first two fields. For the Orders field, click the drop-down list arrow, then select Count. Your grid should look like figure 13.7.

4 Run the query. You'll see orders broken down first by customer, and then by shipper within each customer (see fig. 13.8).

Fig. 13.7
Make sure the fields used for grouping are in the right order.

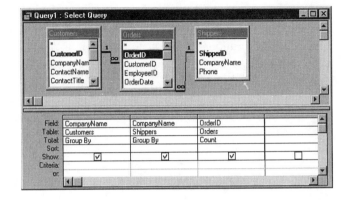

Fig. 13.8
The result values are grouped twice: first by customer, then by shipper.

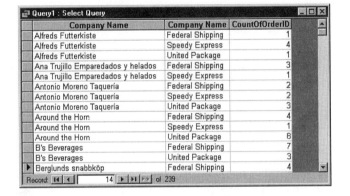

Q&A *What would have happened if I grouped first by shipper, then by customer?*

Nothing too tragic. In fact, if you want to focus on each shipper and see how many orders they've handled for each customer, that would be the way. But if you want to focus on each customer and review which shippers were used for their accounts, then the order we used above is better.

Using criteria in totals queries

There are two kinds of criteria you can use in totals queries. You can use either type by itself, or use both types (in different fields). The first type tells Access, "Before you do any calculating, exclude certain records. Then show me everything you found." The second type tells Access, "Go ahead and calculate based on all the records. But only show me some of them in the datasheet."

Let's go through examples to get a handle on the differences between the two criteria types.

Calculate on some records, then show all of them

To use this criteria type, you have to select Where in the drop-down menu of the Total row. Let's build on the previous example to see how "calculate on some, then show all" works. We'll add criteria that tells Access to include records only if the order date is in 1995 or later:

1 Click the Query View button (if necessary) to return to Design view.

2 Place the OrderDate field from the Orders table on the QBE grid.

3 Click the drop-down menu in the Total row and select Where. Type **>12/31/94** on the Criteria row.

4 Leave the Show box unchecked. Your QBE grid should look like figure 13.9.

5 Run the query. Access excludes records from before 1995 in the calculation, but includes every record it retrieves in the results (see fig. 13.10). If you compare the records in figure 13.10 with those in figure 13.8, you'll see that there are now fewer orders in some of the records. In other cases, a record is gone entirely because there aren't any post-1994 orders for that group.

Fig. 13.9
Make sure the Total row says Where for the field getting the criteria.

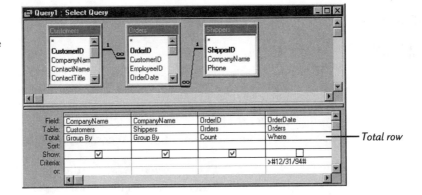

Total row

Fig. 13.10
The count in some records has been reduced because of the added criteria.

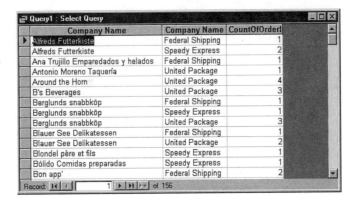

 TIP **Suppose you want to set criteria for the OrderID field—perhaps** include just the records above 10500. But you already have Count in the Total row for that field, and you know you need Where to set the "calculate on some, then show all" criteria. So, what do you do? If you want to set criteria for the same field you're calculating, place the field on the QBE grid again. (That's right, it appears in two separate columns.) Then set your criteria as you would for any other field.

Don't think that setting criteria is just for Count calculations. Remember the example where we simply found the sum of all freight costs? We placed the Freight field on the QBE grid, put Sum in the Total row, and we were done. Suppose we'd only wanted to include records where the freight cost was above $25. We would have placed the Freight field on the QBE grid a second time, selected Where in the Total row, and typed **>25** on the Criteria row.

Calculate on all records, then show some of them

Now, let's meet the second type of criteria using the same example. Make sure you're in Design view. Then, to get rid of criteria you put in for the last example, select the Order Date of the QBE grid, and press the Delete key. You're back where you started, with Access set to calculate all the records.

Suppose you only want to see records where the number of orders for any one customer through any one shipper (the numbers in the last column of the query in Datasheet view) is higher than two. Simply click the Criteria row in the OrderID column and type **>2**. When you run the query, you see that all records with a count of two or less have been dumped.

Using both types of criteria in one query

Finally, let's use both criteria in the same query. Let's leave the query as it was at the end of the preceding section, but include in the calculation only orders where the freight costs are above $25. In the query window, place the Freight field from the Orders table on the QBE grid. Set the Total row to Where, then type **>25** in the Criteria row for that column. Figure 13.11 shows how the grid should look.

Fig. 13.11
You can use both types of criteria in one query.

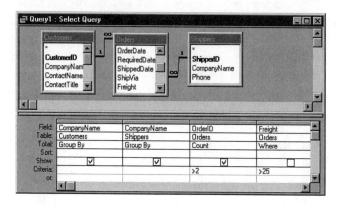

Remember that the criteria you use is specific to a field, not to the query. As the figure shows, one doesn't exclude the other. Here, you're simultaneously making the following limitations part of the query:

What's being limited	What it's limited to
The records Access calculates on	Only those with freight costs above $25
The records shown in the results	Only those with more than two orders

Sorting and the Top Values property

Often, you don't care about every record a query retrieves, and want to see just the ones with the highest or lowest values for a certain field. You can set the Top Values property to view only the extreme records. This property is set in a box located to the right of the Totals button on the Design toolbar; by default, it's set to All. Click the drop-down list arrow to see your other choices.

You can have Access give you records with the highest or lowest 5, 25, or 100 values. You can also ask it to give you records with the highest or lowest 5 percent or 25 percent of all values.

Before you use the Top Values property, you need to tell Access how to sort the records. That will determine whether the highest values or the lowest values are shown in the datasheet. As usual, you select a sort order on the Sort line of the QBE grid.

In the past, you might have used ascending (A-Z) sorts more than descending (Z-A) sorts because you were putting things in alphabetical order. When doing counts, though, you'll often want your values ordered from highest to lowest—a descending sort—so you can see the highest values first.

 CAUTION **Perhaps because the Top Values property box is on the toolbar,** many people forget that they've changed the selection to something other than All. That might not be a problem if you've chosen to view only the five highest records, which is visually rather obvious. If, however, you've chosen the top 100, your results might look like a complete set of records, even though some have been excluded. Be sure you remember to change the setting back to All when you need to see all the records.

How about an example?

Okay, we want to know which of Northwind's customers have made the most orders. We're only interested in the top five, ranked from highest to lowest:

1 Create a new query.

2 Add the Orders table to the query window.

3 Place the CustomerID field in the first column of the QBE grid, and place OrderID in the second column.

4 From the list of Sort options for the OrderID column, select Descending.

5 Choose View, Totals. Select Count in the Total row for the OrderID column. Leave the default Group By in the Customers column.

6 Click the drop-down list arrow in the Top Values box, and then select 5. Figure 13.12 shows how your grid should look.

7 Run the query. You'll see the five customers with the most orders.

Fig. 13.12

As long as you've got a sort order selected, you can use the Top Values property to choose a certain number of records from one end of the sort.

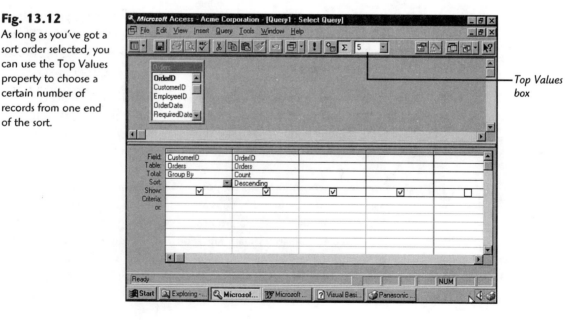

What does Top Values do with more than one sort?

As you know, you can sort on more than one field. How does Access know which one you want the Top Values property to apply to? It doesn't, unfortunately, it just picks the field furthest to the left. For our example, if you had an ascending sort in the Customers column as well as a descending sort in the Orders column, you'd get five customers with names like AAA Groceries and AAAA Distributors, instead of those with the most orders.

The Simple Query wizard and totals queries

Simple Query Wizard can do some calculations. With certain exceptions, which I'll explain, I think you're better off not using the Simple Query Wizard. It won't let you put criteria in, or group values within a field. Of course, you can modify your design after running the wizard, but I'm not sure it's worth the time and trouble of cranking up a wizard when you can quickly design a query from scratch to do the job.

On the other hand, maybe you should use Simple Query Wizard if any of the following are true: this chapter has given you lots of trouble, you really love wizards, or you hate the QBE grid. If you want to find several different totals (for example, Sum, Min, and Avg) for a field, it can really help to use the wizard. Try out the wizard when you have a few minutes; decide how much you like it, and get a sense of which situations it's most useful for.

Part V: Forms

14

Forms: Present Data On-Screen the Easy Way

● In this chapter:

● Create a form with two mouse clicks

● How can I make my form look like a table?

● Some other easy forms to make

● I'm ready for the Form Wizard

● Making forms based on more than one table

How do you give your data some breathing room and make it easier to manipulate? You put it in a form . . . . ●>

Records in a table grid can be like shirts on a clothes rack. Sure, it's convenient to store them that way. But what if you want to take a good look at one of them? All your records are bunched up, squished together, one on top of another. If there are a lot of fields, you never get to see an entire record all at once.

How do you give your data some breathing room and make it easier to manipulate? You put it in a form. But forms are more than just database cosmetics—they're robust objects in their own right. This chapter will discuss the beauty—and the power—of forms.

Can I really make a form with two mouse clicks?

Sure, you can make a simple form that includes all the fields of a given table (or query) with two clicks in the right place. Let's make a new form from the Orders table in the Northwind database (Northwind.mdb in the Samples folder) and see what it looks like. (If you prefer, you can follow the same steps to make a form of any table in any database.)

Open the database, click the Tables tab in the Database window, and select the Orders table. Select Insert, AutoForm from the menu bar. You get a columnar form shown in figure 14.1.

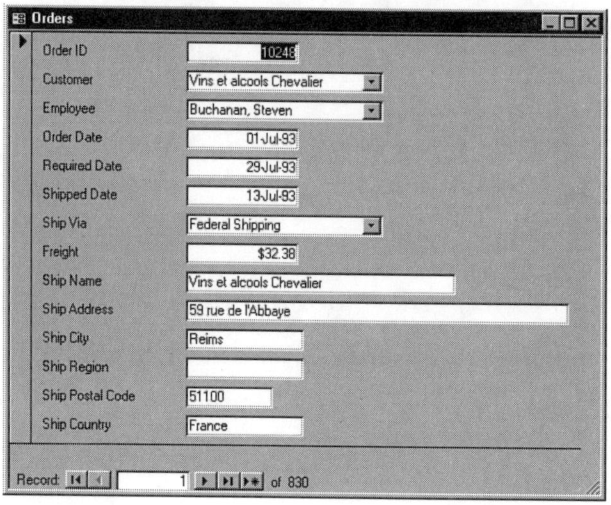

Fig. 14.1
Two clicks is all it takes to make a new form.

TIP **You can also click the drop-down menu of the New Object** button on the toolbar and select AutoForm. Actually, often you just have to click the New Object button, since AutoForm is the default button. But just to be on the safe side, select it from the drop-down menu. Otherwise you could wind up making a query when you want a form.

How to get around in a form

Notice in figure 14.1 that all the fields in the table have been included in the form. Their names are listed vertically in the same order as they appear in the table. To the right of each field name is its value in the first record of the table. In this form, each record of the table has its own page. To see the next record, you can simply press Page Down. To move back a record, press Page Up.

You can move to both adjacent and non-adjacent records by using the navigation buttons at the bottom of the page. The following table summarizes what each button does. You can also use the Record Indicator Box to move to a specific record. Highlight the record in the box, type in the new number, and press Enter.

Go to the record you want using the buttons	
Button	**Where a click takes you**
◀◀	To the first record
◀	Back one record
▶	Forward one record
▶▶	To the last record
▶*	To a blank page where you can enter a new record

How do I move around in a record?

The following table summarizes how to use your keyboard to get around in a record. It's not much different than moving around in a grid.

Moving around in a form using the keyboard	
Key	**Where it takes you**
Tab	Next field
Shift+Tab	Previous field
↓	Next field
↑	Previous field
→	Next field
←	Previous field
Home	First field
End	Last field

In a form, directional keys take you to the next or previous field, regardless of direction.

Can I use a form to edit the table?

Sure, that's why it's there. To select the entire value (to highlight all of it), click on the field name. Or, you can click the value itself, and you'll see the blinking cursor. Now you can simply edit it as you would in any datasheet. Your changes will be reflected in the form and in the underlying table. In the same way, any changes you make in the table will now show up in the form.

Adding a new record

Table 14.1 shows the button you click for a new record. You'll get a blank page that's ready for new entries (see fig. 14.2). Then, simply input your data as you would in any datasheet. When you're finished with a record, just press the Tab key to move to the next blank record. Your record is now saved.

TIP **You can also erase entries as you did in a table. In a new record** you're working on, you can clear all entries by choosing Edit, Undo Current Field/Record. You can delete a record you just saved by selecting Edit, Undo Saved Record.

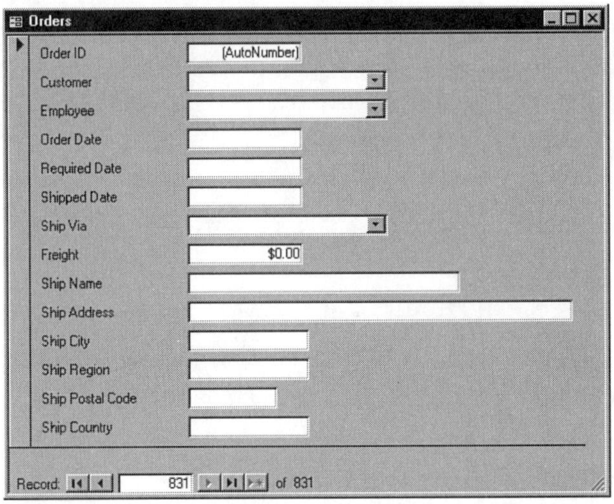

Fig. 14.2
You can easily see the field names of your data with the column format.

Orders		
Order ID	[AutoNumber]	
Customer		
Employee		
Order Date		
Required Date		
Shipped Date		
Ship Via		
Freight	$0.00	
Ship Name		
Ship Address		
Ship City		
Ship Region		
Ship Postal Code		
Ship Country		

Record: 831 of 831

Can't forms look more interesting?

You're not terribly impressed with the form you made? Are you wondering if that is all there is to forms? A look at the Employees form of the Northwind database will give you a little better idea of how elaborate a form can be. If you read Chapter 8, remember you used the Employees table to learn about finding stuff. Now you'll see the same information in a form. Click the Forms tab in the Database window, and open the Employees form (see fig. 14.3).

The first thing you notice, of course, is the photo. You can put other graphical elements in a form, like a chart. Notice that you quickly and clearly see the employee's name in the upper right-hand corner above the photograph. Now press Page Down to see the second page of the record (see fig. 14.4). You still see the employee's name in the upper right-hand corner. Each record is neatly divided into two sections for easy reference—a page for company information and a page for personal data.

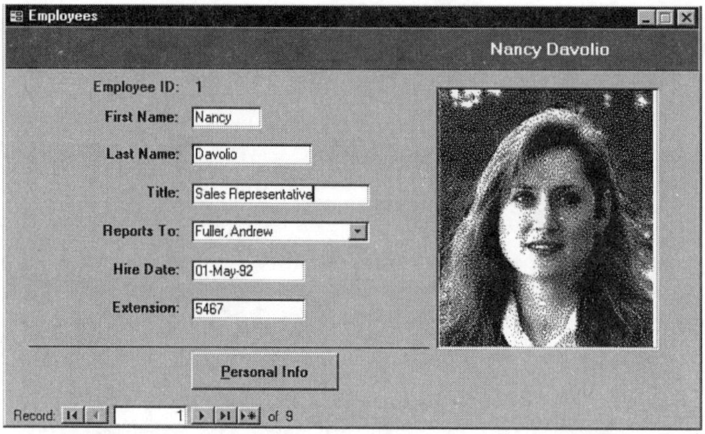

Fig. 14.3

The Employees form presents data elegantly.

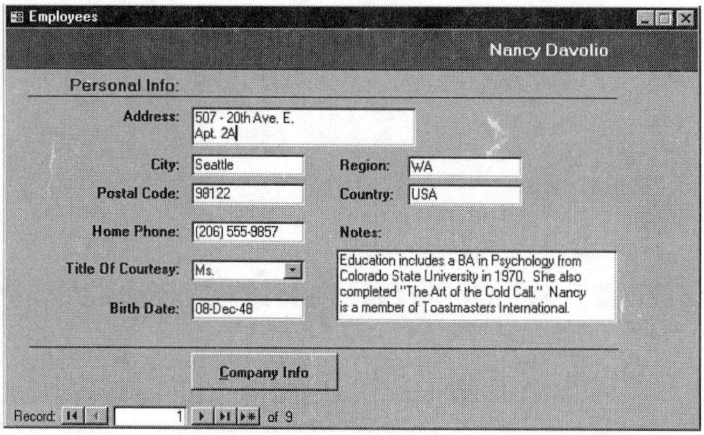

Fig. 14.4

Forms can display Memo fields attractively, like the Notes field at the right.

There are also a couple of drop-down menus among the fields. Because there's less clutter, these will be easier to view compared with lookup columns in a table. Now take a look at the Notes. There's enough space for you to read them without having to Zoom up. You can click the Company Info button to return to the first page of the form.

I don't want to over promise and say you'll be making great forms overnight. Some of this stuff requires practice. A lot of it won't be covered in this book. But this is not impossible stuff. You don't have to be Toulouse-Lautrec. You may need some additional support beyond this book and what Access itself provides. Appendix A will give you an idea of some places to go for more help.

But sometimes I want the records one on top of another

At times you will want to see your data in a datasheet, even if it's easier to view it record by record in a form. For one thing, it's simpler to compare data when it's in Datasheet view. Do you have to go back and look at the table each time to see your data in columns and rows?

No way. You can make your form look like a table by simply selecting Datasheet view. Choose View, Datasheet, and you have something that looks very much like the Employees table (see fig. 14.5). If you want to add (or take away) grid lines, choose Format, Cells; in the Gridlines Shown section, you can change the setting as you like. All the same information is there.

Fig. 14.5

Make your form look like a datasheet by switching to Datasheet view.

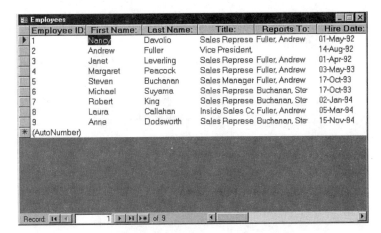

	Employee ID:	First Name:	Last Name:	Title:	Reports To:	Hire Date:
▶	1	Nancy	Davolio	Sales Represe	Fuller, Andrew	01-May-92
	2	Andrew	Fuller	Vice President		14-Aug-92
	3	Janet	Leverling	Sales Represe	Fuller, Andrew	01-Apr-92
	4	Margaret	Peacock	Sales Represe	Fuller, Andrew	03-May-93
	5	Steven	Buchanan	Sales Manager	Fuller, Andrew	17-Oct-93
	6	Michael	Suyama	Sales Represe	Buchanan, Ste	17-Oct-93
	7	Robert	King	Sales Represe	Buchanan, Ste	02-Jan-94
	8	Laura	Callahan	Inside Sales Cc	Fuller, Andrew	05-Mar-94
	9	Anne	Dodsworth	Sales Represe	Buchanan, Ste	15-Nov-94
*	(AutoNumber)					

Record: |◄| |◄| 1 |►| |►I| |►*| of 9

TIP **You can select Datasheet view from the toolbar too. The Form** View button in Form view shows the Design icon. Click the drop-down menu arrow beside it and select Datasheet View.

Now take a look at the toolbar. Looks awfully familiar, doesn't it? In fact, it's the same toolbar you see for a table. That means you can do all the same things you do in a table, like find values, sort fields, and filter records.

In the Format menu you can Hide and Unhide columns, and Freeze and Unfreeze them as well. In other words, you have most of the benefits of a table, without looking at a table at all.

Now choose View, Form to switch back to Form view. The commands in the various menus will change, but you still have the same toolbar. In other words, you have many of the same tools to manipulate your data however you decide to view it. Is it any wonder that many users prefer to work almost exclusively with forms?

How else can I make a new form?

You can quickly make a new form in any open table with one or two mouse clicks. But it's like shopping at the corner grocery—there's that one sad turkey TV dinner in the case, so guess which one you have to take?

It's time to go to the forms supermarket. You could buy the same convenient TV dinner—or you may wind up with something more ambitious and satisfying.

Click the New button in the Forms tab of any Database window to see all the ways you can make a form. Figure 14.6 shows the New Form dialog box.

Fig. 14.6
The description box on the left helps you recall how each selection is used.

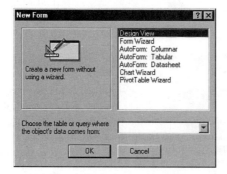

Wow, there are a lot of choices. Let's dispose of the first and last two rather quickly. For now, I would forget about starting from scratch by making a form in Design View. When you become more skilled, maybe you'll want to use it. But even power users like using form wizards—there's nothing wimpy about relying on them. Meanwhile, both the Chart and Pivot Table Wizards can be useful, but they are beyond the scope of this book.

Those hassle-free AutoForms

Now let's look at the other choices. As the name implies, AutoForms are the fastest, simplest way to make a form. First, select the type of AutoForm: Columnar, Tabular, or Datasheet (see fig. 14.6). At bottom, you choose the table or query that will provide all the data. For example, to select the Employees table, click the drop-down arrow, scroll down to the Employees table, and then select it. Then click OK. That's all it takes.

You've already made a Columnar AutoForm from the Orders table. You could have made a similar form by selecting AutoForm: Columnar from the New Form window, choosing the Orders table, and clicking OK. Since you're already familiar with a Columnar AutoForm, let's go ahead and see what the other types of AutoForms offer.

How does a Tabular AutoForm work?

Figure 14.7 shows a Tabular AutoForm based on the Northwind Order Details table. The tabular form includes the best features of the table grid and the column-type form. Field names are on top as in a table, but each value has its own text box for easy viewing. You can fit more than one record on each page, which saves some screen shuffling. And you can easily compare data in two adjacent records.

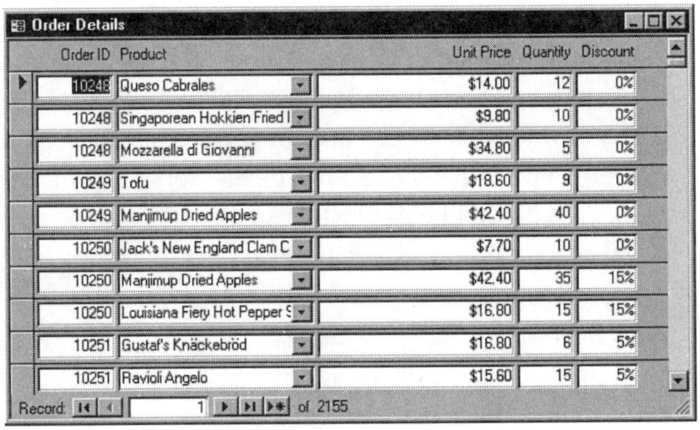

Fig. 14.7
A Tabular AutoForm can show more than one record per page.

The Tabular AutoForm works great when there aren't many fields. But take a look at figure 14.8, which shows a Tabular AutoForm for the Orders table.

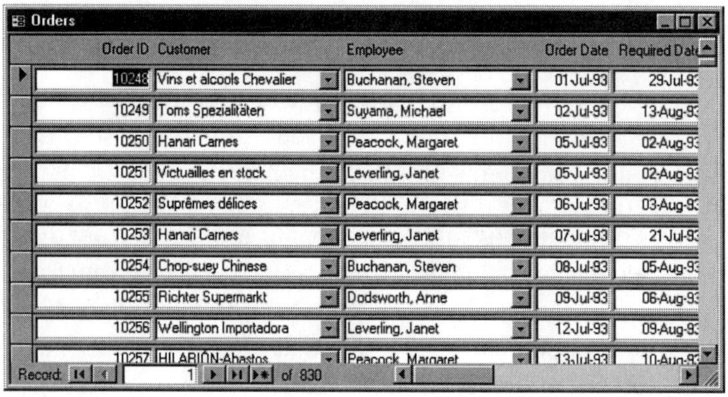

Fig. 14.8
Only a few of the
many fields in the
Orders form can be
seen at one time.

You have the same problem as you do in a table: How do you fit all the fields in one screen and still read them? So the Tabular AutoForm is better when you have relatively few fields.

Why would I want a form that's a datasheet?

A Datasheet AutoForm is an interesting hybrid of table and form. When you open it, the form is in Datasheet view (see fig. 14.9). In Form view, it's similar to a Tabular form—all fields appear in one row on one screen. But unlike a Tabular form, each record appears on a single page. You run into the same problem you did with a Tabular form—too many fields and it becomes a mess. Still, if you like to work primarily in Datasheet view but want occasional access to Form view, this AutoForm may be useful.

Fig. 14.9
Besides the Datasheet view shown here, the Datasheet AutoForm also offers a Form view.

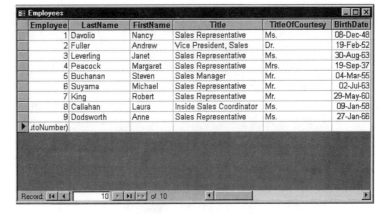

Employee	LastName	FirstName	Title	TitleOfCourtesy	BirthDate
1	Davolio	Nancy	Sales Representative	Ms.	08-Dec-48
2	Fuller	Andrew	Vice President, Sales	Dr.	19-Feb-52
3	Leverling	Janet	Sales Representative	Ms.	30-Aug-63
4	Peacock	Margaret	Sales Representative	Mrs.	19-Sep-37
5	Buchanan	Steven	Sales Manager	Mr.	04-Mar-55
6	Suyama	Michael	Sales Representative	Mr.	02-Jul-63
7	King	Robert	Sales Representative	Mr.	29-May-60
8	Callahan	Laura	Inside Sales Coordinator	Ms.	09-Jan-58
9	Dodsworth	Anne	Sales Representative	Ms.	27-Jan-66
(AutoNumber)					

How can I use the Form Wizard to make a table?

AutoForms work fine but they have their limitations. You get all the fields in that table, whether you want them all or not. You also don't have any choice about the form's style.

You can make better-looking, more sophisticated forms with the Form Wizard. The Form Wizard also offers 10 different styles to satisfy your aesthetic taste.

Let's make another form from the Orders table of the Northwind database. This time, though, you'll use the Form Wizard selection in the New Form window. If you haven't already done so, open the Northwind.mdb database in the Samples folder, and click the Forms tab in the Database window. Then click the New button at right. You'll see the New Form dialog box in figure 14.6.

Select Form Wizard, second on the list. At bottom, click the drop-down arrow, scroll down until you find the Orders table, and select it. Then click OK.

Selecting fields in the Form Wizard

Figure 14.10 shows the first screen of the Form Wizard. The Orders table, selected in the New Form screen, appears in Tables/Queries. Below, all the fields in the Orders table are listed. You can choose fields individually by selecting them and then clicking the single-arrow button. Or, if you want to include all the fields in the form, simply click the double-arrow button. Once chosen, you can similarly deselect fields by using the left-facing arrow buttons.

Click the double-arrow button to select all the fields of the Orders table. Then click Next to move to the next screen.

Fig. 14.10
Choose the fields you want with the arrow buttons.

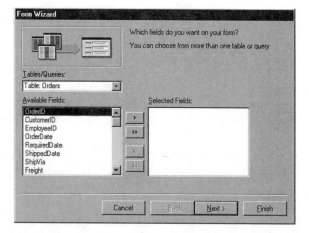

What kind of layout should I select?

In the next screen, you have three choices for the layout: columnar, tabular, and datasheet. You've already seen examples of these when you made AutoForms. The Columnar button should be selected; if not, click it and choose Next.

Choosing a style

In the next screen you can select a style for your form (see fig. 14.11). Choose a style that sounds appealing and select it, then see what it looks like in the preview box at the left. Or start at the top and move down one by one until you find one that suits you.

Fig. 14.11
Pick a style that's
handsome.

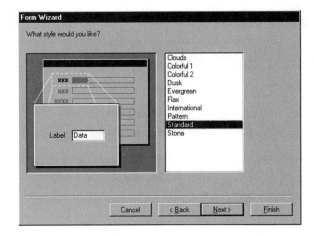

Thus far, all your forms have used the default standard. That works fine, and
you may want to use that all the time. Just for variety, let's choose another
style. Flax looks like it might be attractive, so let's try that. Select it and click
Next.

Choose a name and display the form

Last screen—you're almost done. First you need a title for the form. An
Orders form already exists, so Access suggests Orders1. That'll work, for
now. (You can change the form name or simply delete the form afterward; I'll
go over how to do both in a moment.) Now you decide how you want to open
the form. Let's open it ready to view or enter information. Click Finish, and
you're done. Figure 14.12 shows how your figure will look.

Fig. 14.12
You're not married to
the style you've
chosen. In Chapter 16,
"A Tour of Some
Selected Properties,"
you'll learn how to
change it.

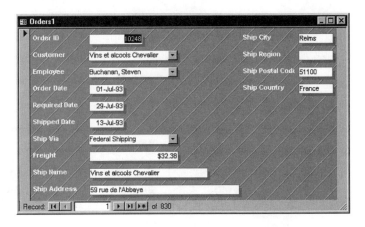

TIP   **Just as in any other wizard, you can go back and forth between** wizard windows. Use the <u>B</u>ack and <u>N</u>ext> buttons liberally to create the form you want. When you've gotten everything straightened out, just click <u>F</u>inish.

I want to include fields from more than one table

When you created tables, you tried to group similar data in each one—the shirts went with the shirts, ties with the ties. But how you actually use your data, how you want to see it, and how you want to input it may be quite different than the way you've stored it in tables. You may want this piece of information from this table next to this other bit from that one. With a form, you include additional fields from other tables in your form.

Try using a Form Wizard instead of a query

One traditional way of bringing information from different tables into a single form is to use a query. You create the query as you always do, and then make the form based on the query. With a query, you are able to use expressions and criteria to define the data you want with precision.

If you don't require criteria, however, a simpler way to create forms with fields from another table is to use the Form Wizard. Let's take a simple example. In the Orders form you created, the employee assigned to the order is shown in the EmployeeID field. Suppose you also wanted to know his or her title, which can be found in the Title field of the Employees table. Follow these steps to create the form:

1 Select the Form Wizard in the New Form dialog box and tell Access to use data from the Orders table. Click OK.

2 Select some or all of the fields from the Orders table for your form, clicking the single or double arrow button as appropriate.

3 Click the drop-down menu of the <u>T</u>ables/Queries box and select the Employees table. The <u>A</u>vailable Fields list will show all of its fields (see fig. 14.13). Click Title and click the top single-arrow button to include it in <u>S</u>elected Fields. Click <u>N</u>ext.

Fig. 14.13
You can select fields from an additional table or query by clicking the drop-down menu again and choosing other fields.

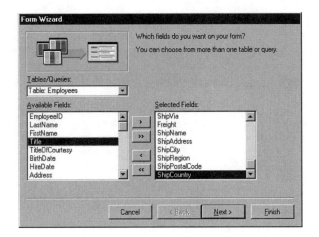

4 You now have a choice of how you want to view your form. You still want to view your form by order—all you wanted was one additional field that told you the Employees title when you viewed the Orders form. Leave the settings as they are. Click <u>N</u>ext.

5 Follow the Wizard's instructions to finish your form.

How can I change the title of a form?

You change a form title just like you did with any other object. Select the form in the Database window, wait a half-second and then click the title. The cursor will be flashing, and you can now rename the form. After you've changed it, click anywhere outside the form to confirm the change.

 The usual caveat about renaming objects applies. Be careful. If you've used an object's name in any other place in the database, that reference will now be invalid. You may also want to be consistent in the naming of tables/queries and the forms (and reports) based on them.

How do I delete a form?

Again, it's the same for any object. Select it in the Database window, choose <u>E</u>dit, <u>D</u>elete (or press the Delete key), and then confirm it when Access asks.

15

Use Form Controls to Improve Your Design

● **In this chapter:**

- **Why is form design tougher than table design?**

- **What are controls all about?**

- **Moving, sizing, aligning, spacing controls**

- **Add a text box and label to your form**

So far as design goes, forms are more challenging than other objects . . . . **➢**

I f you read Chapter 14, you may have wondered, "Gee, with tables and queries, right away I knew how to move and resize stuff. With forms, I haven't even seen the word 'design' yet. What's the big secret?"

There's no secret, just a plain truth: so far as design goes, forms are more challenging than other objects I've talked about. While there were things you could change in tables/queries, ultimately a grid is still a grid: cells, cells, and more cells. With a form, your options have greatly expanded. You can put this box here, make a line over there, and stick a button in between them. It's a little like desktop publishing, if you've ever done any of that.

If you haven't, don't worry. You don't need an MFA from design school. If you keep it simple, the Form Wizards take care of most of your design worries. Occasionally, you might need a little touch-up here and there. I'm going to go over some of the real basics to help you with that part.

If you're wondering about the chapter title, you'll soon see that form design centers on controls. Like the controls of an airplane, they do all the work for you. By the end of this chapter, you'll know how to handle them.

Let's see the Form Design window

If you'd like, you can open the Northwind.mdb database in the Samples folder again so you can follow the figures. Click the Forms tab, and select the Employees form. You open a form in Design view by clicking the <u>D</u>esign button.

 If you're in Form view, you can switch to Design view by choosing <u>V</u>iew, Form <u>D</u>esign; or click the View button on the toolbar. If you're in Datasheet view, you can switch to Form or Design view by clicking the drop-down menu of the View button and selecting the appropriate view.

Figure 15.1 is the Employees table in Design View, while figure 15.2 shows it in Form view. Here are a few things to note about Design view:

- A few of the icons in the first toolbar at the top may look familiar, but the ones in the middle look new.

- A second toolbar underneath it looks like it's for word processing. That's the **Formatting toolbar**, and you can change the style, font, alignment, etc. of your text with it.

- Below the two toolbars is a horizontal ruler, and there's another ruler going down the side of the screen.

- There are more icons in a toolbox sitting in the middle of the screen. (You can move a toolbox by clicking its titlebar, holding down the mouse button, and dragging it.)

- There are a lot of little dots on the screen. That's called the **grid**. This grid isn't for putting data in tables, it's for lining up stuff.

Fig. 15.1
The Employees table in
Design view.

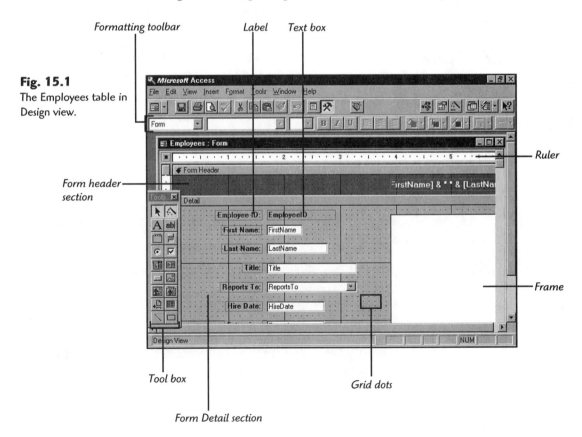

Formatting toolbar   Label   Text box

Form header
section

Ruler

Frame

Tool box

Grid dots

Form Detail section

Fig. 15.2
The same table in Form
view with data
selected.

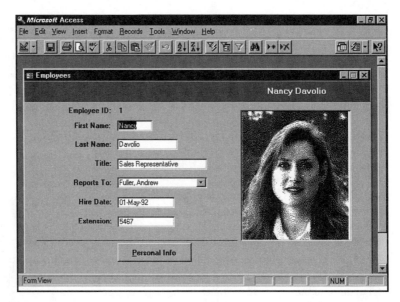

 CAUTION If you can't see the rulers, grid, or toolbox, open the **V**iew menu
to see if there's a check mark beside each one.

It looks like the form has different parts

In figure 15.1, you can see the Employees table has at least two sections, the
Form Header and **Detail**. The Form Header indicates that the name of each
employee will appear in the upper-right hand corner of the screen in Form
view. The employee's name will appear at the top of each page. Your data, on
the other hand, goes in the Detail section.

There are three other sections: the Form Footer, the **Page Header**, and the
Page Footer. The Page Header and Footer appear in the form only when you
print, and I'll discuss them briefly in Chapter 16.

You may find you have a lot of empty space in a section and you need to
make it smaller. Or you may want to add something and you need a little
more space. Move your mouse pointer to the border between sections and
push it around until you see the two-sided arrow with bar. Then click, keep
the mouse button depressed, and drag.

Plain English, please!

> A **page header** displays information that you want on the top of every page, like a title or column headings. A **page footer** shows information at the bottom of each page, such as a page number.

You said controls are important. So what are they?

Controls are the graphical objects that determine what your form does and what it looks like. Take another look at the two views of the Employees table. A control is any of the boxes in the first figure that decides what goes on in the second figure. All the boxes with text in them (Employee ID, First Name) are controls. The big empty frame at right where the employee photo goes is a control too.

 Plain English, please!

> A **control** is any object on your frame that displays your data (for example, an employee's name), performs an action (like a button for opening another form), or decorates your form (such as lines and rectangles to better organize your data).

Why is there two of everything?

No, you didn't suddenly develop an acute case of double vision. In figure 15.1, the boxes running down the left side are **labels**. In Form view, those will tell you the data's title. The boxes to the right are the **text boxes** that store your data. In Figure 15.2, look at First Name, the second data item. The box that says First Name on the left is the label, while Nancy on the right is in the text box.

Designing forms looks complicated!

Making great forms from scratch is not something you do overnight. That's why the wizards are so great for making good forms easily. As you get more proficient, you'll want to experiment and do more on your own. But the wizards get you most of the way there.

Enough background on forms. Let's get to work!

You've learned lots of form vocabulary and have little to show for it. OK, let's see how labels and text boxes work. Labels and text boxes control where your data goes and how it looks—so they're essential.

How do I select a text box?

Before you move or resize a text box, you first have to select it. Click the Last Name text box in Design view of the Employees table (or any other text box) and see what happens (see fig. 15.3). It looks like both the text box and the label got selected. Well, sort of—each has a big square in the upper left-hand corner. The text box also has a bunch of little squares around it. What does that mean?

Fig. 15.3
A text box and its attached label in Design view.

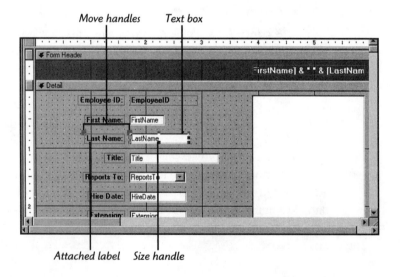

It means that you've only selected the text box—not the label. But the text box and label are **attached**. Both have a (relatively) big square, called a **move handle**, in the upper left-hand corner (see fig. 15.3). Whenever you move the text box, the label gets dragged along with it, and vice versa. If you're going to move a text box, you probably want the label along with it. When you select one, the other comes too.

On the other hand, only the text box has the little squares around it, which are **size handles** (see fig. 15.3). These handles, unavailable on the label, can be used to resize the text box. Just because you want a bigger text box doesn't mean you want a bigger label too. You can only resize the text box when you select it. The label will stay as it is.

Q&A *How come I see all the little squares around the box on the left, not the one on the right.*

You selected the label instead of the text box. You'll still be able to move the two together, but you can only resize the label.

How do I move a text box with its attached label?

Now, if you're thoughtful and reasonable, you think, "Ah, I want to move these at the same time. So, I'll click one of the move handles, keep the mouse button depressed, and drag the pair together." Impeccable logic, but totally wrong. That's exactly what you don't want to do.

Here's what you have to do. Move the mouse pointer to the border of the selected control. In this case, that's the text box. Now move it around until you see an open hand (see fig. 15.4). Now click, hold down the mouse button, and drag. Notice that you see both text box and label moving as you push the mouse. Wherever you stop and release the mouse button, that's where they will both wind up.

Fig. 15.4
Make sure you see the
open hand before you
drag the text box with
its attached label.

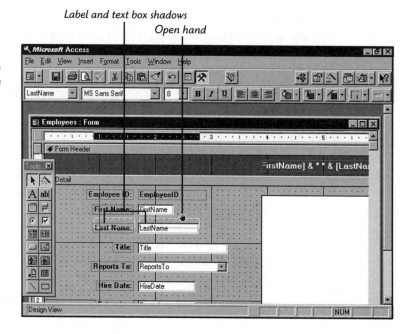

Label and text box shadows

Open hand

What are the move handles good for?

You use the move handles when you want to move either of the attached controls separately. Take a look at figure 15.5. When you move the pointer near the move handle of either the text box or the attached label, it turns into a hand with the index finger pointing up. Now click, hold down the mouse button, and drag. You can see the one control moving, while the other stays put. Now you can drop the control where you want it.

Putting controls in the right place

Access provides a couple of aids to help you drop a control right where you want it. First, you can use the grid. Take a look at Format, Snap to Grid and make sure it's checked; if not, click it. When you drag a control and Snap to Grid is on, it falls smack on the little dots where you put it.

Fig. 15.5

To move a control separately, look for the upward-pointing hand.

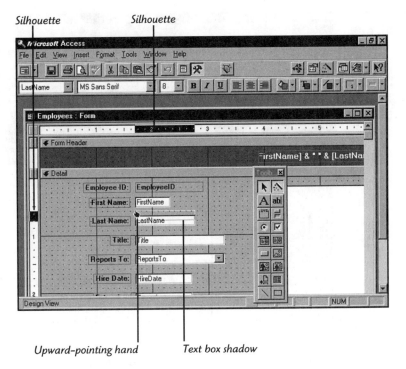

Silhouette   Silhouette

Upward-pointing hand   Text box shadow

Also notice that, as you drag, the silhouette of the control moves along in both horizontal and vertical rulers (see fig. 15.5). So you can use that as a guide as well.

TIP **Do you just want to nudge a control a tiny bit? Select it, hold** down the Ctrl key, and press the arrow keys until the control is correctly positioned.

How do I resize a control?

You resize a control by just grabbing any size handle and dragging it. Move the mouse pointer toward any of the little squares and watch it turn into a double-arrow (see fig. 15.6). Then click, hold down the mouse button, and drag. The box shadow indicates the potential size of the box.

Fig. 15.6
Drag the double-arrow
symbol to resize the
control.

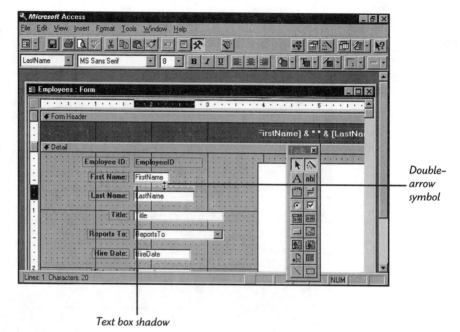

*Double-
arrow
symbol*

Text box shadow

> **TIP** **One of the nice things about forms is that text boxes can hold**
> several lines of text. That's a lot better than zooming things up all the time
> in a table. To see additional lines of text, you simply make the text box
> longer.

Deleting a control

Deleting a text box and its attached label is easy. Just select the text box and
press the Delete key. Want to delete the label? Select the label and press
Delete.

Can I select more than one control at a time?

Suppose you wanted to move several text boxes and their labels together.
You might, for example, want to take all the address fields in a table (Address, State, ZIP) and put them in another part of the form. In that case, you
would want to keep them all together and drag them as one.

You can select two or more controls at the same time. That way, you can move controls in groups or resize several controls at once. What you do is drag the mouse pointer right through the controls.

Suppose you wanted to select the label and text boxes for First Name, Last Name, and Title in the Employees form (see fig. 15.7). Start outside First Name (either above the label or text box, it doesn't matter) and drag through all six boxes, completing a rectangle. All six controls are now selected.

 TIP **You can also select multiple controls by holding down the Shift** key and clicking the controls you want. This comes in handy when there isn't much room to draw rectangles. It's also useful for selecting nonadjacent controls.

Fig. 15.7
Drag the mouse pointer right through the controls to select them as a group.

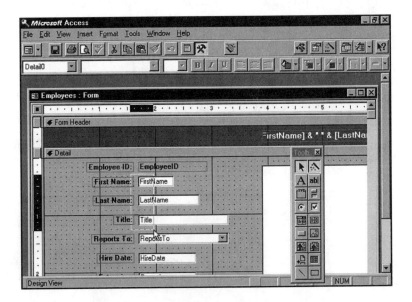

How do I move all of the controls at once?

You move the controls just as you moved a text box and its attached control. Pick any control, move the pointer near the border, and look for the open hand. Then click, keep the mouse button depressed, and drag the controls where you want them.

What if I want to size them?

Again, resize any control as you learned in the "How do I resize a control?" section. Grab one of the sizing handles, drag until the control is the size you want, then release. All the controls will be resized proportionately.

TIP   **If you want to resize a text box with its label, select both of them.** (Remember, that's not the same as selecting the text box with an attached label.) Drag the size handle for one control, and the other will follow suit.

How can I make controls the same size?

Use the Format, Size command to make controls all the same size. Suppose you want the First Name and Last Name text boxes in the Employees table to be as wide as the Title text box. First, select the three text boxes as a group (their labels can be attached for moving, so long as they are not selected for resizing). Then, from the Format, Size menu, choose Widest (see fig. 15.8). The three controls will all be as wide as the Title text box. As you can see from the figure, you can also use the same menu to make text boxes as short, tall, or as narrow as another one.

Fig. 15.8
While you can resize controls one by one, using the Format, Size command ensures uniformity.

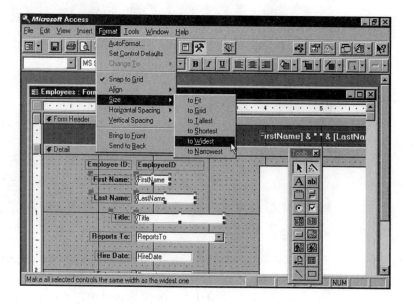

My form is all messed up. Help!

It's easy to make a hash of things when you first start fooling around with controls. Yes, you've used the grid and kept the Snap to Grid command turned on. Yes, you've used the rulers. But things still look like a mess—not a big mess, it's just that when you move one thing, something else got out of whack. Spacing can become uneven. Controls can be too close together. Labels that were flush right are now jagged.

Your first line of defense is the Undo command, easily accessed from the toolbar or by selecting <u>E</u>dit, <u>U</u>ndo. Your second line of defense is to close the form and not save any of your layout changes. But sometimes it's too late for either tactic. Fortunately, you can usually put things right again with a command from the Format menu bar.

Getting controls aligned

It is easy to realign controls that get out of line. In the first page of each record of the Employees table, for example, the labels column is aligned flush right. Suppose a couple of fields got out of whack, both the text boxes and the labels. First, realign the labels. Select the messed-up ones along with one of the labels that is correctly aligned. Then, choose F<u>o</u>rmat, <u>A</u>lign, <u>R</u>ight. Access aligns the controls with the (correctly placed) one that's farthest right. Now repeat the process for the text boxes, but align them left.

As you can see from the <u>A</u>lign submenu, you can align controls left, right, top, or bottom. In each case, the controls line up with the one farthest in that direction. You can also align controls to the grid. That may be helpful if you turned Snap to Grid off at some point.

 TIP **Here's a good rule of thumb when you align controls: Select** controls only in the same "row" or same "column." (That's not a grid column or row—just stuff that happens to be placed that way.)

I'm still having problems with aligning

There's no doubt that aligning controls takes some practice. It gets confusing when you're trying to position stuff both across and down at the same time. That can happen with columns of labels and text boxes. Try experimenting with different combinations and see what happens. (Don't worry about messing up your form—just don't save any design changes when you close it. Or copy the form so you have one you can play around with.)

> **TIP** If you just have one control (with or without its attached label), it can be easier to just move it than to realign it.

Spacing controls evenly

Another mishap of fooling with controls is that the spacing gets uneven. The alignment may be OK—the controls are lined up straight as an arrow, but the space between them varies. Take a look at figure 15.9. Reports To is not evenly spaced between Title and Hire Date. How can you make them even?

First, select the Reports To, Title, and Hire Date text boxes. (For controls with attached labels, you select the text boxes, not the attached labels.) Then, choose Format, Vertical Spacing, Make Equal. The controls will be equally spaced.

Fig. 15.9
Select the text boxes to make the spacing equal.

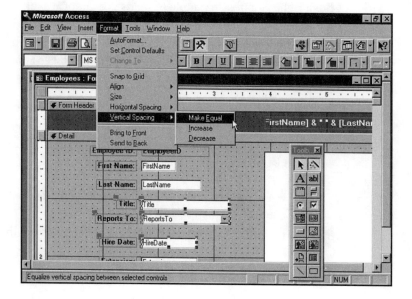

> **TIP** For the equal spacing command, you should always select at least three controls.

Changing the space between controls

You can use the same technique to make the space between controls greater or smaller. Suppose you decide that Hire Date and Extension in the Employees form should have a little more space between them. First, select the text boxes of the two data items. Then, choose Format, Vertical Spacing, Increase (see fig. 15.10).

Figure 15.11 shows the new design. Now look at figure 15.10 and 15.11 together for a before-and-after comparison. Notice that the top item, Hire Date, remained stationary, while the other dropped down a bit. In Vertical Spacing, it's always the control on top that remains put.

Fig. 15.10

Increase the space between fields using the vertical and horizontal spacing commands.

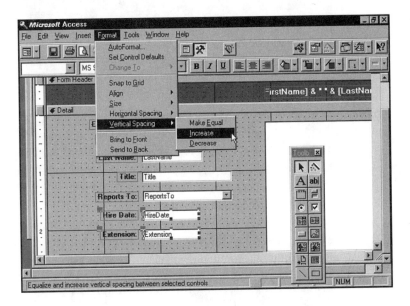

Is your spacing problem between columns, not rows? Select Horizontal Spacing in the same Format menu to increase, decrease, or make equal the space between form columns. When using Horizontal Spacing, it's the control that's farthest left that stays put.

Fig. 15.11
The top field stays
where it is when you
increase or decrease
spacing.

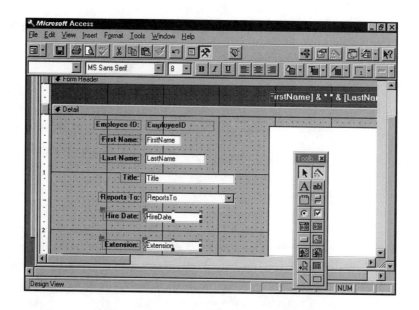

Cutting, copying, and duplicating controls

You can cut or copy a control just like you would anything else in windows. Use Edit, Cut and Edit, Copy, or click the appropriate button on the toolbar. Pasting, unfortunately, is far from an exact science. When Access pastes, it puts the control in the upper-left corner of whatever section you happen to be working in. It's likely that is not the place you want it. There is one exception to this rule: if you select a control before you paste, Access will put the cut object directly beneath it.

Instead of copying a control, you can duplicate it. Select the control, then choose Edit, Duplicate, and the control will be copied directly underneath the original. Do you want another duplicate placed directly underneath the duplicated control? Choose Edit, Duplicate again. All three controls will be aligned and evenly spaced.

I want to add a control to my form

Up to now, I've just been talking about manipulating controls that are already on your form. As I've stressed before, it's best to leave form creation to the Form Wizards (that includes AutoForms). When you open a form a wizard has created, the controls are already nicely in place, and you don't have to worry about making them. So I'm not going to go into most of the different controls you can create, and all your different options when making them.

Occasionally, you might need to add a text box and label to a form you already have. You may need a field you initially left out of your form. You might have added a field to a table or query, and now you want to update the form and include it. So let me discuss how to add an additional field from a table or query to a form.

Bound and unbound controls

It will be helpful if you learn a little bit more about controls. They come in two varieties: bound and unbound. A **bound control** has a specific data source, like a field in a table. In other words, it is **bound** to that field. It can be any field with any Data Type—Text, Number, Yes/No. A text box is very often a bound control.

An **unbound control** has no data source. Unbound controls include lines and rectangles that you use to dress up your form. A label is an unbound control too: it's just several alphanumeric characters—it has no underlying data source.

When a control is bound, all the different characteristics of the data—the way it's formatted, or if it has an input mask, or the description in the status bar—get inherited from the underlying table. When it's not, the control doesn't pick up anything on its own. So if you want a text box to get its information from a specific source, you have to make sure it's bound to it.

How do you do that? If you use the Form Wizards, 99 percent of the time you don't have to worry. If you want to add a field from a table on your own, then you have to consider how it will get its data. Here again, there is an easy out: If you drag the field onto the form design from a field list, then the text box created is bound to that field.

Now show me how to add a text box

In the Employees form, the Extension went right below the Hire Date. Let's suppose you had left out the Extension when you originally made the Employees form. You now decide that you should have included it. How do you put it in there?

The easiest way to create a bound text box is to drag the field from the field list to the form. Both a label and a text box will be created wherever you drop it on the form. Then you can resize it and align it.

How, you may ask, do you see the field list? Select View, Field List, or click the field list button on the toolbar. Figure 15.12 shows the field list for the Employees table.

Fig. 15.12
Use the field list to create a bound text box.

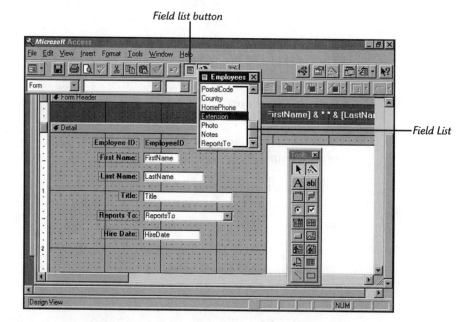

Use the scrollbar to see the Extension field. Click once on it to select it. Now click on it again, hold down the mouse button, and begin dragging it to the form. You want to position it so that the field symbol is aligned and evenly spaced with the Hire Date text box (see fig. 15.13). Then release the mouse button, and see what you've done (see fig. 15.14).

OK, so far so good. The Extension text box looks OK (if yours is a little bit off, use any of the techniques you learned earlier in this chapter to get it in place—move it, align, place it as you see fit). But the type in the Extension label isn't in bold, and it needs to be aligned.

Fig. 15.13
Position the new text box under the Hire Date text box.

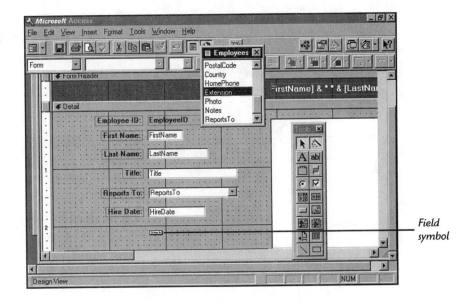

Field symbol

I'll discuss text formatting in Chapter 16. But I don't think I'm giving away any secrets if I tell you to select the Extension label and click the big B on the second toolbar to put it in Bold. Now you need to widen the label a bit so you can see its full name. You can resize it on your own, but it's probably easier to select Format, Size, to Fit. Finally, align it with the Hire Date label, and you're done.

Fig. 15.14
The label needs to be bold and aligned.

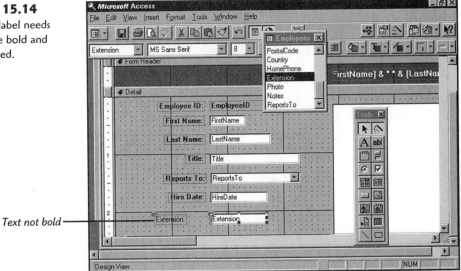

Text not bold

Q&A *My Employees form looks like a mess. How do I get back to where I started?*

Just select File, Close, and click No when Access asks you if you want your changes saved. You're back to where you started.

16

A Tour of Some Selective Properties

● In this chapter:

- A short tour of long property sheets

- How do I make text look the way I want it?

- Hide text boxes you don't need

- How do I keep table and form properties consistent?

- I can't stand this form's style anymore. Change it!

- Exploring several options for printing forms

You can adjust properties—both the substantive and the cosmetic—to make forms work better for you . . . .

"**H**oney, could you get some batteries while you're out?"

"What size?"

"We need C's."

"Alkaline or regular?"

"Alkaline."

"Rechargeables or throw-aways?"

"Umm, throw-aways."

"Eveready or Duracell?"

"Oh, forget it, I'll get them myself!"

Ah, decisions, decisions. There can be so many selections, it makes you nuts. But sometimes the choice is crucial—if you need C batteries, A's won't do the trick. Other times it's less important, but your choice still makes a difference—like deciding to pay more for longer-lasting rechargeables. And sometimes it's just a matter of preference: Eveready or Duracell, both will serve you well.

In Access, as in Windows 95 itself, the choices that determine traits are called properties. You've already set and adjusted table properties in Chapter 7, "Designing Database Tables." This chapter focuses on how to change properties—both the substantive and the cosmetic, the essential and the dispensable—to make forms work better for you.

What kinds of things in a form have properties?

Controls have properties, sections have properties, and the form itself has properties. You'll remember that controls determine most of what is important in a form, the database object that displays your data using graphical elements. So most of your work will be with control properties.

Properties define where the data comes from (for example, which field in which table or query), how data is displayed, where the control is located…there's a property for anything and everything. Some properties can be set or changed through the menu bar and toolbars. Other properties are set directly in a **property sheet**, which lists all the properties of the object and their settings. You can always set properties within the property sheet.

 Plain English, please!

A **property sheet** is a window in which you can assign traits for database objects. In both forms and reports, every control has its own property sheet.

CAUTION **Sometimes you'll think you've selected a property sheet for a** control, and it turns out that you have selected it for a section or the form itself. If you can't find a property you're looking for, make sure you're looking at the right property sheet.

What does a property sheet look like?

You can use any form in Design view to view property sheets. If you want to follow along with the figures, I'm mostly going to use the Customers form in the Northwind database (Northwind.mdb, located in the Samples folder). Open the database, click the Forms tab, select the Customers form, and click the Design button. The Customers form opens in Design view (see fig. 16.1).

 Select the Company Name text box, then click the Properties icon on the toolbar. (You might want to read Chapter 15, "Use Form Controls to Improve Your Design," first if words like "text box" are new to you.) You'll see the property sheet in figure 16.2. Click on the different tabs to see the various categories of properties. The All tab shows all the properties contained in the other tabs. Sometimes you may find that a more convenient way to view properties.

 You can also see the property sheet by selecting the control and choosing View, Properties. A shortcut is supposedly to double-click the control (don't select it first). This doesn't always work that well, and you wind up ready to rename the thing. If you're going to double-click, do it crisply.

Properties button

Fig. 16.1

The Customers form in Design view.

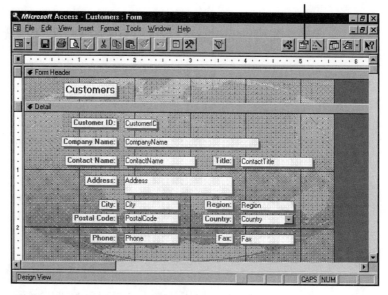

Fig. 16.2

Click the different tabs to see various properties.

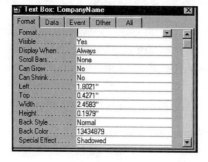

CAUTION A text box and its label are closely related. As you saw in Chapter 15, when you select a text box, a move handle also appears on the label. But when it comes to properties, text box and label are separate entities. Choose only the property sheet of the control you want to change.

These property sheets are too complicated

Property sheets are complex because they list every possible trait of a control. Some of them do apply to the control you're working on. But many others are just listed and don't have any setting. If you happen to need them later on, they're there for you.

Even that makes property sheets sound more overwhelming than they really are. A bound text box inherits the property settings in the underlying table or query. What does that mean? Most of the work is already done! You have already made an input mask for a telephone number. Or set the data type to Currency for a retail price. Or decided to display a date in Long form. As I discussed in Chapter 15, all those settings were carried over into the form when you created it.

So why do I need to know about properties at all?

Once you've made the form, the umbilical cord is cut between the table and the form. Suppose you change the way a date is displayed in a table after you make a form. Nothing happens to the date in the form—it stays the same. The reverse is true, too. When you change the properties of a text box in a form, the field in the underlying table is unaffected.

Usually you want to keep properties consistent between the form and the table. Things like Default Value, Validation Rule, and Validation Text should stay the same. But there will be times when you'll want to know how to change them in a form.

Properties can help you take full advantage of a form's expanded graphical features. For example, you may want to display multiple lines of text in a control—something you couldn't do in a table. You may want to change the style in which controls are displayed. Or, you might choose a different, more attractive font. In these cases, electing property settings that differ (or are nonexistent) in a table makes perfectly good sense.

How do I change the way my text looks?

Suppose you've been using the Customers form for a while. You want to be able to identify the country of a customer more easily. One way to do that would be to change the font in the Country text box from normal to italic. How would you go about changing it?

Figure 16.3 shows what the various boxes and buttons of the Formatting toolbar do. (I've left out the more esoteric ones on the right side.) You can use them to change the way your text boxes and labels look.

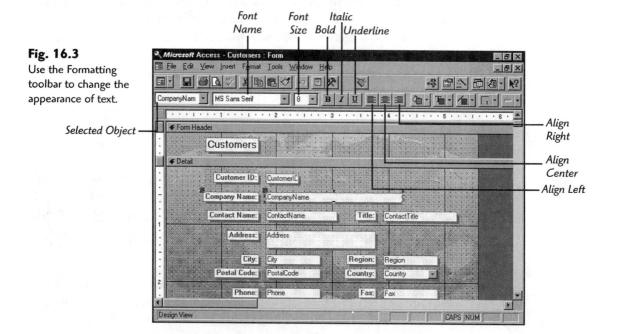

Fig. 16.3
Use the Formatting toolbar to change the appearance of text.

To put the text in the Country text box in italic, first select the control. Then click the *I* button in the toolbar. The text in the Country text box is now in italic. If you switch to Form view (click the Form View button), you can see that the values in the Country text box (Germany, USA, etc.) are now in italics.

If you've spent some time with other Microsoft programs, such as Word, the left side of the Formatting toolbar doesn't hold many surprises. You can select another font by clicking the drop-down list and choosing one you like. You can also make a font bigger or smaller by selecting a bigger or smaller number from the font size drop-down list.

Apply bold type and underlining with the **B** and <u>U</u> buttons, just as you did for italic: select the control, and click the button. If you just want to change a few letters within the control, select it, highlight the target text, and click the appropriate button. You can center the text within the text box or make it flush right by choosing the appropriate button on the toolbar.

TIP **Don't go wild changing fonts around. If you used a Form Wizard,** your form already looks good. A little goes a long way in this area. Touch up one or two controls as you see fit and leave the rest alone.

Try working with any font change for a while in Form view to see if you like it. If it's OK, click Yes when Access prompts you to save your changes at closing time. If not, click No. The font will be back to its old self next time you open it.

Is there any way to "hide" a field on a form?

You can "hide" a field (i.e., label and text box) so it won't show in Form view. You'll still see it in Datasheet view, but then you can use Format, Hide Columns to hide it there, as you would in any datasheet. Here's how to do it:

1 Select the Region text box (or any other) and click the Properties icon.

2 Click on the Format tab.

3 Click the Visible property, second from the top.

4 Click the drop-down menu button (see fig. 16.4). Choose No, and both the label and text box will be hidden in Form view.

Fig. 16.4
You can "hide" a field
in the Format section
of the property sheet.

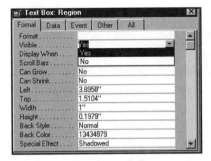

How can I change several controls at once?

If you need to change the same property in several controls, you can save time and avoid mistakes by changing them together. First, select the controls you want to change by holding down the Shift key and selecting them. Then click the Properties icon on the toolbar.

Suppose you have a temp in who's working on the Northwind database. You don't want him to see customers' addresses or phone numbers. Here's how to make sure they're not visible:

1 Select the Address and Phone fields by holding down the Shift key and selecting the text boxes.

2 Click the Properties icon on the toolbar. You get a Multiple selection property sheet (see fig. 16.5).

3 Click the Visible property in the Format tab. It says Yes. Change it to No.

4 Close the property sheet. The two fields will be hidden from view.

Fig. 16.5

You can change several controls at once using a Multiple Selection property sheet.

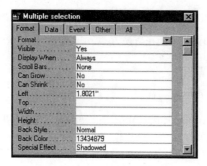

The Visible property initially showed Yes because both of the selected controls had that setting. If the two controls had different settings, the property would have simply been blank. That doesn't mean too much: Once you have the Multiple Selection property sheet in front of you, you can change it to whatever you want.

TIP **You can deselect a selected control in a multiple selection by** holding down the Shift key and clicking it again.

Q&A *I selected several text boxes at once, but then I didn't see the property I wanted to change listed in the property sheet.*

You'll only see (and be able to change) those properties that are common to all the controls you selected. For example, you may have selected, along with the text boxes, a stray line or rectangle somehow. Those don't have the same properties as text boxes. So, you won't see the properties exclusive to text boxes listed in the Multiple Selection property sheet. Look over your control selection, and deselect any unneeded controls.

I want a message to help me put data in the field

One of the prime functions of a form is data entry. When putting data in a text box, you may want a message in the Status Bar to help you out. It can remind users just what the text box is for, or give them some special instructions about it.

When you create a bound control, the message in the Status Bar is the field's Description in table design. If there's no Description, there's no message. You can change the form's message using the Status Bar Text property.

Suppose you wanted to put a message in the Contact Name text box asking that the contact's first name be typed first. Here's how you'd go about it:

1 Select the Contact Name text box.

2 Choose <u>V</u>iew, <u>P</u>roperties.

3 Click the Other tab.

4 Click on the Status Bar Text property, and type **Type first name first**.

5 Close the property sheet.

When you are in that text box in Form view, the message will be displayed in the Status Bar.

TIP **You can invoke the Zoom window while viewing the Status Bar**
Text property by pressing Shift+F2. That way you can see the entire message
you are typing.

I renamed a field in my table. What about my form?

If you change the name of a field in an underlying table, you'll need to change
the Control Source property of the text box in the form. Otherwise, Access
can't tell where the data is supposed to come from. Let's say you changed the
name of the Region field in the Customers table to *Area*. You would then
want to change the control source for the Region text box to the same name.
Here's how you would do it:

1 Click on the Region text box to select it.

2 Click inside the box. The cursor should begin to blink.

3 Backspace to erase the old Control Source, and type **Area**
(see fig. 16.6).

4 Click outside the text box to enter the change. You can change the label
name by following the same procedure for the label box.

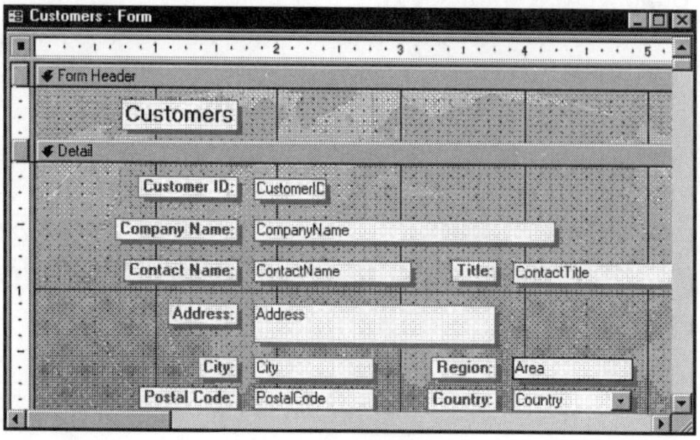

Fig. 16.6
You can change the
Control Source directly
in the text box.

I want to make sure I enter information correctly

Usually you set properties to ensure correct data entry in table design. I discuss these—default value, validation rules, input masks—in Chapter 7. As shown in figure 16.7, these properties are in the Data tab of a text box's property sheet. When you create a form based on the table, the field properties are inherited by the form's controls. You will usually want to keep these properties consistent between form and table.

Fig. 16.7
Change data entry properties in the Data tab.

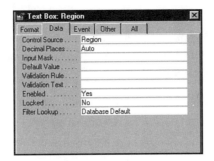

I want to change the way a date or number looks

Once again, it's a good idea to keep formatting consistent between a form and its underlying table. You can change the formatting for a date or number in the Format property, which is the first property in the Format tab. Figure 16.8 shows the property sheet for the Hire Date control in the Employees form of the Northwind database. The drop-down menu for the Format property is open. If you need to change the date format, simply choose one of the other selections. (For a more extensive discussion of date and number formats, see Chapter 7.)

Fig. 16.8
Change the format in
the Format property of
the Format tab.

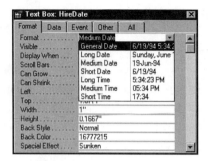

I can't take this style anymore

When you select a style pattern, be it for drapes or a form, often you choose
something that excites you at the moment. But sometimes actually having to
live with it, day in and day out, can become excruciating. You wonder, "Why
did I have to be so imaginative?"

You can forget about taking back the custom-made love seats—you're
probably stuck with them. But you can return a form style and get a new one
as often as you like. If you made your form with a Form Wizard, you may
remember that you had several styles to choose from—Dusk, Leaves, and so
forth. With AutoFormat, you can change to one of these other styles anytime
you want.

1 Select the form by choosing Edit, Select Form.

2 Choose Format, AutoFormat, or click the AutoFormat button on the
toolbar.

3 The AutoFormat window appears. Select any styles that look appealing
and see what they look like in the Preview screen on the right (see fig.
16.9).

4 When you find a style that suits you, choose OK. The form style will
change accordingly.

Fig. 16.9
Get a form make-over
in the AutoFormat
window.

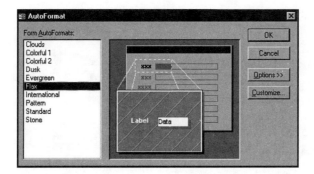

What about printing a form?

You have a lot of printing options for forms. You can hide data on the screen
but include it when printing, or vice versa. You can print all of a multiline
text box when only part of it is visible in Form view. You can print certain
records, certain pages, or the entire report. Let's take a look at some of these
choices.

How can I tell what my printed form will look like?

Print Preview does that. You can select it from either Form or Design View.
Select File, Print Preview or click the Print Preview icon. Figure 16.10 shows
Print Preview for the Customers table. Notice that Access has put a little over
three records on each page.

You can move from page to page (not record to record) by using the navigation buttons at the bottom of the page. If you want to magnify any part of the
page, move the pointer to it and click. To return to full-page view, point
anywhere on the page and click again. You can return to Design or Datasheet
view by clicking the Close button.

In Datasheet View, Print Preview shows the form as a datasheet. If you print
from Datasheet view, you will get a datasheet.

TIP **Use the Last Page navigation button to see how long the entire**
printed form is.

Fig. 16.10
You can see as many as 12 form pages in the Print Preview window. Choose View, Pages and select the number of pages from the submenu.

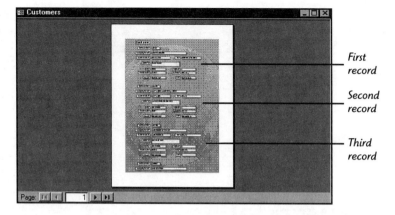

First record

Second record

Third record

I want only one record on a page

An entirely reasonable printing request is that each page have only one record on it. You may remember that all the data in your form goes in the Detail section. So you need to change a property in that section.

1 Click on any open space in the Detail section or on the Detail header to make sure the Detail section is selected (see fig. 16.11).

2 Select View, Properties, or click the Properties icon.

3 Figure 16.12 shows the Properties sheet for the Detail section. The Force New Page property in the Format tab is highlighted when you open it. If it isn't, select it and click on the drop-down menu.

4 Choose After Section and close the Properties box.

I'm ready to print!

From Form view, Design view, or Print Preview, select File, Print. Figure 16.13 shows the Print dialog box. Click OK to print the entire document. To print only selected pages, insert page numbers in the Print Range area, then choose OK.

Fig. 16.11
Select the Detail
section to print a
record on each page.

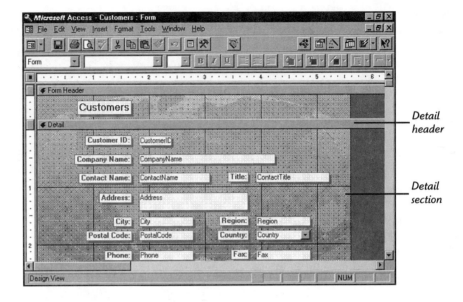

Detail
header

Detail
section

Fig. 16.12
The Force New Page
property may already
be highlighted for you.

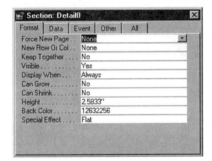

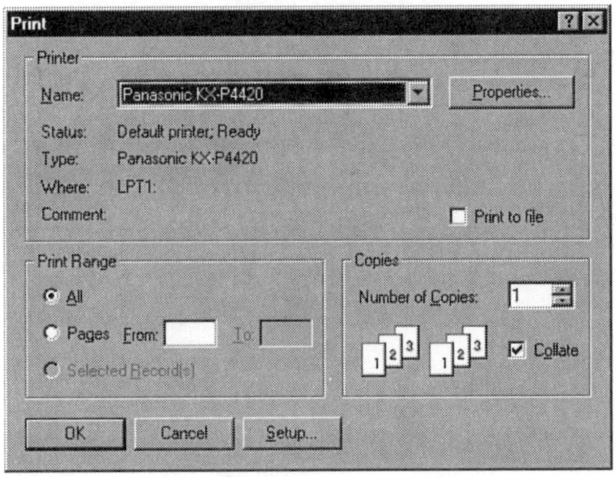

Fig. 16.13
Use the Print Range
settings to print only
selected pages.

I just want to print the current record

That's simple enough. Choose Edit, Select Record in Form View. Then choose File, Print. In the Print dialog box, click on Selected Record(s) in the Print Range Box, and choose OK.

Page numbers would be nice

Naturally, you expect to be able to put page numbers on your printed form. Choose Insert, Page Number in Design view. The Page Numbers dialog box appears (see fig. 16.14).

Fig. 16.14
If you want a Page One, check the Show Number on First Page box at the bottom.

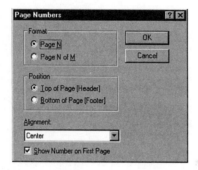

You have several choices to make:

- Do you simply want the page number, or do you want it to read, for example, "Page 7 of 19," with 19 being the total number of pages?

- Do you want the page number at the top of each page or the bottom?

- Do you want to put the page number in the center, the middle, or the inside of each page?

Depending on your choice in the second option, Access will create either a Page Header or a Page Footer section for the page number (see fig. 16.15). The number will appear in Print Preview and, of course, when printed, but not in Form view.

Page number control

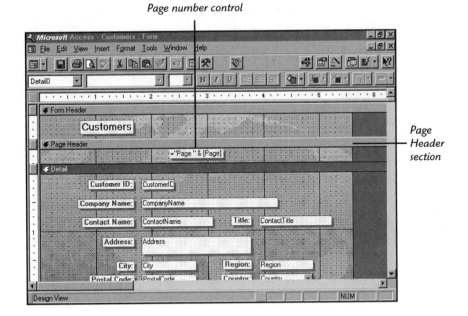

Fig. 16.15
The Page Header section is only for printing.

Page Header section

I don't want this label and text box printed out

You can have data visible in Form view but not when you print, and vice versa. Select any text box and click the Properties icon. The Display When property is the third from the top in the Format tab. The default is Always—that means you always see the text box, whether on the screen or when you print. To change the setting, click the drop-down menu. Choose Screen Only or Print Only as you wish. The changed setting will apply to the label as well.

Part VI: Reports

17

Reports: Data Quick and Easy

● **In this chapter:**

● **Make a report with just a few mouse clicks**

● **What'll my report look like? Print Preview at your service**

● **Make your reports more useful and more readable by sorting and grouping fields**

● **Report design made easy with the Report Wizard**

● **Use the wizard to make great mailing labels too!**

Not only do reports make your data look more attractive—they also make it more meaningful through better organization. . . . . ▶

You've probably heard the sayings, "Beauty's only skin deep," "You can't judge a book by its cover," and "Appearances can be deceiving." Folk wisdom like this reminds us to search for the substance and to ignore the superficial.

But what's the first thing we notice about a restaurant, a book, or a CD? We notice what it looks like. An attractive appearance won't make bland food exciting, boring books interesting, or rotten music hummable, but it does invite us in, and it makes us willing to give the thing a chance.

In Access, you've printed your data in tables, and it hasn't looked too bad. But when you want people's eyes to pop open—when you want to say, "You've *got* to see this"—do it with a report. A report organizes your information according to specifications you set. It can include special formatting, graphics, and layout that make the difference between data that is merely readable and data that is compelling.

A good report is not only attractive, but also functional. Reports are powerful objects in their own right; they sort and group data better—far better—than any other objects.

Designing effective reports from scratch is not easy. That's why Access provides powerful wizards to help you make great-looking reports fast. In this chapter, you learn how to create stunning reports with very little effort.

I want to make a report as fast as I can

You can make a report with just a few mouse clicks. Open any database, and click the Reports tab, and click New. The New Report dialog box appears (see fig. 17.1). At the top, select AutoReport: Columnar; at bottom, click the drop-down list arrow and select the table or query the report's data will come from. (For this example, use the Suppliers table of the Northwind database, Northwind.mdb, in the Samples folder.) Click OK. Access makes a report of the table that you selected and opens it in Print Preview (see fig. 17.2).

Fig. 17.1
The New Report dialog
box offers many ways
to create a report.

Fig. 17.2
Create a new report
with just two mouse
clicks.

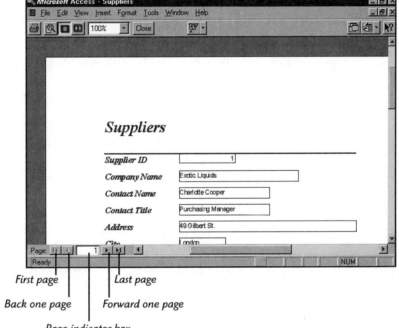

First page · Last page
Back one page · Forward one page
Page indicator box

The report Access made is a columnar AutoReport. Later in this chapter, you learn how to make a tabular—all the data is in a column. AutoReport, as well as more exciting, more customized reports with the Report Wizard. Right now, though, let's take a short walk around the report to get a feeling for what's in one.

I want to see what my report looks like

When you want to see your report, you view it in Print Preview (you can also see your report in Layout view; you'll learn about that in the next chapter, but for the moment, don't worry about it). Unlike a form, which has a Form view, there is no "Report view" as such. Reports are all about making things look the way you want them, and Print Preview shows you the key factor: how your report will look when it's printed. Every page of the report and all your data are here in Print Preview. If you want to change the data in a report, you don't do it in the report itself—you do it in the object (table/query) on which the report is based.

When you want to open a report in Print Preview to view it, click the Reports tab in the Database window, find and select the report you want to open, and click the <u>P</u>review button at the right of the window.

Moving around in Print Preview

You can move from page to page by using the navigation buttons at the bottom of the window, as shown in figure 17.3. (If you can't see them, maximize the report window.) They work the same way they do in a form (see the figure). To move to a specific page, highlight the number in the Page Indicator Box, type a new page number, and press Enter.

 CAUTION   **Remember that when you work in forms, the indicator box is for** *records*. **When you're working in reports, the indicator box is for** *pages*. **That's because a report is specifically created for the purpose of printing it.**

Viewing an entire page

When you move the mouse pointer to the report page, it turns into a magnifying glass. Notice in figure 17.2 that the magnifying glass has a minus sign inside it. When you click the page, the magnification is reduced, and you can see what the whole page looks like (see fig. 17.3). Move the mouse pointer over the page again, and the magnifying glass has a plus sign in it. Click the area that you want to magnify (don't click randomly), and you're back to close-up view.

Fig. 17.3
Use the magnifying
glass for a better view.

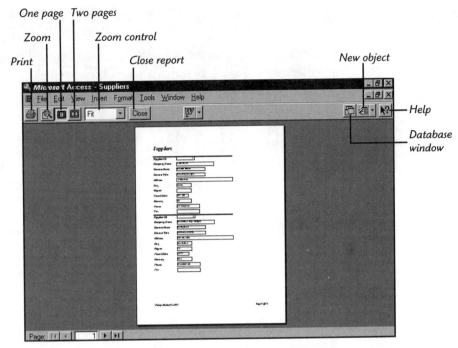

One page Two pages

Zoom   Zoom control

Print   Close report

New object

Help

*Database
window*

Looking at two or more pages side by side

Figure 17.4 also shows how buttons in the toolbar can make your life much easier. You can, for example, see two pages of your report by clicking the Two Pages icon in the toolbar. This procedure can be useful if your report is going to be bound in book form, and you want to see what two pages look like side by side.

You can see as many as 12 pages on-screen at one time—not very well, but you get an idea of what they look like (see fig. 17.4). Choose View, Pages, and then select the number of pages: 1, 2, 4, 8, or 12.

Fig. 17.4
You can view up to 12
pages at the same time.

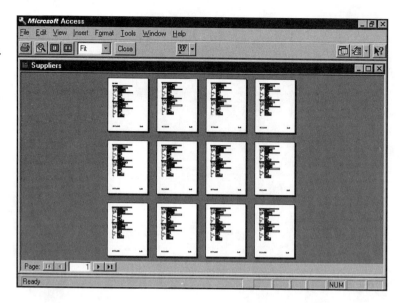

I can't see what the entire page looks like

Use the Zoom control to see your report at various levels of magnification, ranging from 10 percent to 200 percent. The Fit to window (shown in the list box as "Fit") setting is a good choice for both close-ups and the big picture.

Q&A *I changed the magnification, and now my report's gone!*

Nah, it's around somewhere. This situation is like when your contact lens slips off your eyeball. You can't find the lens anywhere, and you're sure that it's floating around inside your head (apologies to the squeamish). But it's *somewhere* in your eye; you've just got to hunt for it. Fortunately, finding a report is much easier than locating a contact lens. Just click one or both of the scroll bars until it comes back into view.

A short walk around a report

Focus, for a moment, on the report itself. (If your Print Preview window now shows 12 little pages, choose View, Pages, 1 to get back to a single page.) The title is nice and big at the top, so you know what you're looking at (if you need to, click on the title to make it larger). The date is at the bottom (use the scroll bar to see it). The date is updated whenever you open the report, and it'll be there when you print—a useful feature, because it enables the reader to know the date of the report.

The fields are listed vertically in a column (hence this report is a columnar report). Each field has a box around its name, and another box appears around the data. Notice also that Access has put more than one record on each page.

TIP **Forms and reports are a great deal alike, especially when it comes** to designing them. In fact, if you know forms, you know about 80 percent of what there is to know about reports. So you may want to read the chapters on forms—especially on controls (Chapter 15, "Use Form Controls to Improve Your Design,") and properties (Chapter 16, "A Tour of Some Selective Properties")—before you tackle report design.

How else can I make reports?

You can make a report from a table or query with a couple of mouse clicks. But if you can spend a few extra seconds, you'll want to enjoy the riches offered by the New Report dialog box (see fig. 17.1). If you're in any object, click the New Object drop-down menu and select New Report. You also can click the Report tab in the Database window and then click New.

Another report that you can make quickly

As you saw in figure 17.1, you have several choices for a new report. Report design is too difficult and the wizards are too powerful for you to even *think* about making a report from scratch in Design View. You'll learn about the Report Wizard and the Label Wizard later in this chapter.

You have already made a columnar AutoReport; let's see what a tabular AutoReport looks like.

Create the report using the Suppliers table, as you did before, so that you can compare the two types of AutoReports. Choose AutoReport: Tabular at the top of the New Report dialog box . Then choose a table/query from the drop-down menu at the bottom. Scroll down the menu until you see the Suppliers table, and select it. Then click OK. Access does the rest. As in the AutoForm: Tabular, the field names are strung across the top of the page (see fig. 17.5).

Fig. 17.5
The tabular format follows the layout of a table, with the fields at the top of the page.

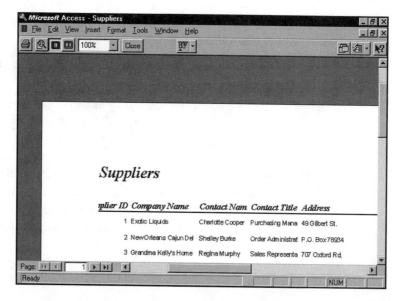

The tabular format offers significant advantages over the columnar one that you saw in figure 17.1. One advantage is that you get more records on fewer pages. In addition, tabular format more closely follows the format of a table, with field names at the top of the page and records at the bottom, so comparing data among records is relatively easy (at least if the records are on the same page). And if you're using the report as a checklist, you may not need every piece of data in every field.

Q&A *I don't see how you got all the fields on one page. On my screen, it looks like they're spread over two pages.*

No, they're one page; you can tell by using the navigation buttons. Because the orientation is landscape, the page is wider than your screen. You can use the horizontal scroll bar to see all the fields, or you can zoom down to 50 percent magnification to make the report look like figure 17.5. Ultimately, the important thing about reports is the way that they print, not what appears on-screen.

Can I sort fields in a report?

Sure. In fact, sorting and grouping are the areas in which reports really shine. (If you have no exposure to sorting or want a refresher, refer to Chapter 8.)

By now, you have the skills to organize and view data in Access in many ways. You've learned about Find, Sort, Filter, and Query. So if the information that you need isn't on-screen, you know how to slice and dice it so that you get what you need.

With a printed report, you can't do any of those things. What's there is there. Remember that other people are going to use this report, so you want to make sure that they can get what they need with minimal hassle. That's where sorting and grouping become important.

 In Print Preview in the Suppliers report, choose <u>V</u>iew, Report <u>D</u>esign to get to Design view. Then choose <u>V</u>iew, <u>S</u>orting And Grouping, or click the Sorting and Grouping button in the toolbar. The window shown in figure 17.6 appears.

Fig. 17.6
In the Sorting and Grouping window you can choose the fields which you want to sort.

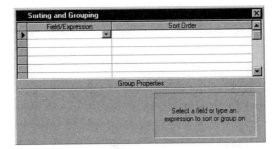

Take a three-second tour of this window. You should see an arrow for a drop-down menu in the first row in the Field/Expression column (if you don't, click in the cell). Click on the arrow, and you'll see all the fields in the Suppliers report. Then click the Sort Order column, and click the arrow in that cell. You have the usual choice of Ascending (A to Z, earliest to latest, smallest to biggest) or Descending (Z to A and so on).

Suppose you want to sort suppliers by country and then by company name. Select Country from the drop-down menu in the first column of the first row. The Sort Order column automatically displays Ascending. (You can change that option to Descending, if you want Zambian suppliers to precede those from Argentina.) Then click the cell below Country and select Company Name from the drop-down menu. Again, the Ascending option appears in the Sort Order column.

I'm not sure what "grouping" is in a report

As soon as you select a field to sort on, the bottom half of the Sorting and Grouping window comes to life. There are a bunch of boxes for Group Properties. So the most sensible question is: What does it mean to group in a report?

Open your morning paper to the sports pages. Let's say it's June, and the NBA and NHL playoffs are going on. If labor peace reigns, the baseball season also is under way. As any fan knows, the majors are divided between the National and American leagues, and within each league are the Eastern, Central, and Western divisions.

Suppose that you want to see how the Pirates are doing. First, you find the baseball standings; then you find the National League; then you look for the Central Division; and finally, you find Pittsburgh. You can say that the team standings are *grouped*—first by sport (baseball, hockey, or basketball), next by league, and finally by division. Sport is the first group, league is the second group, and division is the third.

I still don't get the difference between sorting and grouping

Two pictures are worth a thousand words. Compare the datasheet shown in figure 17.7 with the report shown in figure 17.8. Both items contain the same information. In the datasheet, the records are sorted first by category and then again by product. In the report, the records are grouped by category and then sorted by product.

What's the best way to do grouping?

Simple sorting isn't hard to do in the Sorting and Grouping window, and you can change your sorts at any time. When you start mixing in grouping, though, the procedure becomes a little tougher. Most of the time, you'll want to use the Report Wizard for sorting and grouping. That way, you build it into your report from the get-go by answering a few questions in plain English. You may want to modify your sorting and grouping after you create a report; you learn how to do that in the following chapter.

Fig. 17.7
In the datasheet, the records are sorted on two fields: category and product name.

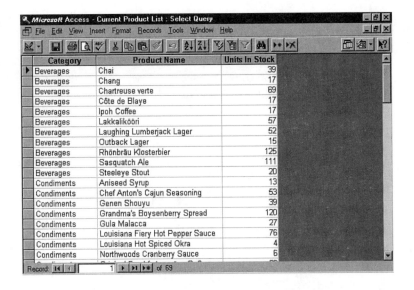

Fig. 17.8
In the report, the records are grouped by category and sorted by product name.

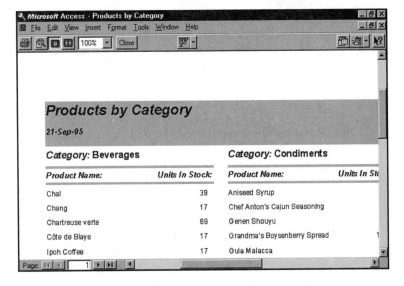

The Report Wizard isn't only good for grouping, of course; it's also great for creating any report in which you want more flexibility and more features than the AutoReports provide.

Creating a report with the Report Wizard

Let's use the Report Wizard to make a report of the Orders table. Click the Reports tab in the Database window, click <u>N</u>ew, and select the Report Wizard in the New Report dialog box.

As before, at the bottom of the box, you select the table/query that will provide the information. Click the arrow for the drop-down menu and find the Orders table (use the scroll bar, if you need to). Select it and click OK.

How do I select the fields for my report?

If you used the Form Wizard in Chapter 14, "Forms: Present Data On-Screen the Easy Way," the first screen of the Report Wizard should look familiar. You can choose fields for your report one at a time by selecting a field and then clicking the single-arrow button. To choose all the fields, click the double-arrow button. If you want to remove fields after you select them, click the buttons that face in the opposite direction.

Select all the fields in the Orders table by clicking the double-arrow button. Then click <u>N</u>ext to move to the next screen.

How to create grouping levels

Now group the orders by country. Select ShipCountry (use the scroll bar to find it on the list), and click the top button. At the right of the screen you'll see the scheme shown in figure 17.9. Notice that ShipCountry is listed separately on top and all the other fields are listed together below.

Suppose that instead, you want to group twice. You want to group orders by country first; then, within each country, you want to group by postal code. You would select Country first, and click the top button; then select Ship Postal Code, and click the top button again.

To make matters simple, however, let's just group by country. Then click <u>N</u>ext to move to the following screen.

Fig. 17.9
The wizard asks you to select grouping levels. Make your choices, and the right side of the screen shows how your data will be grouped.

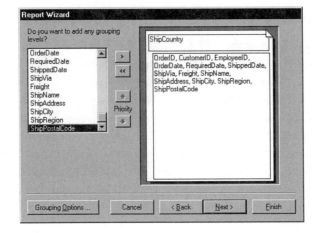

How do I use the sort window?

In the sorting screen, you can select fields for ascending and descending sorts. If you want an ascending sort on a field, just click the arrow for the drop-down menu and select the field. If you want a descending sort, select the field and click the Sort button to the right of the box. The A–Z button becomes the Z–A button. If you want another sort, click in the box below and make another selection.

How many fields you decide to sort and how you sort them depend on your table. In the Orders table, for example, you may first want to sort by date in descending order, so that the most recent orders come first. Then, within each day's sales, you can sort by customer name in ascending order, so that the As come before the Bs (see fig. 17.10).

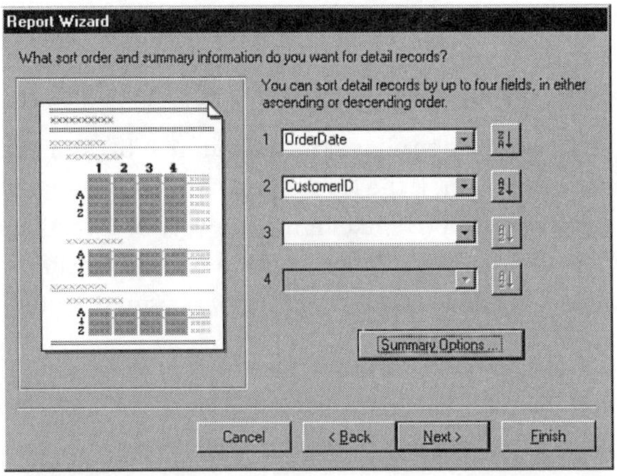

Fig. 17.10
You can sort fields in either ascending or descending order. In this example, the first sort is descending; the second, ascending.

What's the Summary Options button for?

Click the Summary Options button. In Chapter 13, "Totals Queries Add Things Up—and More," I discussed totals queries. In this screen of the Report Wizard, you can choose the calculations you want Access to perform and print by checking the appropriate box. As you can see in figure 17.11, under the Field column are the names of fields (in this case, just one, i.e., Freight) on which you can perform calculations. You can have Access print the sum, average, minimum value, and maximum value for these fields—simply click the boxes for the ones you want. If you want to see all the records in the fields and not only a summary total, make sure the Detail and Summary option is selected. You can also get percent-of-total figures, if you want them.

Click the Sum option in the Summary Options dialog box to sum the freight costs, and leave the Detail and Summary option selected at right (see fig. 17.11). Click OK; then click Next to move to the following screen.

Fig. 17.11
Access lists all fields on which it can perform calculations in the first column at the left of the screen. In this example, the totals options are only available for the Freight field.

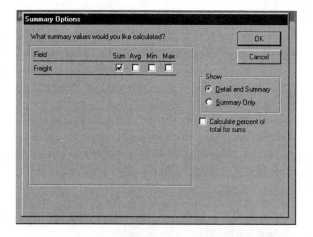

What are my layout choices?

The next screen determines the appearance of your report. In the middle of the window, you pick the layout you like. You can move down the list and see what each option looks like in the preview box on the left side of the window. The various options show grouping slightly differently, but which option you select is mostly a matter of personal preference.

You also can choose Portrait (the way that you normally print) or Landscape, in which the page is wider than it is long. You can get more fields on the page with landscape printing, but fewer records.

A check box below the layout choices allows you to indicate whether you want all fields on one page. If you have many fields and limited space, something has to give—some data will be left out. But at times, you may want to see an overview of a page, even though the data in some fields is abbreviated.

Note that your layout choices will be different if you don't have any grouping. You can choose Vertical (single-column) or Tabular layout. You saw examples of each type of layout in the first two AutoReports that you made in this chapter.

Choose the Outline1 layout with Landscape printing. Don't check the box for putting all fields on one page. Then click Next.

What do "label" and "control" mean in the style window?

In the next screen, you choose a style for the report. You can press the arrow keys to see different selections in the preview window. If you read Chapter 15, you've probably had your fill of labels and controls. Here, *label* refers to the name or title of the field, and *control* refers to the data.

Compared with form styles, report styles are a little dull. But, remember, this report is going to be printed, and what looks inviting on a 256-color screen may not look as great in black-and-white print. Choose the default style, Corporate, and then click Next to move to the last screen.

Finally, the last window!

You're almost finished. At the top of the final screen, choose a name for your report. At the bottom of the screen, specify how you want to view the new report. You'll probably want to look at the report in Print Preview before you consider making any design changes.

Click the Finish button, and you're done. Access has totaled freight charges for all orders in each country group (see fig. 17.12). At the end of the last page, which shows the Freight field, a grand total for all freight costs appears.

Fig. 17.12
Access shows the totals for each Country group in the Freight field.

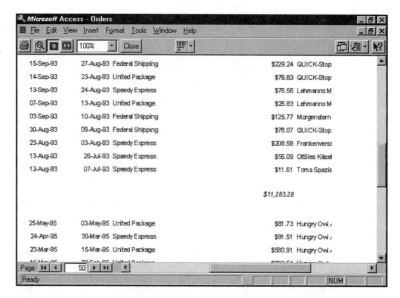

Q&A ***You make it sound so simple, but when I use the Report Wizard, I always have some problem. Sometimes the report or field titles are truncated, or a total of three words appear on a single page. What do I do?***

Sorry about that; you have to monkey around with the report design. The next chapter should give you some help on how to tailor your report in Design view. But it does take practice, and at times, you will be frustrated. Most of the time, though, the Report Wizard takes you pretty near to what you want.

Let's print!

Because printing is the *raison d'être* of a report, let's spend a few minutes going over your printing options. Among your various choices, you can print only certain pages, make multiple copies, choose a different print orientation (i.e., Portrait versus Landscape), adjust your margins, and change the resolution of your printer.

If you don't want to fool with any of that, though, you can just go ahead and print right now. Click on the Print icon and your report prints immediately.

I want to print only certain pages

If you have a 645-page report, you probably don't want to print out the whole thing most of the time. In the Print dialog box you can select just certain pages to print. Choose File, Print to get there, and then go to the Print Range section of the lower left-hand corner (see fig. 17.13). . In the From box, type the number of the page at which you want to start printing; in the To box, type the number of the last page that you want to print.

Fig. 17.13
Use the Print dialog box to tailor your print order.

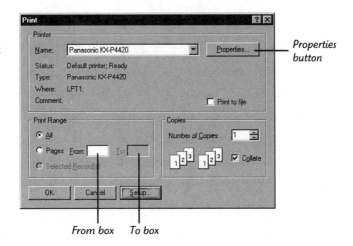

Properties button

From box   To box

I want to make more than one copy

In the Copies section of the Print dialog box, click the up and down arrows to specify more or fewer copies, or simply highlight the number in the box and type the number of copies that you want to print. You also can specify whether the pages should be collated with a check mark in the Collate box.

Portrait versus Landscape printing

We've already discussed the difference between Portrait and Landscape printing in this chapter and at other points in this book. If, up to now, you've used a computer mostly for word processing, you might not have much experience with short-height, long-width Landscape printing. When you want to fit more fields on a page—and are willing to endure the trade-off of fewer records—you'll want to select Landscape printing. Reverse the requirements, and Portrait's the ticket.

To change your selection, click the <u>P</u>roperties button at the upper-right of the Print dialog box. The Paper tab should already be selected; click on it if it's not. Choose Portrait or Landscape printing in the Orientation section, and then click OK.

CAUTION **Changing the orientation can result in some weird stuff—for** example, fields may be sliced in half between pages. If you change the orientation, check the report in Print Preview again to see what it looks like.

I want to change my margins

Go back to the Print dialog box, and click the <u>S</u>etup button at the bottom of the window. The Margins tab should be selected. Highlight the measurement that you want to change, and type a new one (in inches). A decimal entry, such as 1.25, is fine.

Q&A *I changed my margins and now every other page on my report is blank!*

The total width of your report, plus the widths of the margins, exceeds the paper size specified in Print Setup. There are a variety of ways to tackle this problem. You can: first, reduce the margins; second, change the orientation; third, change the paper size; or fourth, reduce the report width. You already know how to do the first two items. As for the third item, you can change the paper size in the Paper tab of the Properties dialog box (remember to change the paper too!). In the next chapter, you'll learn how to change report width.

I want to change the resolution on my printer

With today's laser printers, you get excellent resolution at a reasonable price. You may be able to print at levels of up to 600 dots per inch (dpi) or more, although 300 dpi is likely to be your top setting. (The higher the dpi, the higher the definition and the better your printing looks.) Even at 300 dpi, your reports will be very attractive. If your report contains photos or other graphics, you'll get a fine picture.

You should, however, remember a few things about printing at high resolution:

- High-resolution printing takes longer than printing at a lower resolution, such as 150 dpi or 75 dpi.

- You may not have enough memory in your printer to print some heavy-duty reports at high resolution.

- You may not see much or any difference at higher resolutions if all you're printing is simple text.

You can change the resolution of your printer easily. Click the Properties button in the Print dialog box; then click the Graphics tab in the Properties window. Near the top of the tab, click the arrow for the Resolution box and change the resolution.

How do I print mailing labels?

For some tasks, Access is a godsend. I'd put making mailing labels in that category. A separate wizard exists for that very purpose; you may remember seeing it in the New Report dialog box.

Select the Label Wizard at the top of the window; then select the Suppliers table from the drop-down menu at the bottom. You're on your way.

Choose a mailing-label size

In the first screen, you choose a mailing-label size (see fig. 17.14). The Avery label numbers are listed, with their dimensions, in the first column; to see all of them, use the scroll bar. The third column tells you how many mailing labels will be printed horizontally across the page.

Despite efforts to get Americans to go metric, we still use the English system—pounds rather than kilos, quarts instead of liters, and so on. If you measure things in millimeters rather than inches, click the Metric button in the Unit of Measure section. You get the appropriate Avery numbers, along with metric-style dimensions.

Fig. 17.14

Choose a size for your
mailing labels.

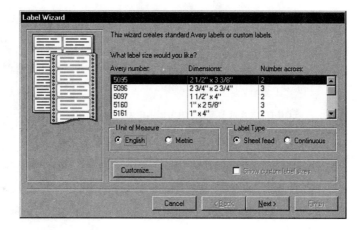

Finally, if you're using a printer in which the paper hangs out like an accordion (a dot matrix printer), click the Continuous button. If your printer sucks in paper sheet by sheet (a laser printer), leave the Sheet feed setting selected.

Choose Avery No. 5095 (the first label size in the list) and sheet-feed printing; then click Next to move to the following window.

Selecting a font

As always, Access gives you plenty of choices when it comes to making things look good. Use the drop-down menus to select the combination of font, font size, and font weight that you find best. Check out what your font will look like using the Sample screen on the left side of the window. You also can add italics or underlining by clicking the appropriate boxes. For this example, keep the default settings, and click Next.

 CAUTION **Depending on your printer, you may not be able to tell the** difference between, say, Extra Light and Light text. Also, Access can't get your black-and-white printer to print color. Access is good, but not *that* good.

Putting in text for the label

Figure 17.15 shows the key screen, where you create the address by selecting fields and adding spaces and commas to make the address readable.

Fig. 17.15
Create the text for
your labels here.

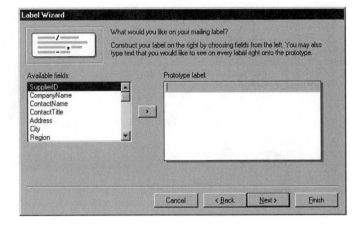

The following list explains a few essentials:

- You choose fields for your address by selecting the field and then clicking the single-arrow button.

- Nothing is in the address until you put it there. Want a comma somewhere? Type that comma. Need a space? Press the space bar. Anything that you want to see in the mailing label, you have to put there yourself.

- Press the up- and down-arrow keys to move from line to line. Don't press the Enter key; that action takes you to the next screen.

- You can type a message (Personal and Confidential, or whatever) anywhere in the label.

I'm confused! Show me how to make the label

Suppose that you're trying to create the label shown in figure 17.16. The person's name goes on the first line, so you select the Contact Name field in the Available fields column and then click the arrow button. The only thing in the first line is the name, and the information for the person's name comes directly from the field. Because there's a space between the first and last name in the ContactName field of the Suppliers table, a space will appear between them when you print the mailing label. If there was no space in the table, there would be no space in the label.

Fig. 17.16
Don't assume that
Access knows where
to put in spaces and
punctuation on your
label. If you want, say,
a space between the
City and State fields,
you've got to put it in
yourself.

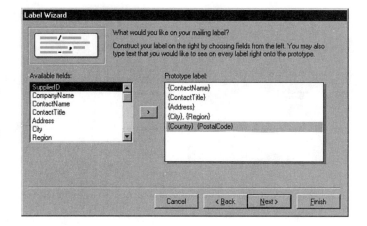

Press the down-arrow key to drop to the next line. Select the Contact Title
field, and click the arrow button to include it in the label. Press the down-
arrow key, select the Address field, click the arrow button, and press the
down-arrow key again.

On the next line, you want to put the city and state (or, for international
suppliers, the region). The state is included in the all-inclusive Region field.
Forget about the wizard for a moment; ordinarily, how do you put a city and
state in an address? First, you type the name of the city, followed by a
comma; then you press the space bar and type the name of the state.

You do the equivalent thing in Access. Select the City field and click the
arrow button to include it in the label, type a comma, and press the space
bar; then select the Region field, click the arrow button, and press the down-
arrow key to move to the next line.

How do you handle the country and postal code? Select the Country field and
click the arrow button. What do you put between the country and the postal
code? Usually, just a space; maybe two. Press the space bar once or twice;
then select the Postal Code from the field list and put it in the label. Click
Next to move to the next screen.

Sorting the labels

In the next screen, you decide how you want to sort the labels. Usually, you
want to sort by ZIP or postal code. Because this mailing list is international,
sort by country first, and then sort within each country by postal code. Select
the Country field (use the scroll bar, if you need to) and put it in the Sort By

window by clicking the single-arrow button; do the same for the Postal Code field. Then click the <u>N</u>ext button.

Name your label report and you're done!

Select a name for your report in the final screen (yes, it is a report, and it will appear as such in the Database window). You also can choose how you want to view your newly made report—do you want to see what your labels look like, or do you want to make design changes in Design view? Let's see how the labels will look when they are printed. When you click the <u>F</u>inish button, Access makes your labels.

Figure 17.17 shows the first page of the label report. As you see by the top two labels, they are sorted by country and then by postal code—the very instructions you gave the wizard. You can also customize the sort—for example, change a sort from ascending to descending. Choose <u>V</u>iew, <u>S</u>orting and Grouping and manipulate the settings as you learned earlier in this chapter.

Fig. 17.17
As you commanded the wizard, there are two mailing addresses in each row, sorted per your instructions.

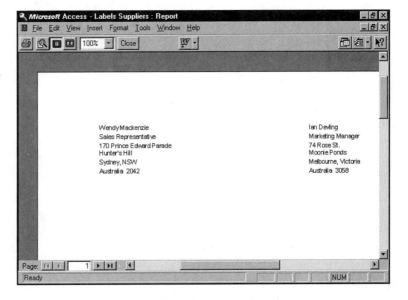

18

How to Change the Look of Your Report

● **In this chapter:**

- **What does my report look like in Design view?**

- **Layout view versus Print Preview**

- **Put in page numbers and reformat the date**

- **Give your report a new look with a different style**

- **I don't want a record split between two pages**

- **Add a group header on your own**

Your report needs some touching up—you want page numbers, a different date format, and an additional group. You can make these and other improvements without much fuss. . . . . ❯

I n the previous chapter, you learned most of what you need to know about creating reports. If you stick with the wizards and carefully answer their questions, you can't go wrong.

But using a wizard to make a report is a little like ordering your groceries by phone. You ask for skim milk, but get whole milk instead; the peanuts come honey-roasted instead of dry-roasted. Asking other people—or a computer—to pick stuff out for you is never quite like doing it by yourself.

In this chapter, I'll show you how to make design changes on your own. Among other things, you'll learn how to change the date/time format, add page numbers, and give your report a different style. Don't get discouraged; report design can be a hassle. If you can't get the date to read just the way you want, or if you have some extra white space on your page, don't obsess over it. As long as your report looks good, that's what counts.

What a report looks like in Design view

It's time we take a look at a report in Design view—the beast's innards, so to speak. You can click the Reports tab of any database, select a report to open, and then click the Design button at the right of the Database window.

The example in this chapter uses the Suppliers report that you created at the beginning of the preceding chapter. (If you happened to have made and saved the report, it will be in the Northwind.mdb file in the Samples folder.) Figure 18.1 shows the Suppliers report in Design View. Compare it to the same report in Print Preview in figure 18.2.

First, tell me how can I switch to Print Preview

Before you look at Design view in depth, get comfortable switching back and forth between it and views that show the report itself. In Design view, you can choose View, Print Preview to see the report as it will be printed. Notice, however, that a view called Layout Preview also appears in the View menu. What's the difference between the two views?

Fig. 18.1
The Suppliers report in
Design view.

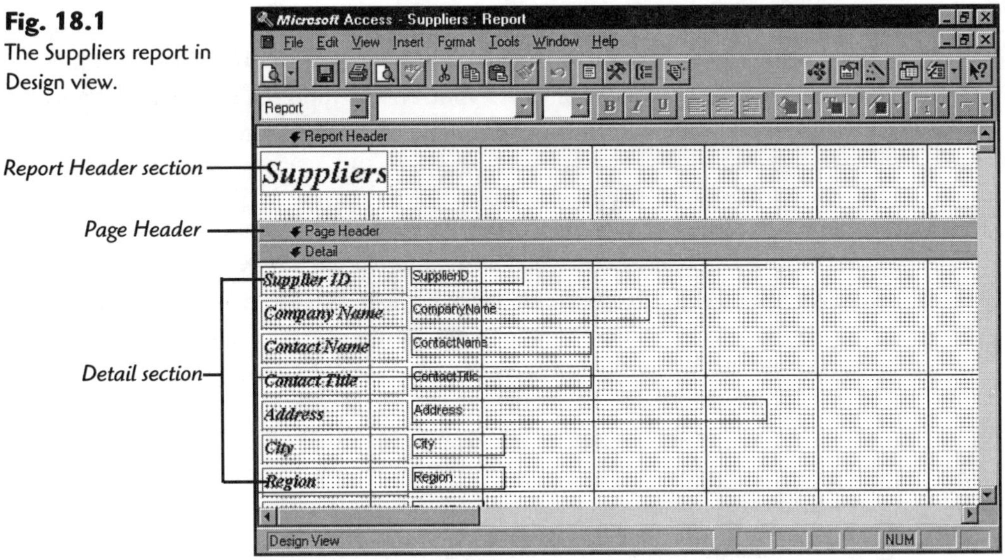

Report Header section

Page Header

Detail section

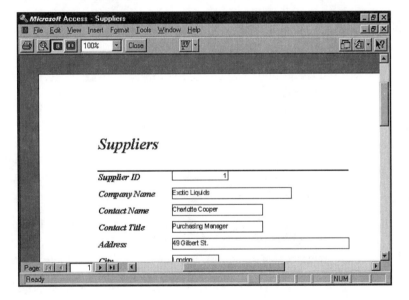

Fig. 18.2
The Suppliers report in
Print Preview.

Print Preview gives you access to the entire report. You can use the navigation buttons at the bottom of the Print Preview screen to move to any page and give it careful inspection. In Layout Preview, on the other hand, you can see only a few pages of your report. You use Layout Preview to check out fonts and other design elements. But don't go hunting for record 1188 on page 345, because it isn't there.

Why would you want to use the abbreviated Layout Preview if you can look at any page in Print Preview? Because it's usually faster. When you have a long report, Access takes a while to get all the pages formatted. So if you just want to see the format, and you're not interested in looking at the information on page 387, the faster method is to switch to Layout view. If your report is short, you may not notice much difference between the two views.

 TIP **Use the Report View icon (the first button in the** toolbar in Design view) to switch quickly between Design view and the two preview screens. Click the button's drop-down menu to select Layout Preview or Print Preview. To get back to Design view, you need to choose Y̲iew, Report D̲esign, since the View button is unavailable in either preview screen.

Hey, this design looks a lot like a form!

If you spent some time learning about forms, report design holds no big surprises. In the Design window, dots and boxes that make up the grid are the labels and text boxes—the controls—that represent field names and their data.

Also, like a form, a report is divided into sections. In figure 18.1, you see the Report Header, Page Header, and the Detail section. At the bottom of the page, out of sight, are two more sections, the Page Footer and the Report Footer.

Controls in the Page Header direct Access to print information or graphic elements at the top of each page of your report; those in the Page Footer are printed at the bottom of each page. Similarly, controls in the Report Header will be printed only on the first page; those in the Report Footer, on the last page. If your report has groups, you can put in a Group Header and Group Footer that will appear at the beginning and end of each group. Later in this chapter, there's an example that creates a Group Header.

 TIP   **If the Design view of a report looks complicated, that's because it** *is* complicated. As an aide to learning the intricacies of Design view, you might want to print a page of your report and compare each item—the title, the date/time, the field names, and the data—with its counterpart (that is, its control) in Design view.

What goes in the Page Footer?

If you have the Suppliers report open in Design view, use the Page Down key or click on the scroll bar to move to the bottom of the page (see fig. 18.3). In the Page Footer section, there is a box on the left that says =Now(). That mysterious combination is an expression that provides the current date.

Fig. 18.3
The Page Footer contains expressions for the date and page number. Don't worry that they look complex; you can use them without knowing what each symbol means.

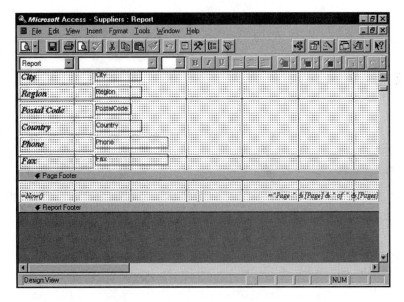

In Chapter 10, "It's Only an Expression," I explained that expressions represent a kind of language that you use to communicate with Access. The Now expression shows the current date and, if you want, the time. Thus, when you print a report, you know as of what date the data is accurate.

To the right of the date control, there is another complicated expression that is used for numbering pages. We'll talk about page numbering a little later.

What does the Page Header do?

Right now, the Page Header isn't doing anything; it's flush against the Detail section (see fig. 18.1). If you look at figure 18.2, you see only empty space between the title and the data below it. Later in this chapter, you'll add page numbers to your report on your own, so you can see how the Page Header works.

It looks like all the fields go in the Detail section

Again, the Detail section is much like that in a form. You select controls in the same way. Ditto moving and sizing them, changing fonts, and centering. The label and text boxes have separate property sheets, just like those in a form, which you select in the same way. To display the property sheet for the Supplier ID text box, click it with the right mouse button and then choose Properties at the top of the context menu (see fig. 18.4). You can close the property sheet by clicking the X in the upper-right corner.

The same rules for inheriting properties also apply, so bound controls inherit the properties of the field in the underlying table. If you change the name of a field in a table, you have to change it in the report as well.

Not everything is the same, of course; one big difference is sorting and grouping. That topic is discussed in more detail near the end of this chapter.

Fig. 18.4
Each control in a report has a property sheet, just as it has in a form.

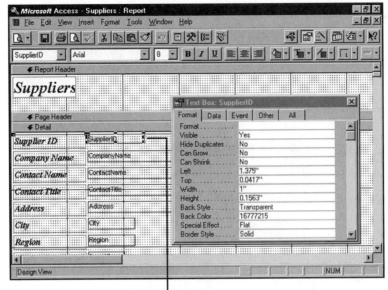

Supplier ID text box

Change the dimensions of sections and your report

You can change the height of any page section to eliminate extra space. The procedure mirrors that of the many times you have changed the dimensions of columns and rows in Access. For example, in figure 18.1 there's some blank space in the Report Header underneath the title Suppliers. Move the mouse pointer to the top border of the Page Header until you see the double arrow with bar symbol. Press the mouse button and drag upward until you eliminate the additional space.

You can also change the width of any section using the same basic method. Move the mouse pointer to the right border, see the double-arrow with bar symbol, and depress the mouse button. Then drag to the left to make the width smaller, or to the right to make it bigger. A report only has one width, however, so if you change the width for any section, you, in effect, change the width of the entire report.

I'd like to add a page number...

As we've seen, the Suppliers report already has page numbers at the bottom of each page. But suppose it didn't and you wanted to put them in your report. Choose Insert, Page Number and use the Page Numbers dialog box to create a page number control for you (see fig. 18.5).

Fig. 18.5
The Page Numbers dialog box creates a control for page numbers.

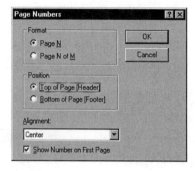

The dialog box contains the following options:

- *Format.* You can select Page N (plain old page number) or Page N of M, with M being the total number of pages in your report.

- *Position.* You can put the page number at the top of the page or the bottom. If you put it at the top, in Design view, you see the page-number control in the Page Header section. If you put it at the bottom, the control goes into the Page Footer.

- *Alignment.* Choose Center, Right, or Inside.

- There's also a check box (Show Number on First Page) for putting a page number on the first page.

Let's put a page number at the top of the page. Choose Page N for the Format, Top of Page, and Center for the alignment. Then click OK to close the dialog box.

Figure 18.6 shows what happened in the Page Header. It now contains a control in the form of an expression that tells Access to put page numbers in your report. The control is in the middle of the Page Header because you chose Center alignment. Of course, now you have page numbers in both the Page Header and Page Footer. Select either control and delete it so you don't see the page number twice.

Fig. 18.6
The Page Header now contains a page-number control.

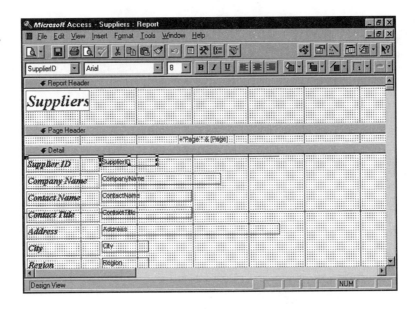

I'd like the date and time to appear in a different style

The date/time format should be appropriate to the report. When you print the standings of your local bridge club, you probably don't want to show the time down to the second.

It's a minor point, but you'd be surprised how many people are still intimidated by computer-made reports. There's no reason to make them feel more insecure than they already do. (Of course, if that's *exactly* what you want to do, by all means keep the format as is.)

The date expression in the Page Footer has the name of the month written out. If you want to change to a short date format (e.g., 11/16/95), follow these steps:

1 Click the Date text box (the text =Now() appears inside it) in the Page Footer section with the right mouse button.

2 Choose Properties from the context menu.

3 In the Format property of the Format tab, click the arrow for the drop-down menu (if you can't see the arrow, click the Format property box first). You see the selections shown in figure 18.7.

Fig. 18.7
If you can't see the date formats in their entirety, just widen the window.

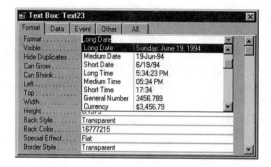

4 Now you can choose any format that you like. For this example, choose Short Date.

5 Close the property sheet.

TIP **If you don't like the position of the date/time control, you can** move it to another section of your report. Select the control, move the mouse pointer to the top or bottom border until you see the open-hand symbol, and drag-and-drop the control to another location in your report. (Be sure you see the open-hand symbol, and not the symbol with one finger pointing upward.)

How can I change the overall style of my report?

You can change the style of your report if the current style has become wearisome. Choose Format, AutoFormat; the properties sheet shown in figure 18.8 appears. Preview the styles by selecting them. When you find a style that you like, select it and then choose OK.

Fig. 18.8
Select a style and preview it in the Sample screen, and then choose OK.

How to keep all the record's data on one page

The Suppliers report we've been looking at has two complete records on each page, nothing more. You probably prefer to keep records together—not to have six fields on one page and three on the next. But in a draft copy, you may not care. You may be able to reduce the number of pages by 15 or 20 percent by *not* keeping records together.

Whichever method is good for you, follow these steps to change the property setting:

1 Click on any empty space in the Detail section with the right mouse button and choose Properties from the short menu.

2 Click the Format tab, if it's not already selected, and look for the Keep Together property (see fig. 18.9).

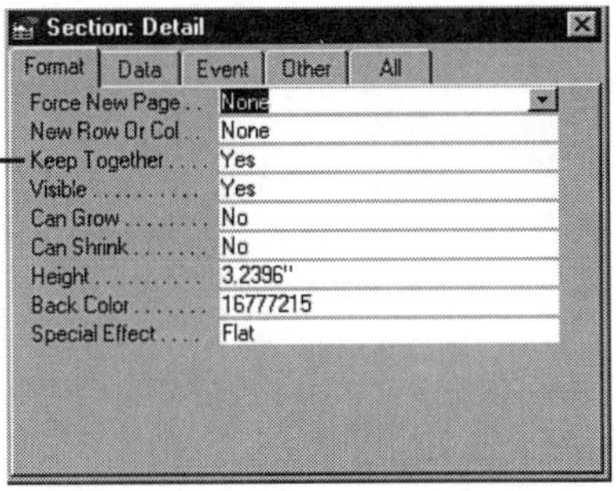

Fig. 18.9
Use the Keep Together property to keep fields on the same page.

Keep Together property

Section: Detail
Format | Data | Event | Other | All
Force New Page . . None
New Row Or Col . . None
Keep Together . . . . Yes
Visible . . . . Yes
Can Grow . . . . No
Can Shrink . . . . . . No
Height . . . . 3.2396"
Back Color 16777215
Special Effect . . . . Flat

3 Choose Yes to keep fields together on the same page. Choose No to let them run over to the following page.

4 Close the property sheet.

 TIP **You can also put just one record on a page. On the Format tab of** the Detail section's property sheet (the same one we just used), click on the Force New Page property near the top. Select After Section from the drop-down menu, and close the property sheet.

I want to add a group

In Chapter 17, "Reports: Data Quick and Easy," you used the Report Wizard to sort and group records. You didn't have to fool around with the Sorting and Grouping window or worry about group properties; all you had to do was answer the wizard's questions.

But suppose that you decide to group on a field *after* you create the report. Perhaps you want to group the records of the Suppliers report by country. Then, within each country group, you want to sort the records by company name, as shown in figure 18.10.

Fig. 18.10
The report is grouped by country and sorted by record.

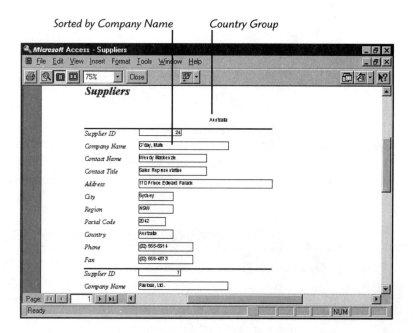

Sorted by Company Name   *Country Group*

To do that, start by choosing View, Sorting and Grouping. Click the drop-down menu in the first cell of the first column, and select Country. Ascending is chosen for you in the Sort Order column.

Create the group

At the bottom of the window is the Group Properties section. Click in the Group Header box, click on the arrow, and select Yes from the drop-down menu. This action creates a Group Header for the Country field. Notice that a Group icon now appears in the field-selector box of Country (see fig. 18.11).

Group icon

Fig. 18.11
The Group icon appears in the field-selector box when you create a group.

Group Header property

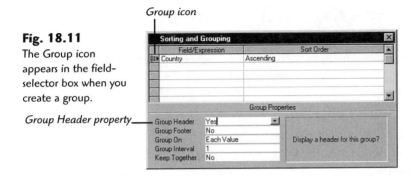

Now you want to sort by Company Name, so go back to the top of the screen and click the cell directly below Country. Click the arrow for the drop-down menu, and select Company Name. The selection in the Sort Order column is Ascending.

Is that all there is to it? Not quite. Look at the Suppliers report in Design view (see fig. 18.12). You see a new section for the Country Header (i.e., the Group Header for the Country field), but there's nothing in there. So if you left things the way they were, you wouldn't see country titles, such as Australia and Austria, at the start of each group—which would defeat the purpose of grouping them in the first place.

Fig. 18.12
The Country Header has been added to the report's design, but there's no control for the country name.

Country Header section

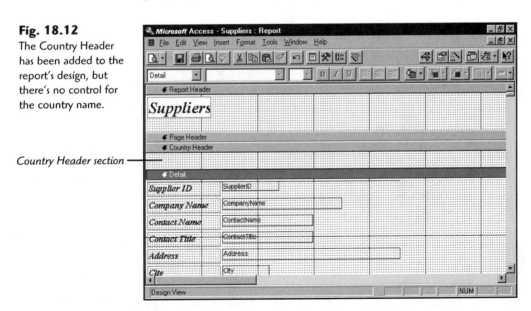

How do I give each group a title?

Probably the easiest way to give each country group a title is to drag the Country field from the field list over to the Country Header. Follow these steps:

1 Choose <u>V</u>iew, Field <u>L</u>ist.

2 Find the Country field in the list (click the scroll bar), and drag it over to the Country Header. In figure 18.13, the mouse cursor is centered in the section.

Field list

Fig. 18.13
Drag the Country field
to the Country
Header.

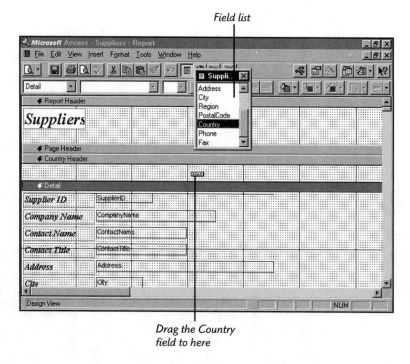

*Drag the Country
field to here*

3 When you drop the Country field, two controls are created: a label (on the left) and a text box (on the right). You don't need the label, so select it and then delete it (see fig. 18.14).

Fig. 18.14
Delete the label for
the Country field.

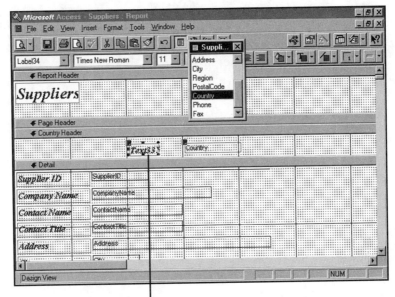

Delete the selected label

You're done. You can switch to Print Preview to see what your report looks like.

Q&A *I'm not sure why you had me delete the label instead of the text box. These country names are really just titles; they don't provide any data.*

If you used the label, all you would see is Country at the start of each group, rather than the name of the individual country. The text box is bound to the Country field, which supplies the individual country names.

That was a lot of work to make a group!

Yeah, it was. That's why the wizards are so great. Sometimes it may pay to simply create a new report with the groups you want, rather than hassle with adding groups on your own.

How do I delete a sort or grouping?

Click View, Sorting and Grouping. Select the field you grouped or sorted on by clicking its selector box. Then simply press the Delete key. Click Yes when Access asks you to confirm the change.

Part VII: Finishing Touches

19

Negotiating Exports and Imports

● **In this chapter:**

● **Use Cut and Paste to move Access tables and records**

● **Export to databases, spreadsheets, and word processing programs**

● **When should I import, and when should I link?**

● **Wizards make it easy to import and link data**

It's time to start exporting and importing data. Lift the barriers to data protectionism—get free trade information here . . . . ❯

Eighteenth-century Japan was a closed society. All foreigners were banned from her islands, and there was little contact between Japan and the outside world.

That's a far cry from today's Japan, where young women wear the latest in European fashions, and children are surprised to learn that America has McDonald's, too.

So far, this book has considered an Access database to be like 18th-century Japan. Each database has been its own hermetically sealed package, with nothing coming in and nothing going out. But that arrangement doesn't reflect reality. You may want to put an object from one Access database into another. You may want to use Access data with another application, like Word or Excel. Or you may want to open and manipulate a table that was created in another database program.

It's time for Access to come out of isolation. It's time to bring down the walls of data protectionism. Access stands ready and able to trade information freely with the other applications of the world.

How to move an object to another Access database

This chapter starts with Cut and Paste, because these commands are already familiar to you. Let's begin by cutting a table and pasting it into another Access database.

1 Select the table in the database window.

 2 Choose Edit, Cut or click the Cut button in the toolbar.

3 Open the database in which you want to paste the table, and select the Tables tab.

 4 Choose Edit, Paste or click the Paste button. The Paste Table As dialog box appears (see fig. 19.1).

5 Type the name that you want to give the new table. (If an existing table has that title, Access asks whether you want to replace it.)

Fig. 19.1

In the Paste Table As dialog box, you choose a table name and select among paste options. You can keep the old table name or choose a new one.

6 The Structure and <u>D</u>ata option should be selected; click its radio button if it isn't.

7 Click OK. Your table is pasted in the new database.

 TIP **You can cut and paste other database objects besides tables.** Because tables form the foundation of any database, this chapter concentrates on tables. If you have the information in your tables, you can always create an appropriate object.

 Q&A *Can't I use Copy the same way that I use Cut?*

You can, but it's probably easier to use the Export command for importing entire tables from another Access database. (Is that confusing? If you import from one place, you have to export from another.) Exporting is discussed in detail a little later in this chapter.

Using the Structure Only option

Another paste option in the Paste Table As dialog box is <u>S</u>tructure Only. Sometimes, you want to copy only the design of the table, without all the accompanying data.

That's what the <u>S</u>tructure Only option is for. You get all the field names, field properties, and even the descriptions that you had in the original table, but none of the data. This option is an excellent way to create a new table that you can modify.

Using the Append Data option

When you choose the <u>A</u>ppend Data to Existing Table option in the same dialog box, Access attempts to paste all the records from the cut table into the new table. That process can be tricky. Access may not paste records because of primary key violations, or it may delete records because of conflicts in data type. Figure 19.2 shows the warning that you see.

Fig. 19.2
Access issues a complex message stating the reasons why it couldn't append data.

I don't want to issue a hard-and-fast rule and say don't use the Append Data option, but please be careful about how you do it. Consider alternatives, such as using an append query (discussed in Chapter 20, "Change Your Data with Action Queries"). That alternative is especially helpful if you have many records to paste. If you have only a few records, consider pasting selected records, as explained in the following section.

Pasting selected records into another Access database

You don't have to cut and paste an entire table. You can simply cut (or copy) selected records and then move them to the target table.

1 Select the records that you want to copy from a table (or another datasheet).

2 Choose Edit, Cut (or Copy) or click the Cut (or Copy) button on the toolbar. The records are placed on the Clipboard.

3 Open the Access database that contains the table into which you want to paste the records. (If the table is in the same database, ignore this step.)

4 Select the target table in the Database window, and click the Open button.

5 Click in the first field of the first empty row.

6 Choose <u>E</u>dit, Paste Appe<u>n</u>d. Access appends the records to your existing table.

 TIP **When you paste, you can also highlight rows that contain existing** data. Click the Paste button, and Access pastes the records from the Clipboard right over the existing records.

 Q&A *When I try to paste, nothing happens; I just hear that "you can't do that" chime.*

Did you select a destination for Access to paste to? Access has to have a destination. You can highlight and paste data in cells that contain existing data, or you can paste data into the first empty row.

Why am I getting so many error messages?

Cut and Paste work best when the fields in the source and target tables are exactly the same—same number of fields, same names, same field order, same data type, and so on. But that assumption is more than optimistic. Sometimes, the fields in the source and target tables have different field sizes. Sometimes, an extra field exists in either table. And sometimes, an otherwise matching field has a different data type.

What rules does Access follow for pasting?

Following are some key things to remember about the way that Access puts data in the target table:

- Access pastes according to the column order of the source table. Column 1 of Table A gets copied into Column 1 of Table B. Access doesn't care what the names of the fields are.

- A value in Column 1 in Table A cannot match the primary key of Column 1 in Table B.

- If the source table contains more fields than the target table does, Access doesn't paste the extra fields. If the target table contains more fields than the source table, Access leaves the extra fields empty.

- Data types must be compatible. You can't paste text into a number field.

- Access may not paste a value because it violates settings in certain properties, such as Validation Rule and Input Mask.

- The Field Size property determines the maximum size of a field value. The text you're pasting must not be longer than the field size allows.

This list by no means covers all the rules and all the mishaps that can occur when you try to paste data. So don't get discouraged; you won't have a successful paste operation every time. You may have to modify your source or target tables for the paste operation to work; or you may need to use a different strategy, such as creating a new table.

Where did the table called Paste Errors come from?

When Access pastes, it pastes the records that it can; the others are thrown into a table called Paste Errors. When you see that unfortunate (but not uncommon) message, go to the Datasheet window, select the Tables tab, open the Paste Errors table, and see what records Access didn't paste. Then you can troubleshoot your mistakes.

Using the Export command to copy a table

If you want to copy an entire table, use the Export command. You can copy to another Access database or to a different application. Try to copy to another Access database first.

1 In the Database window, select the table that you want to export.

2 Choose File, Save As/Export. The Save As dialog box appears.

3 Select the option To an External File or Database, if it isn't already selected.

4 Click OK. The Save Table In dialog box appears.

5 In the Save as Type box at the bottom of the dialog box, Microsoft Access should be selected, as shown in figure 19.3. If it's not, select that option.

Fig. 19.3
Select Microsoft Access in the Save as Type field.

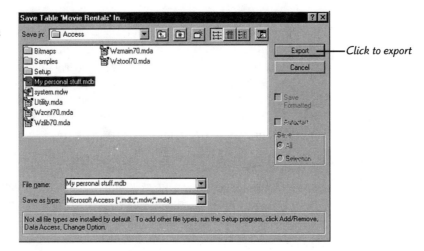

—*Click to export*

6 Select the drive or folder that contains the Access database file in which you want to save the table. Select the destination datbase.

7 Click Export. The Export dialog box appears.

8 At the top of the box, you can elect to keep the current name of the table, or you can type a new one.

9 At the bottom of the box, specify whether you want to paste the entire table by choosing Definition and Data; if you want to paste just its structure, select Definition Only.

10 Click OK. Your table is exported to the target database.

The obvious advantage of this method over the Clipboard method is the fact that you don't have to bother opening the other database. The name of the table can be retained in the new database, provided that no existing table has the same name.

TIP **If you want to import or export more than one table, you'll find** the Import Wizard to be easier to use and more robust. This wizard is discussed toward the end of this chapter.

Exporting to a database or spreadsheet application

You can export an Access table into another database application (e.g., Paradox or dBASE) or spreadsheet (e.g., Excel or Lotus). You use the same Save As command and the same general procedure as you did when you exported to another Access database. However, you specify the file type of the target database or spreadsheet in the Save as Type box.

When you export to a spreadsheet, the field names become the first row, and the records appear in the succeeding rows below.

CAUTION   **The manual of the destination database should tell you how to** import from outside sources, including Access. Needless to say, those instructions are of primary importance, and you should follow them carefully. Not all export operations are completely successful. A foreign database may, for example, decide to truncate the titles of your Access field names.

Excel is a popular spreadsheet application in the Microsoft Office suite. The following example for exporting a table uses Excel as the destination (i.e., target) application.

1 Open the database that contains the table you want to export and select that table.

2 Choose File, Save As/Export.

3 In the Save As dialog box, select To an External File or Database.

4 In the Save Table In window, click the Save as Type drop-down menu at the bottom of the screen. Select Microsoft Excel 5-7 (*.xls) from the list, as shown in figure 19.4.

5 At the top of the window is the Save In box. Click the arrow for the drop-down menu and select the drive or folder that you want to save the file to.

6 In the File Name section, use the file name that Access recommends or type a new one.

7 Select the Save Formatted check box if you want to save the formatting.

Fig. 19.4
You can put an Access table in a new Excel file.

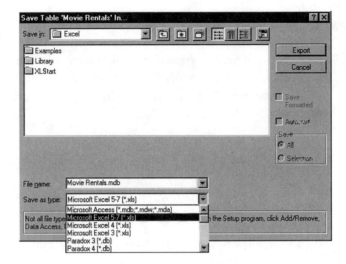

8 Click the Export button at the top right of the window. Access saves your table in a new Excel file.

CAUTION

Don't choose an existing file to export to, unless you don't care about the data in that file. Access dumps whatever's in the existing file and puts in the data you're exporting. One major exception: in Excel versions 5.0 and later, Access puts the data in the following worksheet.

Use Rich-Text Format (.rtf) for Word Processing

At times, you may want to open an Access table, with all its formatting, in a word processing program. An excellent way to do that is to save the Access file in rich text format. The table's formatting (type style, borders, shading, and so on) is saved along with the text.

You use the same export procedure as you've been using, but in the Save Table In window, you save the file as a Rich Text Format file. Click the Save as Type drop-down menu, and use the scroll bar to see the selections near the bottom; choose Rich Text Format (*.rtf) from the list. Select the appropriate folder or drive in the Save In box at the top of the window, and click Export. When you open the file, it looks comparable to the way it did in Access, provided that your word processor has all the formatting features Access enjoys.

Text Export Wizard

Often when you export, you don't need or want all the formatting that you have in an Access table. You may want only the data, or you may want the data arranged in a different way. To help you, Access provides the Text Export Wizard. Here's how you can use it:

1 Select the table in the Database window.

2 Choose File, Save As/Export.

3 In the Save As dialog box, choose To an External File or Database.

4 In the Save Table In window, select the drive or folder you want to save to. Click the Save as Type drop-down menu and choose Text Files (*.txt, *.csv, *.tab, and *.asc). In the File Name box, you see the name of the table you're exporting with a .txt extension. Keep this name or type a new one.

5 Click Export. Access starts the Text Export Wizard.

What the heck is a text delimiter?

I think that you'll be able to handle the Text Export wizard with few problems. But there a couple of items that may require explanation that I'll go over.

First, at the top of the first screen, don't get hung up on the Delimited and Fixed Width choices (see fig. 19.5). Somehow, you need to separate the series of values in a record so that they're readable to you and others. In a delimited text file, that separation is accomplished by putting a comma, semicolon, or similar character between records. (The form of punctuation that you use to separate values is called the *delimiter*.) In a fixed-width file, you put the values in columns with some space between them—like a table, but without the grid lines.

In the second screen, you can designate a Text Qualifier (see fig. 19.6). Selecting a text qualifier amounts to choosing to put double, single, or no quotes around each value—in other words, "measles" versus 'measles' versus measles. Big deal, huh? (I suggest you put either single or double quotes, unless you have a particular reason to use no quotes.)

Fig. 19.5
The Delimited and
Fixed Width options
sound harder than they
are. Choose each
option and view the
Sample Export Format
box at the bottom of
the screen to under-
stand the difference.

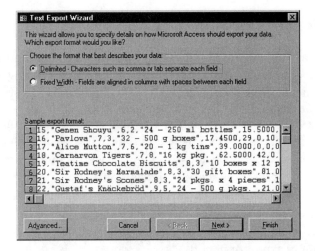

Fig. 19.6
Choosing a delimiter at
the top of the screen,
and the selection of a
Text Qualifier on the
right, are usually just
matters of personal
preference.

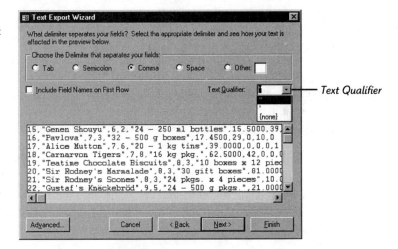

Text Qualifier

In figure 19.6, notice that you have the option of including the field headings
in the first row of the new text document by selecting the First Row Contains
Field Names check box.

TIP **Sometimes, you want to do a large mailing of a form letter. Access**
can help. First, create the form letter in a word processing program, such as
Microsoft Word; then get all the names and addresses from an Access table.
This procedure is known (generically, not just in Access) as a *mail merge.*
You can start a mail merge in Access, but if you're using Word, it's probably
better to use Word's Mail Merge Helper.

Bringing data into Access

So far, this chapter has discussed exporting Access information; this section discusses bringing data into Access. You might be asking yourself, "Haven't I been importing data all along?"

The crucial factor in determining whether you're exporting or importing is, as in other endeavors, where you start. When you transfer data between formats, it's fairly obvious whether you were importing or exporting. When you exported from Access to Excel, you weren't using Excel at all; everything was done in Access. When you exchange data between Access files, however, you can get confused about which procedure you're using. The following section may make the difference clearer and help you decide whether you want to export or import.

What's the difference between importing and linking?

An imported table in Access no longer is connected in any way to the database that you imported it from. The imported table is exactly the same as any other table in your Access database. The table still exists in the external source; importing a table doesn't delete it under any circumstances.

A linked table, however, is not fully imported into Access but remains in the other database or data format. Nevertheless, most of the things you can do in a full-fledged Access table you can do in a linked table. You can edit the data; you can even make forms, queries, and reports that use the data. But the table remains in the original database or its original format.

When should I import, and when should I link?

Suppose that you're a stamp collector. You buy a stamp collection from a friend, who created a database for it in Paradox, another database program. You don't have Paradox and have no interest in learning it. You want to import those tables and make them part of your My stamp collection.mdb file in Access. The imported tables are indistinguishable from those created within Access.

On the other hand, suppose that the Guatemalan Philatelic Society wants to create a database for all the country's stamps. You agree to supply pricing data for post-1940 air-mail stamps. The club president mails you the floppy disks for the entire database, which is in Excel. All you have to do is type the prices in the appropriate field. First, you check the floppy disks for viruses and make copies. (That procedure has nothing to do with Access per se; I just thought I'd throw in a little database hygiene.) Then you link the required files to Access. That way, you can make your changes without changing the format of the files.

Tell me some more about linked files

Linked tables have distinctive icons that tell you where they came from. In figure 19.7, for example, the linked table with the arrow came from Excel. (Had the table been imported, you would see the plain old Access table icon.) When you link the tables, that icon stays in the Database window. You can delete the link, if you want to, but that's all you'll be erasing—just a link. The original table, in its foreign format, remains secure and unaffected.

You can't change the way that a linked table is stored in the foreign database. But you can change a few of the table properties in Access, including format, number of decimal places, input masks, and captions. To repeat, any changes that you make in these properties don't affect the way that they're stored in the original database.

Fig. 19.7
Linked tables get icons that reflect the source of their data. In the figure, the linked table is an Excel file.

Linked file

Importing and linking tables

Access has a host of features to help you import and link. Let's go through some examples that will help you understand how exporting and linking work.

Importing from one Access database to another

Earlier, you learned how to export an Access table to another Access table. Importing has the advantage of allowing you to transfer several Access tables at once.

To import a table from another Access database, follow these steps:

1 In the Database window of the database into which you want to import the table, click the New button in the Tables tab.

2 Select Import Table and click OK.

3 In the Import window, make sure that the Files of Type setting is Microsoft Access (.mdb).

4 In the Look In section, select the drive or folder that contains the Access database that has the tables you want to import.

5 Select the file, and click the Import button. The Import Objects window appears.

6 Click the Options button. Notice that you also can import any relationships that you created between the tables (see fig. 19.8). As before, you have the choice of importing the entire table or just its structure (its *definition*).

7 Select the table or tables that you want to import. You can select more than the one table; just click the ones you want. If you don't like your selections, click the Deselect All button to start all over. You can also use the Select All button to choose all tables. When you're satisfied with your selections, click OK. Access imports your data.

Fig. 19.8
Be sure to click the Options button for additional choices. You can, for example, elect to import the relationships between tables.

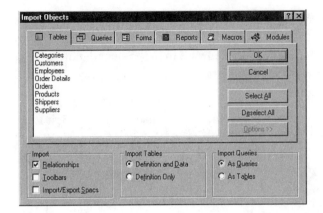

CAUTION **I don't want to leave the impression that importing is a slam-dunk.** Bringing in tables from Access or from a spreadsheet program such as Excel usually is a straightforward process. But importing from other database applications, which go about accomplishing database tasks differently, can be trickier. If you have problems, Appendix A discusses some places where you can go for advice.

TIP **You also can begin importing or linking by choosing File, Get** External Data and choosing Import or Link Tables.

Show me how to link a spreadsheet

Now that you imported tables from another Access database, let's try linking an Excel spreadsheet. To keep matters simple, the following example assumes the Excel file has only one worksheet. (If your file has more, it's no big deal—just follow the instructions in the Link Spreadsheet Wizard and those given here, and you should have no problems.) Here's how to link your Excel file to an Access database:

1 In the Database window of the database to which you want to link the table, click the Tables tab.

2 Click the New button.

3 Select Link Table and click OK. The Link window appears.

4   In the Files of Type box at the bottom of the window, select Microsoft Excel (*.xls). In the Look In box at top, select the drive or folder that has the file you want to link. Select the file you want to link and click Link. Access starts the Link Spreadsheet Wizard.

5   If you want to use column headings in the spreadsheet as field headings, check the Include Field Names on First Row box (see fig. 19.9). Click Next.

Fig. 19.9
You can view your data at the bottom of the window. Use the scroll bar to see additional rows.

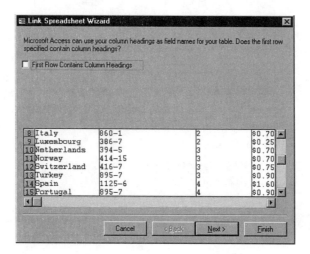

6   In the second screen, give the linked table a name and click Finish. Access links the spreadsheet to your database.

I want to import a table from a word processor

So far, you have imported tables from a database application and linked a table from a spreadsheet application. In this section, you import a delimited text file from Microsoft Word. First, save your document in Word as Text Only with Line Breaks. Then follow these steps:

1   In the Database window of the database into which you want to import the file, click the Tables tab.

2   Click the New button at the right of the window.

3 Select Import Table. The Import window appears.

4 Select Text Files (*.txt, *.csv, *.tab, and *.asc) in the Files of <u>T</u>ype: box at the bottom of the screen. Find the drive or folder that contains the file you want to import in the Look <u>I</u>n box on top. Select the file and click Import. Access starts the Text Import Wizard.

5 Make your selections in the first three screens of the wizard (click <u>N</u>ext to move from screen to screen). If you've read the rest of this chapter, these screens should give you little trouble.

6 In the fourth screen, you have options for the fields you are importing. First, select the field in the bottom of the screen by clicking anywhere in its column. In Field Na<u>m</u>e, you can change the name of the field. In the <u>I</u>ndexed box, you can elect to index the field. And in Data <u>T</u>ype, you can select a data type from a drop-down menu, as shown in figure 19.10. After you're satisfied with your selections, click <u>N</u>ext.

Fig. 19.10
To select a field, click anywhere in its column. Then make your selections in the Field Options section in the upper right-hand corner.

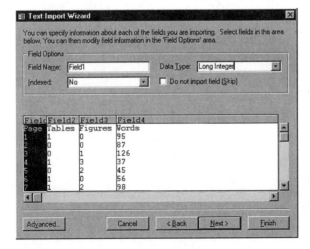

7 Choose among the primary key options, and click <u>N</u>ext.

8 In the final screen, choose a table name and click <u>F</u>inish. Access imports the data and creates the table.

20

Change Your Data with Action Queries

● **In this chapter:**

- **Change many records at the same time with an action query**

- **Can a query make tables and delete records?**

- **Tack on hundreds of records to a table with an append query**

- **Use an update query to change many records by the same factor**

- **How can I tell one dialog box from another?**

You use action queries to change large numbers of records in your tables in one fell swoop. Action queries are big time-savers and help ensure data accuracy . . . . ➤

By now, you might have some pretty hefty tables in your databases, containing hundreds or even thousands of records. You might need to make changes that affect many records at the same time. You might want to get rid of all records before a certain date or store them in a separate table. You might want to increase prices in a table of products by a certain percentage. Or you might need to add a group of records from one table to another.

These kinds of tasks are the forté of the action query. By now, you're accustomed to using select queries to retrieve information from tables and display it. By contrast, you use action queries to change large numbers of records in your tables at the same time. This chapter shows you how action queries can save you time and spare you frustration.

What kinds of action queries are there?

Four types of action queries act on table records: make table, delete, append, and update. The queries' names pretty much reflect what each one does. Each query has practical uses. This chapter explains all four types. Along the way, the chapter also discusses the Archive Query Wizard, which can save you a great deal of time and trouble.

How do you start to make an action query?

 To state the sort-of obvious, an action query still is a query. So you start by creating a query, using the table or tables that contain the records that you want to manipulate. Then click the arrow next to the Query Type button in the toolbar to get a drop-down menu. You see the choices in figure 20.1, the last four of which are action queries. The big exclamation mark after each query tells you, "Hey, be careful what you're doing. You're not dealing with a spirited but ultimately harmless select query. You're dealing with a query that can make important, irreversible changes to your database."

 CAUTION   **Before running an action query, I strongly urge you to back up** your data. Hopefully you have a complete backup procedure for all your work in place, Access and non-Access data included. If you don't want to do that, as a precaution consider merely copying the tables, as you learned in Chapter 19, "Negotiating Exports and Imports."

Fig. 20.1
The Query Type drop-down menu lists the four types of action queries.

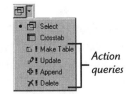

Action queries

TIP **The Query Type icon is specifically for select queries, not for query** type. But in Design view, this icon is the one to look for in the toolbar. Click on the arrow next to it for a drop-down menu, and select an action query from the list. Just remember that the icon itself is for select queries, and if you click it, that's what you get.

Make-table queries

As the name implies, make-table queries are for making tables. You can make a new table that contains some or all of the fields from a table in your database. You can put the new table in your current database or in another database.

When should I use make-table queries?

Make-table queries have a couple of advantages over alternative data-replication methods, like copying and exporting. But make-table queries have a couple of advantages. First, you can use criteria. Thus, you can better define the records to be included in the new table. So even though you will usually want to make select queries and leave your underlying tables intact, in some cases, you want to create a new table from an existing one and use criteria.

Second, a report based on a query includes up-to-date values from the underlying table. If you want a report that is, in effect, frozen in time, you need to base it on records that haven't been updated. So use the Make Table query when you want to see information just as it was at a particular moment.

Beginning the query

Suppose that you want to make an abbreviated table from the Employees table of the Northwind Traders database (Northwind.mdb in the Samples subfolder within the folder you installed Access). This table will have some of the same fields as the Employees table and will just be for U.S. staff. (This example is just for illustrative purposes. It's conceivable that you would make this table and put it in another database, but probably not in the same one.)

You start to create a make-table query just as you would a select query.

1 Click the Queries tab in the Database window.

2 Click the <u>N</u>ew button. The New Query dialog box appears.

3 Select Design View, and click OK. The Show Table dialog box appears.

4 Add the table or tables that you want to use in your query. In this case, double-click the Employees table.

5 Click <u>C</u>lose.

6 Double-click the fields you want to use in your new table. Figure 20.2 shows the fields chosen for the abbreviated Employees table on the QBE grid.

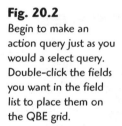

Fig. 20.2
Begin to make an action query just as you would a select query. Double-click the fields you want in the field list to place them on the QBE grid.

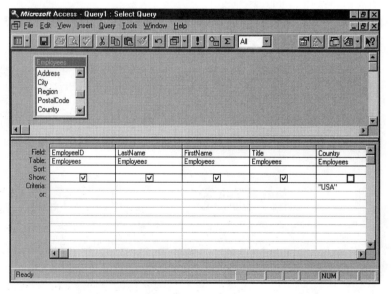

7 If necessary, enter criteria for the fields. In the figure, USA is entered in the Country field. You don't need to see the field in the new table, so the Show box has no checkmark.

Select a table name and a database

Now comes steps that are specifically for Make Table queries.

1 Click the arrow next to the Query Type icon (refer to fig. 20.1), and select Make Table from the drop-down menu. You see the Make Table dialog box, shown in figure 20.3.

Fig. 20.3

Type in a name for your new table. You can also replace an existing table by selecting it from the Table Name drop-down menu. (Be sure you want to do that!)

TIP The action-query choices are also available in the Query menu.

2 Access first asks you for a Table Name, where you can enter a new name for a table. For this example, type **Staff**. You also can select an existing table from the drop-down menu; Access replaces the old table with the new one. Obviously, be sure you no longer need the original table before you replace it.

3 Next, select where you want to put the new table. The Current Database is the default, which is where we'll put the new table. If you want to put it in Another Database, select that option in the Make Table dialog box. If you do select another database, type the full path name of the destination database. For example, if you want to add the table to the Test.mdb database in the My Documents folder (assuming you have created such a file), type **C:\My Documents\Test.mdb**. Then click OK.

Preview your table and create it

You probably will want to preview your table before you create it. Choose View, Datasheet, or click the Query View icon in the toolbar. Then click the Query view icon again to return to Design view, and make any changes that you want.

Finally, click the Run icon in the toolbar to create the table. If you chose the name of an existing table for your table, Access displays a warning that the existing table will be deleted. Even if you didn't choose the same name, you still get a message that *X* number of records will be pasted into a new table. Click Yes, and Access creates your table.

Modifying your table in Design view

Switch to the Tables tab of the Database window, and you'll see your new table, Staff, listed. Select the table, and then click the Design button to see what it looks like in Design view. Notice that the data type and the Field Size property for each field are the same as they were in the original table (see fig. 20.4). But the new table doesn't have a primary key. Also, none of the other field properties has been inherited, and none of the Descriptions has been inherited either, so you have to put those things in on your own. Don't worry about the field properties, but go ahead and make the Employee ID the primary key.

Microsoft Access - Staff : Table
File Edit View Insert Tools Window Help
Field Name
Data Type
Description
EmployeeID
AutoNumber
LastName
Text
FirstName
Text
Title
Text
Field Properties
General
Lookup
Field Size
Long Integer
New Values
Increment
Format
Caption
Indexed
No
A field name can be up to 64 characters long, including spaces. Press F1 for help on field names.
Design view. F6 = Switch panes. F1 = Help.
CAPS NUM

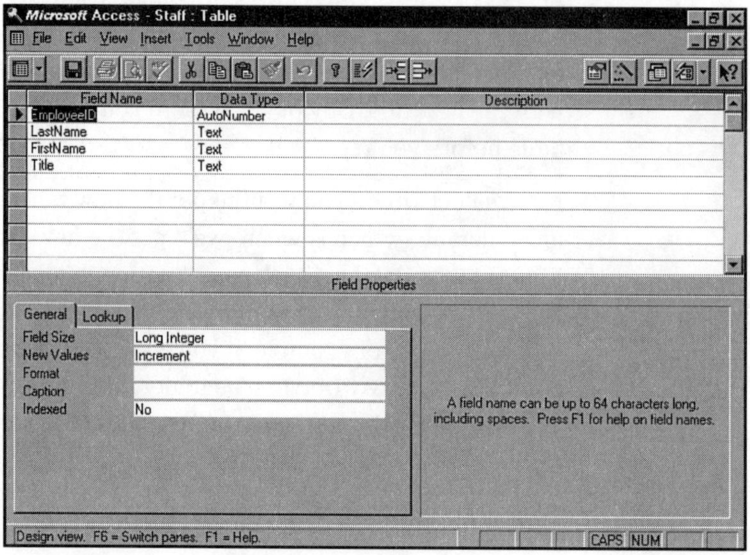

Fig. 20.4
The primary key and most field properties are not inherited.

Do you need to save the query?

Review for a moment what you have done. You designed a make-table query. You previewed the results in Datasheet view. When you ran the query, you made a table. But you've still got a real live, honest-to-goodness query. You can save the query; make changes in the design, if you want to; and run it again when you need to.

If making the table was a one-shot deal, you can politely decline when Access asks you about saving it. Your table has been made, and Access can't take that away from you. In other cases, however, you may want to run the query again at a future date. Click File, Save; give your query a name (for this example, name it Staff Names and Titles); and click OK. (The name of a query cannot duplicate that of a table.) As always, the name should be apt, but it doesn't have to scream that the query is a make-table query. Access puts the Make Table icon (with the exclamation mark) next to the query name in the Database window, so you'll know what it is.

When you click Open in the Datasheet window for a make-table query (or any action query), you don't see a datasheet displaying records. Rather, Access gets ready to run the query, gives you the proper warnings, and then creates the table.

If you want to change anything in the query, select it in the Database window and click the Design button. Do you need to see the Make Table dialog box to change the table name or the target database? Choose Query, Make Table. You can have the query replace the table that you made; you also can make a table with a new name and save it separately.

After you have the query just the way you want it, click the Run icon (the big exclamation point), and Access makes your table. The records reflect the current data from the underlying table.

Delete queries

 You use delete queries to delete large numbers of records. You could highlight a group of records with your mouse and then press Delete, but if you have a few hundred records to get rid of, that procedure would be a pain. Equally important, delete queries allow you to dump records that meet only certain conditions. However, in a delete query, you can't remove selected fields. Either the entire record goes or nothing at all.

Warning: delete queries can be harmful to your database

Deleting records carelessly can really mess up your database when both of the following are true:

- The table is on the "one" side of a one-to-many relationship.

- Referential integrity is set with the Cascade Delete option.

Why is using a delete query a problem under these conditions? Look at the Relationships windows for the Northwind database, shown in figure 20.5. Suppose that you decide to stop doing business with all suppliers in Japan because the high yen has made Japanese goods too expensive. You want to eliminate all records of Japanese suppliers in the Suppliers table. You'll use a delete query and set the criteria in the Country field of the Suppliers table to Japan.

Fig. 20.5

Relationships determine the full consequences of a delete query. You can unintentionally delete records you want to keep if you're not careful.

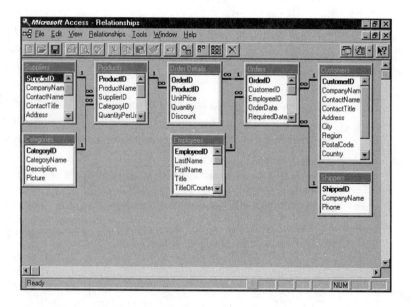

But the Suppliers table and the Products table have a one-to-many relationship. If you set Referential Integrity with Cascade Delete, running the query is going to wipe out the record for any product that came from a Japanese supplier. (Refer to Chapter 6, "Relationships: How Database Tables Relate to Each Other" if any of this discussion is hazy for you.)

In addition, the Products table has a one-to-many relationship with the Order Details table. You just eliminated several products in the Products table. Again, assuming that the Cascade Delete option is on, if those products were included in orders, the records in Order Details would be wiped out, too.

Is using a delete query with Cascade Delete good or bad?

If you eliminate all the records that you want to dump, using Cascade Delete is good. That's exactly what it's there for: to get rid of all the related records in other tables. If you delete records that you want to keep, though, then using Cascade Delete is bad. (Brilliant analysis, huh?) You may, for example, want to retain order details for all products in all orders, even for products that are discontinued.

None of this information is new or shocking to you; you come up against the same law of unintended (or intended) consequences whether you delete one record or a thousand. But re-creating a few records takes a few minutes; creating a few thousand takes days. That's why you need to be especially careful when you use a delete query. Consider all the potential outcomes of eliminating any records. You may want to modify your settings for referential integrity accordingly.

 CAUTION **When the Cascade Delete option is set and you try to delete** records within a datasheet, you get a warning about the possible effect on other tables. When you use a delete query, though, you get no warning. Access does display a message that tells you how many records you're about to delete, but it says nothing about cascading deletes. You're on your own.

I don't want to lose any records that I need

The preceding discussion wasn't meant to keep you from using the delete query; I just wanted you to be aware of the danger. You don't want to be deleting information from a datasheet record by record. You don't have to be afraid to use delete queries if you follow two precautions:

- Make backup copies of your data.

- Preview, in Datasheet view, the records that you'll be deleting.

Enough lectures; let's make a delete query

Suppose that you want to dump all the records from the Orders table that have an order date before August 1, 1993. Here's how to set up and run the query:

1 Create a query.

2 In the Show Table window, double-click the Orders table (the table from which you want to delete records) to add it to the Query window. Click Close.

3 Choose Query, Delete.

4 Double-click the asterisk at the top of the Orders field list.

5 Double-click the OrderDate field (the field for which you'll set criteria) to place it on the second column of the QBE grid.

6 In the Criteria row below Where, type **<8/1/93**. Your window should look like figure 20.6. Notice that the window is titled Delete Query.

Fig. 20.6
The field you need to use for criteria is in the second column.

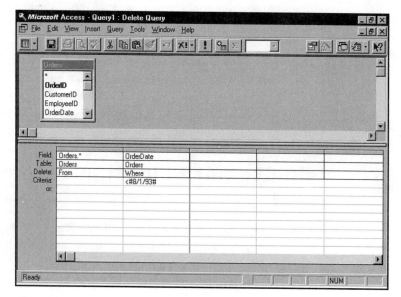

7 Switch to Datasheet view to see the records that will be deleted, and make sure that you set the criteria correctly.

8 Switch to Design view, and click the Run icon (the big exclamation point).

9 Access tells you how many rows you're about to delete. Click Yes to delete the records or No to cancel. (For this example, click No to leave the records alone.)

10 Decide whether you want to save the query for future use, or whether it can be discarded. Save the query by choosing File, Save; naming the file in the Save dialog box; and clicking OK. Alternatively, tell Access that you don't want to save the query when you are prompted.

Append queries

 You use an append query to add records from an Access table to another existing table. The target table can be in the same database or another database. Like a delete query, an append query allows you to use criteria in designating records—definitely a big plus.

You don't have to have the same number of fields in the source and target tables. If you have 12 fields in one table and 10 in the other, Access matches the fields that have the same names and ignores the rest.

The first steps to making an append query

Figure 20.7 shows the Staff table that you created with a make-table query. Suppose that you now want to add records for staff in the United Kingdom. Let's add the records with an append query.

1 Create a query.

2 In the Show Table window, select Employees and click Add.

3 Choose Query, Append, or click the arrow next to the Query Type button and select Append from the drop-down menu. The Append dialog box appears.

4 In the Table Name section, choose Staff (the table to which you want to attach records).

5 In the lower half of the Append dialog box, choose Current Database.

6 Choose OK.

Fig. 20.7
You created the Staff table with the make-table query. You can add records to this table using an append query.

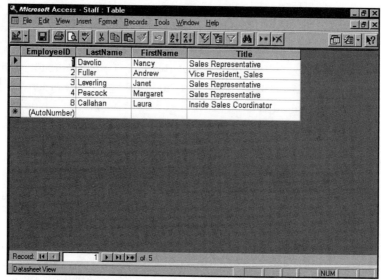

Put fields to the QBE grid

Now you want to put fields on the QBE grid. You need to include the fields that you want to append and any fields that you need for setting criteria. You also need to include the field that corresponds to the primary field in the target table. (Remember that you set Employee ID as the primary key in the Staff table when you made the table in the section, "Modifying your table in Design view.") Figure 20.8 shows how to set up the QBE grid.

TIP **Including the primary key in the grid may not be necessary (or desirable)** when the key is an ID field (i.e., AutoNumber type). If you want Access to add ID values in the target table automatically, you don't want to include the ID field. If the last value in the target table has an ID of 217, for example, and you want the first appended record to be 217 plus 1, or 218, don't include the primary key. The primary key is included in this example so that the records retain the ID that they had in the original table.

Fig. 20.8

Remember to include the field that corresponds to the primary key of the table to which you are appending records. In this case, that's Employee ID.

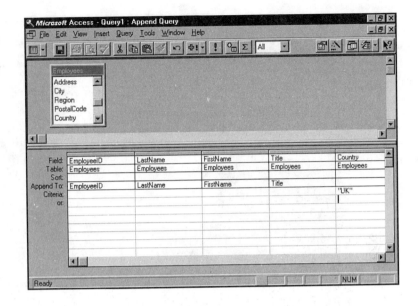

Because the field names in the target table are the same as those in the source table, the field names appear in the Append To row automatically. Otherwise, you need to select the field in the target table to which you want to append the information. The Append To cell for the Country field is empty; that field is used only for setting criteria.

TIP If you drag the asterisk (*) to the Field cell, Access chooses the asterisk selection in the Append To cell. Access appends all fields that have matching names and forgets about all nonmatching fields.

Finishing the append query

When you get your QBE grid squared away, preview the query by switching to Datasheet view (click the Query View button). You see the records that will be added to your table. Then switch back to Design view, and click the Run button (the exclamation mark) to run the query.

Your updated table doesn't open and appear automatically. If you want to see what the table looks like, select the Staff table in the Tables tab, and open it. You see that the table now contains all records for both U.S. and U.K. employees (see fig. 20.9).

Fig. 20.9
The records for U.K. employees have been added, and they retain their original ID numbers.

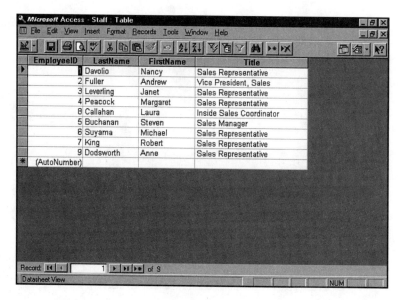

If you want to save the query, choose File, Save, and give the query a name in the Save dialog box. Otherwise, tell Access that you don't want to save the query when it asks you.

Update queries

Update queries are great when you want to change many records in a field. Once again, because you're dealing with a query, you can set criteria to change only the records that you want to change.

Creating an update query

Suppose that you decide to put up with higher prices from your Japanese suppliers after all. All the suppliers are raising their prices by 15 percent, so you need to raise the prices for Japanese items in the Products table by the same percentage. Let's raise all the prices in one stroke with an update query.

1 Create a query.

2 In the Show Table dialog box, select Suppliers, which contains the Country field (the field for which you need to set criteria). Then select Products, which contains the Unit Price field (the field that you want to update). Note that the fields are joined in a one-to-many relationship. Close the Show Table window.

3 Choose Query, Update, or click the Update Query icon.

4 Double-click the Unit Price field from the Products table to put it in the first column of the QBE grid. The double-click the Country field of the Suppliers table to place it in the second column.

5 In the Update To row of the first column, type **[Unit Price]*1.15**. That tells Access to raise unit prices by 15%.

6 In the second column, type **Japan** in the Criteria line and press Enter. Your QBE grid should look like figure 20.10.

Fig. 20.10
In the Update To row of the Unit Price field, put in the calculated expression. In the second column, type in the Country criteria.

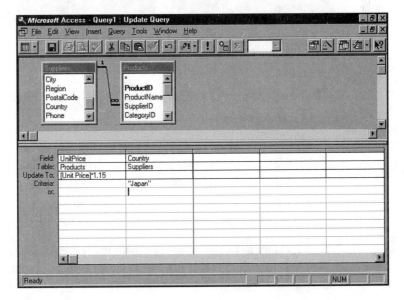

7 Switch to Datasheet view to see the prices that will be updated (see fig. 20.11).

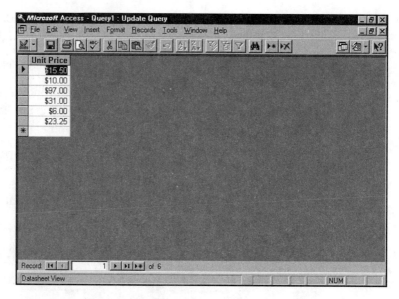

Make the Update Query more informative

As the query stands now, all you have is a list of prices —you have no idea who the suppliers are or which product prices you're updating. Suppose that you had a fit of absent-mindedness and typed **France** instead of **Japan** in the Country field criteria line. You would have no way of knowing that you were changing prices for Brie and pâté rather than for tofu and soy sauce.

Let's fix that. In Design view, double-click the Product Name field from the Products table and the Company Name field from the Suppliers table to put them on the QBE grid. In the Update To row, type these field names, in brackets, in their respective columns (see fig. 20.12). Now, when you switch to Datasheet view, you have some confidence that you're updating the correct fields.

TIP The prices that you see when you switch to Datasheet view are *not* the updated prices. You need to run the query to actually change the values in the table.

Fig. 20.12
Additional fields help guarantee that your update query will be correctly executed.

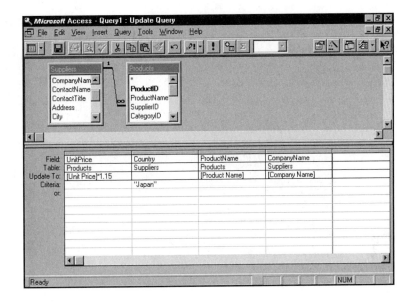

Finish updating the records by clicking the Run button in the toolbar. Ordinarily, Access displays a message saying how many records will be updated, and you can click OK and run the query. Unfortunately, the Northwind database has something called a parameter query for the Unit Price field, so Access first asks you to put in a value before it runs the query. Parameter queries are simply time-savers, but they are beyond our scope and weren't covered in this book. In your own database, assuming that it has no parameter queries, the update query would run after you tell Access it's OK to add the records.

As always, you can delete any of the tables and queries from the Northwind database that you created in this chapter.

Part VIII: Appendix

Appendix A: **Where to Go for More Help**

A

Where to Go for More Help

● **In this chapter:**

● **Access is a lifelong learning experience**

● **Is a users group for someone like me?**

● **How to go on-line for convenient help**

● **I'd like some other stuff to read**

If you have questions about Access that this book didn't answer, here are resources to turn to for help?. . . . .

had a dream the other night. I was on the old *Tonight Show* with Johnny Carson. Johnny was the beturbaned Karnak, and I was Ed McMahon. I was giving Johnny a copy of this book and saying: "You know, I think everything, *everything* you could ever want to know about Access is in here, in this one small book. It's all in there, I've put it *all* in."

And Johnny looked at me, paused, and said "Wrong, Corrupted Databreath."

You could spend a lifetime learning everything there is to know about Access. Certainly, you'll have questions that this book and Access Help can't answer. Where should you turn for help? This appendix offers a few ideas for expanding your knowledge of Access.

Who can use users groups?

I think a lot of people are turned off by the idea of users groups. Some of that is perfectly legitimate. People simply don't have the time or the energy to traipse off at night to learn about computers. And, when you do have some free time, you'd probably rather be anywhere but stuck inside talking about Table Wizards.

I think there's another reason you might shy away from user groups. You may believe users groups are just for the super-proficient, the most powerful among the power users.

That was my own prejudice, which turned out to be completely wrong. I found an extremely warm welcome when I walked into a beginner's meeting of the San Francisco PC Users Group and asked how to start Windows. (OK, I wasn't quite that ignorant, but pretty close to it.) The knowledge and support these people provided was invaluable.

Here are a few things that a local users group may be able to offer you, specifically in terms of Access support:

- *Volunteers* who will answer your questions about Access by phone during designated hours.

- *Special interest groups (SIGs)* dedicated to Access alone or databases in general. A SIG is made up of a few people who might meet regularly at someone's house, a local church, or any number of places.

- *General meetings* where you can ask questions of the entire club. There's usually a speaker, sometimes from Microsoft and other database vendors, who will show off the company's products.

- The opportunity to get free software by agreeing to write a review for the club's magazine.

As with anything else, where you live will determine the resources available. In reality, many clubs don't offer all or even most of these features. There may be no one else who knows anything about Access (or is at least willing to share it) in your area. The San Francisco Bay Area is obviously a world technology center, so local groups have an unusually large pool of enthusiastic, talented people to draw on.

Even with all those caveats, I still think it's worth trying to find a group in your area. There's usually a cycle to member participation—people join when they buy a new computer, or get new software and need help. After a couple of years they become reasonably proficient and quit attending the users group. But there's usually a core of members that stay on year after year. They are constantly looking for new blood, and that means they are interested in you.

If you're interested, here's a few ideas on how to find a local group:

- Call the User Group Locator hotline operated by the Association of PC Users Group at 914-876-6678. Follow the prompts and you'll get the names and telephone numbers of groups in your area.

- Microsoft's customer service line can also give you information on local groups. Their number is 800-426-9400.

- Ask your local computer dealer or computer-literate friends.

Aren't on-line services expensive and difficult to use?

Just a few years ago, going on-line was mostly for businesses and power users. With more computers in the home with faster modems, all levels of users are subscribing to on-line services. Like so many other computer tasks, windows-based GUIs have taken most of the pain out of using on-line services. You won't be left stranded at a command line trying to think of arcane instructions to type.

On-line services do cost money, but it's not prohibitive. Much depends on what service you use and how you use them. Pricing plans change constantly and can be as difficult to understand as the tax code. I'd say an investment of $15 to $30 a month will serve you nicely. Competition is becoming more severe, which helps keep prices down. More powerful modems means information is retrieved faster, which means less time spent on-line (which often means lower bills).

TIP **If you live in a relatively remote area, you may have to pay** extra for telephone-connect charges.

Of course, getting Access support would be only one of many, many ways to take advantage of your membership. The point is when you include *everything* you do on-line, you'll find the cost is relatively low.

What are the major on-line services?

You might divide on-line services into three areas: the established commercial services, including CompuServe, America On-line, and Prodigy; the Microsoft Network; and the Internet. These can overlap—all of the major commercial services now offer some Internet access. You'll need to have a **modem** in your computer to connect to any service.

 Plain English, please

Modems allow distant computers to communicate by converting their information into sounds that can travel through telephone lines. A modem can be installed inside your computer (an internal modem), or it can be a separate device (an external modem). If you purchased your computer recently, it's likely there's a modem already installed inside. **99**

Things are changing *very* fast in the on-line world. I don't want to tell you a bunch of stuff that will be out of date when you read it. But I do want you to think about how going on-line can help you learn and use Access. Let me give you just a little taste of what they're about and how they work.

Plain English, please!

> You hear a lot about **flaming** in cyberspace. That's writing a nasty—very nasty—message to someone. It happens sometimes to newbies who don't know they're doing anything wrong. It particularly happens on the Internet, where people make a big deal about netiquette. I can think of few things less meaningful than getting flamed. Who cares? Try to learn the rules, but don't be scared off by them. Everyone was a beginner once.

CompuServe

In mid-1995, CompuServe was the only one of the major commercial services (excluding MSN) that offered a specific **forum** dedicated to Access and monitored by Microsoft staff. While you can learn about databases on the other services, CompuServe offers specific, extensive support in using Access. What's involved in getting started? And what does CompuServe offer Access users?

 TIP **If you are already using CompuServe, type msaccess at the Go** dialog box to use the forum.

CompuServe will give you the software, called the CompuServe Information Manager (CIM), for using the service. You'll need to spend a little time learning about it, but it's pretty intuitive. Believe me, if you can tackle Access, this is nothing. Everything is in plain English, and there are no special commands to learn. Starting off is easy. With today's GUIs, all the work of dialing into a service, signing on, putting in your password, and so on, is automated.

Once you're in CompuServe, you can visit the Access forum. Here's where beginners (and anyone else) can post **messages** about any questions they may have. Figure A.1 shows a simple sample message. Compose your message off-line, go on-line to post it, and sit back and wait for an answer.

 Plain English, please!

> A **forum** is a special interest group within the CompuServe community. By sending **messages**, you can ask questions and share your ideas with others who have similar interests. You can also retrieve files containing information and programs.

Fig. A.1
You can ask questions about Access in a discussion group known as a forum.

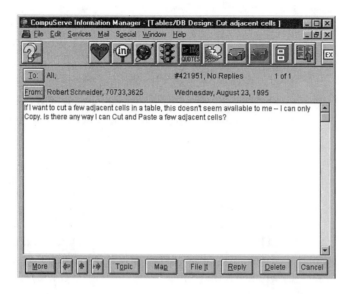

You should receive a reply in a couple of days (see fig.A.2). Often you will receive a reply from a "Most Valuable Professional" (MVP)—Access professionals who voluntarily share their knowledge and experience. Whenever you visit the forum, you're told if you have messages waiting. Open and read them. You can reply if that's necessary. You also can save them for future reference.

Fig. A.2
You can ask questions on anything related to Access. This is a response to a message about cutting adjacent cells in Access.

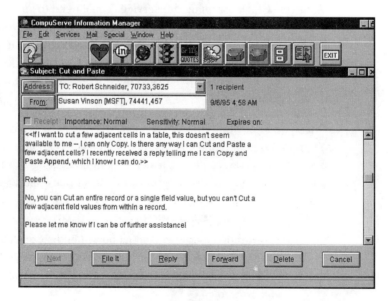

The Messages area is not only for asking specific how-do-I-do-it questions. You can post a message to say what's on your mind. At first, other forum members just see the subject of your message, not the contents. If they decide it looks interesting, they can open and read it. It may rouse them to reply. You reply back. And so it goes, back and forth.

You, of course, can read messages too. A lot of the subjects get rather technical, but all of the messages are usually informative and interesting. "What do you think of the new Filter by Form?" "I don't like the way they changed the Database window." "I think Access handles the Find function better than other database programs." Stuff like that.

If you want to **lurk**—just hanging out to hear what others are saying—that's no problem. The Access forum isn't free—while you're on it, the meter is running. Sending a couple of messages and receiving them won't break you— leisurely reading through dozens of messages will. Be careful.

 TIP　**What many users do to avoid hefty charges is use a navigator.** That's software that goes into forums you select, gets all the messages there quickly (that can include everybody's, not just those to you), and disconnects. Then you can read them off-line when you want.

If you have questions or would like to subscribe to CompuServe, you can reach them at 1-800-609-1674.

The Microsoft Network

 As you've probably heard by now, access to The Microsoft Network (MSN) is just one mouse click away. The icon for The Microsoft Network resides right on your Desktop. Click it, and follow the series of directions on the screens to sign up. Reviewers have said MSN is easy to learn and easy to use.

Perhaps at some point the MSN will make other on-line services passé. In 1995, however, this is still very much of an open question. First and foremost, the MSN does not provide significant support for Access as compared to CompuServe's Access forum. Second, overall content is relatively sparse— user support for most software, even Windows 95 itself, has not provoked cries of hurrah. Third, Microsoft initially will limit the number of subscribers to 500,000, so don't be surprised if you can't even sign up. As for cost, the pricing plans announced appear in line with those of other services.

However, all of this may radically change by the time you read this book. Since on-line services now receive significant attention in the popular press, you should be able to monitor developments and determine what service is best for you. Of course, you can always hook up to a service (sometimes for free) and then cancel later.

The Internet

By now, most everyone has heard of the Internet. In terms of the total information available, it may be equivalent to 100 or 1,000 times what CompuServe has, which is already massive. Using the World Wide Web, you can see pictures from the Louvre or from Uranus. You could easily spend your whole life doing nothing but "cruising the Net."

None of this is relevant for someone who has basic questions on Access and wants them answered correctly and reasonably quickly. There is a newsgroup—similar to a CompuServe forum—devoted to Access. But it's not monitored by anyone from Microsoft. While GUIs have made navigating the Internet easier, it still isn't particularly user friendly—certainly not like the Microsoft Network or CompuServe. So for Access help, I think CompuServe is a better choice than the Net. On the other hand, if you are a subscriber to America Online or Prodigy, the Access newsgroup can be a convenient source for you.

 TIP   **If you have access to the Net, check out the Access newsgroup.**
The Access newsgroup is not monitored and can be reached at
comp.databases.ms-access.

What else can I read that's worthwhile?

William F. Buckley Jr. tells a wonderful story about a conversation he had several years ago with a waiter. The waiter told him he enjoyed reading Buckley's *National Review*—but why did it have to have so many big words? A year later, Buckley met the waiter again, who thanked him for taking his advice. Of course, Buckley had done no such thing—the waiter had simply learned the "big" words.

On that note, I would bypass the computer magazines aimed at the true beginner. Instead, I'd look for both *PC Computing* and *PC World*, which are written and edited for a readership with a wide range of computer ability.

Of particular interest are the help sections that offer valuable tips. Both magazines discuss issues of interest to database users, and often there is a question-and-answer, or a short piece on an Access topic.

TIP   **The number to call to subscribe to *PC World* is 1–800–825–7595.** *PC Computing* can be reached at 1–800–365–2770. A year's subscription to either runs around $15 or $20. If you want to check out an issue, you can usually find them in the big book chains.

I'd also try to pick up the free computer newspapers available in newsracks in many cities. Hey, it's free, right? Moreover, at times the editorial quality equals or exceeds the glossy magazines you have to pay for. Checking out the ads of local dealers is fun and informative, and the classifieds often let you know about computer-related organizations and events in your area.

Finally, I'd like to put in a word for another Que book, *Special Edition Using Access 7 for Windows 95*. It's clearly written and well-organized; you can find what you need easily. This 1,300-page tome truly has a wealth of information. Now *here's* a book which one might say has everything you always wanted to know about Access 7.

Index

Symbols

- sign (table relationships), 187
! icon (Run command), 341
* (multiplication symbol), 167

* (query asterisk), 162-163
< (less than sign)
  date expressions, 159-160
  equal sign with, 161
  record selection criteria, 160-161
= (equal sign) in expressions, 161
> (greater than sign)
  date expressions, 159-160
  equal sign with, 161
  record selection criteria, 160-161
? (wild cards), 162-163
1 sign (table relationships), 187

A-B

Access
  CompuServe forum about, 359
  exiting, 21
  starting, 14
  welcome screen, 15
    Blank Database button, 16

action queries
  Append queries, 345
    adding fields to QBE grid, 346-347
    previewing, 347
    saving, 348
  Delete queries, 341, 344-345
    Cascade Delete, 343
    hazards of, 342-343
    saving, 345
  Make Table queries, 337-339
    criteria, 337
    modifying in Design view, 340
    previewing new table, 340
    saving, 341
  types, 336-351
  Update queries, 348-350
Align commands (Format menu), 247-248
aligning form controls, 242-243, 247-248
alphanumeric text, 40
And criteria in expressions
  filters, 176-180
  multiple fields, 164
  Or criteria and, 179
Answer Wizard, 29
Append command (Query menu), 345

Append dialog box, 345
Append queries, 336, 345
  adding fields to QBE grid, 346-347
  previewing, 347
  saving, 348
appending
  records to other tables, 320-321
    rules for pasting, 321-322
  tables to other tables, 319-320
arithmetic operations
  averaging single fields, 206
  counting single fields, 205-206
  null values, 205
  in queries, 165-167
  summing single fields, 203-206
Association of PC Users Group, 357
asterisks (*) in queries, 162-163
AutoForm command (Insert menu), 220-221
AutoFormat command (Format menu), 266
AutoFormat window, 266-267
AutoForms, 227-228
  Datasheet, 228
  Tabular, 227-228

PLUG YOURSELF INTO...

THE MACMILLAN INFORMATION SUPERLIBRARY™

Free information and vast computer resources from the world's leading computer book publisher—online!

FIND THE BOOKS THAT ARE RIGHT FOR YOU!

A complete online catalog, plus sample chapters and tables of contents give you an in-depth look at *all* of our books, including hard-to-find titles. It's the best way to find the books you need!

- STAY INFORMED with the latest computer industry news through our online newsletter, press releases, and customized Information SuperLibrary Reports.

- GET FAST ANSWERS to your questions about MCP books and software.

- VISIT our online bookstore for the latest information and editions!

- COMMUNICATE with our expert authors through e-mail and conferences.

- DOWNLOAD SOFTWARE from the immense MCP library:
    - Source code and files from MCP books
    - The best shareware, freeware, and demos

- DISCOVER HOT SPOTS on other parts of the Internet.

- WIN BOOKS in ongoing contests and giveaways!

TO PLUG INTO MCP: → **WORLD WIDE WEB: http://www.mcp.com**

GOPHER: gopher.mcp.com

FTP: ftp.mcp.com

User-Friendly References for All Your Computing Needs

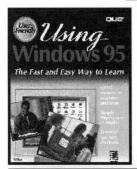

Using Windows 95
0-7897-0092-1, $19.99 USA
Publication Date: 8/95

Using The Microsoft Network
0-7897-0398-X, $19.99 USA
Publication Date: 9/95

Using PowerPoint for Windows 95
0-7897-0365-3, $19.99 USA
Publication Date: 11/95

Using Excel for Windows 95
0-7897-0111-1, $19.99 USA
Publication Date: 9/95

The new *Using* series gives readers just the information they need to perform specific tasks quickly and move on to other things. *Using* books provide bite-sized information for quick and easy reference, along with real-world analogies and examples to explain new concepts.

For more information on these and other Que products, visit your local book retailer or call 1-800-772-0477.

Source code ISBN: 0-7897-0185-5

Complete and Return this Card
for a *FREE* Computer Book Catalog

Thank you for purchasing this book! You have purchased a superior computer book written expressly for your needs. To continue to provide the kind of up-to-date, pertinent coverage you've come to expect from us, we need to hear from you. Please take a minute to complete and return this self-addressed, postage-paid form. In return, we'll send you a free catalog of all our computer books on topics ranging from word processing to programming and the internet.

Mr. ☐   Mrs. ☐   Ms. ☐   Dr. ☐

Name (first) ☐☐☐☐☐☐☐☐☐☐☐   (M.I.) ☐   (last) ☐☐☐☐☐☐☐☐☐☐☐☐☐☐☐☐☐

Address ☐☐☐☐☐☐☐☐☐☐☐☐☐☐☐☐☐☐☐☐☐☐☐☐☐☐☐☐☐☐☐☐☐☐☐☐
☐☐☐☐☐☐☐☐☐☐☐☐☐☐☐☐☐☐☐☐☐☐☐☐☐☐☐☐☐☐☐☐☐☐☐☐

City ☐☐☐☐☐☐☐☐☐☐☐☐☐☐☐☐☐☐   State ☐☐   Zip ☐☐☐☐☐ ☐☐☐☐

Phone ☐☐☐ ☐☐☐ ☐☐☐☐   Fax ☐☐☐ ☐☐☐ ☐☐☐☐

Company Name ☐☐☐☐☐☐☐☐☐☐☐☐☐☐☐☐☐☐☐☐☐☐☐☐☐☐☐☐☐☐☐☐

E-mail address ☐☐☐☐☐☐☐☐☐☐☐☐☐☐☐☐☐☐☐☐☐☐☐☐☐☐☐☐☐☐☐☐

1. Please check at least (3) influencing factors for purchasing this book.

Front or back cover information on book .... ☐
Special approach to the content .... ☐
Completeness of content .... ☐
Author's reputation .... ☐
Publisher's reputation .... ☐
Book cover design or layout .... ☐
Index or table of contents of book .... ☐
Price of book .... ☐
Special effects, graphics, illustrations .... ☐
Other (Please specify): _____ ☐

2. How did you first learn about this book?

Saw in Macmillan Computer Publishing catalog .... ☐
Recommended by store personnel .... ☐
Saw the book on bookshelf at store .... ☐
Recommended by a friend .... ☐
Received advertisement in the mail .... ☐
Saw an advertisement in: _____ ☐
Read book review in: _____ ☐
Other (Please specify): _____ ☐

3. How many computer books have you purchased in the last six months?

This book only .... ☐   3 to 5 books .... ☐
2 books .... ☐   More than 5 .... ☐

4. Where did you purchase this book?

Bookstore .... ☐
Computer Store .... ☐
Consumer Electronics Store .... ☐
Department Store .... ☐
Office Club .... ☐
Warehouse Club .... ☐
Mail Order .... ☐
Direct from Publisher .... ☐
Internet site .... ☐
Other (Please specify): _____ ☐

5. How long have you been using a computer?

☐ Less than 6 months   ☐ 6 months to a year
☐ 1 to 3 years   ☐ More than 3 years

6. What is your level of experience with personal computers and with the subject of this book?

	With PCs	With subject of book
New	☐	☐
Casual	☐	☐
Accomplished	☐	☐
Expert	☐	☐

Source Code ISBN: 0-7897-0185-5

7. Which of the following best describes your job title?

Administrative Assistant .... ☐
Coordinator .... ☐
Manager/Supervisor .... ☐
Director .... ☐
Vice President .... ☐
President/CEO/COO .... ☐
Lawyer/Doctor/Medical Professional .... ☐
Teacher/Educator/Trainer .... ☐
Engineer/Technician .... ☐
Consultant .... ☐
Not employed/Student/Retired .... ☐
Other (Please specify): _____ ☐

8. Which of the following best describes the area of the company your job title falls under?

Accounting .... ☐
Engineering .... ☐
Manufacturing .... ☐
Operations .... ☐
Marketing .... ☐
Sales .... ☐
Other (Please specify): _____ ☐

9. What is your age?

Under 20 .... ☐
21-29 .... ☐
30-39 .... ☐
40-49 .... ☐
50-59 .... ☐
60-over .... ☐

10. Are you:

Male .... ☐
Female .... ☐

11. Which computer publications do you read regularly? (Please list)

_____
_____
_____
_____
_____
_____
_____
_____
_____

Comments: _____
_____
_____

Fold here and scotch-tape to mail.